TOPPLING THE FIRST MINISTRY

TOPPLING THE FIRST MINISTRY

Kerala, the CIA, and the Struggle for Social Justice

T. M. Thomas Isaac and Richard W. Franke

MONTHLY REVIEW PRESS
New York

Copyright © 2025 by T. M. Thomas Isaac and Richard W. Franke
All Rights Reserved

Library of Congress Cataloging-in-Publication Data
available from the publisher

ISBN 978-1-68590-107-3 paperback
ISBN 978-1-68590-108-0 cloth

Typeset in Minion Pro

MONTHLY REVIEW PRESS, NEW YORK
monthlyreview.org

5 4 3 2 1

Contents

Acknowledgments | 7

CHAPTER 1
Introduction: A Lingering Mystery | 9

CHAPTER 2
Policing the Empire: The U.S. Central Intelligence Agency | 24

CHAPTER 3
How the Communists Came to Power in Kerala in 1957 | 61

CHAPTER 4
Reform within the Constitution: The Communist Ministry in Kerala, 1957–1959 | 81

CHAPTER 5
Ousting the Communist Government: A Fruitless Two Years and a New, More Violent Strategy for the Anticommunist Opposition | 103

CHAPTER 6
The Fateful Months of June and July 1959: The Anticommunist "Liberation Struggle" and Dismissal of the Government | 123

CHAPTER 7
Creating Anticommunist Hysteria: The Christian Anti-Communism Crusade and Moral Re-Armament | 147

CHAPTER 8
    Through CIA Eyes: Information and Instructions for
    Toppling the Ministry| 174

CHAPTER 9
    The Aftermath of the Dismissal of the EMS Ministry | 218

CHAPTER 10
    Conclusions of the Study | 241

Glossary and Acronyms | 249
Notes | 252
Index | 287

Acknowledgments

At one level, our book constitutes a wide-ranging overview of and search for an understanding of the vast sources and patterns of historical change and development in the southwestern corner of India. At another level, it is a search for the proverbial suitcase full of money.

It was in 2007 on the fiftieth anniversary of the first Communist ministry of Kerala that we started work on this book. The initial data collection was largely limited to sources in Kerala and was undertaken primarily by Thomas Isaac. This included the collections of legislative records of the period at the Kerala Legislative Library, and the Kerala collection of the newspapers *The Hindu* and *Malayala Rajyam* at the Kerala University Library. We are grateful to the management of the *Kerala Kaumudi* and *Deepika* newspapers for giving access to their records. For the other newspapers and periodicals, we are grateful to Dr. Sushamakumari and Dr. C. N. Somarajan, who provided detailed notes collected as part of their doctoral dissertations on related themes. The pamphlets of the period were primarily collected from M. A. John's home library, Mangalappuzha Pontifical Seminary Aluva, Janakeeya Vayanasala Ponkunnam (Ponkunnam People's Reading Room), and many other rural libraries in Southern Kerala. Extensive discussions with the late P. Govinda Pillai, a Communist legislator during 1957–59, were also very useful.

The initial documentation and analysis resulted in a Malayalam book titled *Vimochana Samarathinte Kanappurangal* (the unknown faces of the liberation struggle) by Thomas Isaac on the occasion of the fiftieth anniversary celebrations. The book proved to be popular and is currently in its sixth printing. The current book has borrowed some of the arguments and analyses from the Malayalam book. However, it has finally come out as an entirely independent exercise, particularly reflecting the vast material collected from the United States on Kerala—especially the voluminous materials recently made available to the public through the Freedom of Information Act and the FOIA Electronic Reading Room.

In May 2007 Thomas Isaac visited the United States. This provided an opportunity to discuss the project, to visit the Columbia Center for Oral History Research, to examine the Ellsworth Bunker records. and also to initiate the search of the CIA records.

The late P. Krishnakumar, Thomas Isaac's personal secretary at the Finance Ministry in the Kerala government for part of the time, played an anchor role in systematically tracking the documents and pamphlets and making them available. Prof. J. Prabash of Kerala University collected and analyzed the electoral data of the 1957 and 1960 Kerala elections.

In August of 2016 we made a three-day visit to the Dwight D. Eisenhower Presidential Library in Abilene, Kansas, where the staff received us cordially and provided assistance with our work. It was at that library that we accidentally discovered the empty box described in chapter 8.

Our drafting of the manuscript was improved by many helpful ideas from copy editors Susie Day, Erin Clermont, and Emily Natsios. Sociologist Barbara H. Chasin made numerous improvements to the research and in drafting the manuscript.

We are especially grateful to Michael Yates at Monthly Review Press for his many contributions in all aspects of the project.

—T. M. THOMAS ISAAC AND RICHARD W. FRANKE

CHAPTER 1

Introduction: A Lingering Mystery

> I told the CIA to go to hell.
> —David Burgess

For David Burgess, his five years—1955 to 1960—as a labor attaché at the U.S. Embassy in New Delhi were "almost idyllic."[1] He traveled widely at U.S. Embassy expense, met with labor leaders and activists across the country, and lived in relative opulence with servants to take care of much of his family life and an international school for his children. Like most, or possibly all U.S. State Department personnel, Burgess was strongly anticommunist. In Atlanta, Georgia, in 1951, he had even joined a fellow union activist in physically blocking a Communist organizer from entering a meeting.[2]

But Burgess was not fiercely blinded by his ideology. During his years in India, he had noticed that many U.S. officials, rather than respecting their Indian colleagues' intelligence and acknowledging their right to hold more nuanced views of international relations, preached hysterical anticommunist sermons. Burgess sent memos back to Washington advising greater tolerance of India's then philosophy of positive neutralism. He never received an acknowledgment.

In 1959 Burgess got an unexpected chance to play a more

significant role in Indian history. In an interview about his life, he recalled that "a CIA staff member at the U.S. Embassy wanted me to take some bribe money to the state of Kerala in order to pay off some labor officials . . . during the election there. I told the CIA to go to hell."[3]

Burgess's recollections put the cap on a long-simmering discussion in Kerala history—what role, if any, did the CIA or other U.S. agencies play in toppling the 1957–1959 elected Communist Party ministry?

Testimonies of the Ambassadors

Part of the story has been known for some time. In 1978, Daniel Patrick Moynihan, U.S. ambassador to India from 1973 to 1975, had already spilled the beans. In connection with a discussion with some Indian officials, Moynihan recalled:

> In New Delhi I had pressed the [U.S.] Embassy to go back over the whole of our quarter-century in India, to establish just what we had been up to. In the end I was satisfied we had been up to very little. We had twice, but only twice, interfered in Indian politics to the extent of providing money to a political party. Both times this was done in the face of a prospective Communist victory in a state election, once in Kerala and once in West Bengal, where Calcutta is located. Both times the money was given to the Congress Party, which had asked for it. Once it was given to Mrs. Gandhi herself, who was then a party official.[4]

In 1979 a further acknowledgment appeared when Ellsworth Bunker, U.S. Ambassador to India (1956–1961), remarked in an oral history interview at Columbia University that the CIA had funneled money to the Congress Party during his tenure through S. K. Patil, a Congress leader from Maharashtra, to support activities to undermine the Kerala Communist Ministry, and not through Indira Gandhi.[5]

These high-level acknowledgments come to life when considering Burgess's account of being asked to actually carry the money. Presumably, this would leave higher-level officers the option of deniability—a common feature of secretive bureaucratic organizations. It is also significant that Burgess wrote down his experiences, because the actions and the philosophy behind them offended him. His refusal to carry out a request from the CIA may also have undercut his career—in 1960, after five years of service, he did not get renewed for another term at the embassy. Kerala's history moved along without him.

Whether he realized it or not, Burgess had been asked to join what turned out to be a massive campaign of subversion that the CIA unleashed immediately after the Second World War against Communist and other left groups. The postwar period had seen an upswing of left movements the world over and several left governments came to power, many of them through democratic elections. Almost all these left governments—including Kerala, an exceptional case of the Communist Party, rather than a broad left party, coming to power through the ballot—were toppled through violent means with active involvement of CIA. We shall notice differences and similarities in the ways the CIA drew upon or created allies within various populations to help carry out their covert plans to topple democratic governments and replace them with pro-U.S. dictatorships.

The Case of Kerala

This book is an attempt to document how one of the most popular state governments in India was toppled through mass agitation and covert operations. None of the existing narratives of the events in Kerala during 1957–1959 have attempted to chronicle the CIA's role in the dismissal of the elected left government by the central government in India. Among other cases of government-toppling, Kerala is a distinctly different case: the CIA has never publicly claimed credit for undermining Kerala's Communist government.

The Kerala case study is interesting for many reasons. Unlike other CIA toppling projects, which targeted sovereign nations, this project targeted Kerala, a state within India. Therefore, CIA intervention strategies would need to include influencing the federal government to take a stern stand against Communists in Kerala, and strengthen Kerala's local internal political opposition to the state government. There was no question of direct overt action.

Kerala, the homeland of Malayalam-speaking people, is one of the twenty-eight states of India. It was formed nearly a decade after India's national independence by integrating the erstwhile principalities of Travancore and Cochin with the Malabar district of Madras province. Located in the southwestern corner of the Indian subcontinent, it is a geographically compact, narrow strip of 560 kilometers in length between the Western Ghats Mountains and the Arabian Sea, with rolling hills and valleys in the midland. Blessed with two monsoons and fertile soil, the state has high agricultural potential and its numerous ports, because of the favorable monsoon winds, played an important role in the Indian Ocean trade. From the Middle East, Judaism, Christianity, and Islam came to Kerala in early times, so that today Kerala has large communities of Christians (18.4 percent) and Muslims (26.6 percent). Hindus, with 54.7 percent of the population, constitute the major religious community. The state has a long tradition of social harmony and religious tolerance, which survives today, in contrast to the polarizing and majoritarian tendencies gaining strength in India.

At the time of its formation, Kerala was one of the poorer states in the country. In 1961 the per capita income of an average Keralite was ₹259 (259 Indian rupees), while that of an average Indian was ₹306.[6] Yet Kerala was distinct from the rest of India by its relatively higher social indicators. In 1951, for example, soon after India became an independent nation, Kerala's literacy rate was 50 percent for males and 31 percent for females, versus all-India figures of 25 percent for males and 8 percent for females.[7] Many development experts have traditionally considered the infant mortality rate (IMR) to be the most reliable overall statistic, reflecting diet, housing conditions, and access to health care in low-income countries. In 1951 Kerala's infant mortality rate was 153 per 1,000 children below one year of age, while in India it was 192. Kerala's life expectancy was 48.1 years, while in India it was lower at 41.9 years. In India the number of women per one thousand males was 941, while in Kerala the ratio was 1022. These educational and health advancements were achieved despite the lower economic growth in Kerala.

Kerala's remarkable achievements were made possible by social reform movements from the latter half of the nineteenth century, and the demand for education that these movements generated from below.[8] The spread of education proved to be a prime mover, creating positive impact upon health and demographic variables. This process of creating demand for education and health services was strengthened by the political process in the post-independence period. As a result, in the subsequent decades, the differences between Kerala and the national average continued to widen until around the turn of the twentieth century.

By 1991 Kerala's adult literacy rate was 91 percent, while the national average was 52 percent. Kerala's life expectancy increased to seventy-two years, while the national average was sixty. The infant mortality rate was 17, while the national average was 85. The per capita income, at ₹4,207, was still lower than the national per capita income of ₹6,126.[9]

By the 1970s almost all of Kerala villages were electrified. Over thirty-five Malayalam newspapers were being published and over 3,700 village libraries were functioning, with over 700,000 reading room memberships.[10] On a list of twenty-two infrastructural amenities within two kilometers—paved roads, bus stops, post offices, schools, hospitals, railway stations, and so on—Kerala ranked first on 17, and above the all-India average on the remaining ones.[11]

Kerala's development experience, which ensured a higher quality of life for ordinary citizens even at a relatively lower level of economic income, spawned a large body of development literature, which has come to be called by some scholars the Kerala Model of Development. This model[12] has been characterized as the outcome of a redistributive strategy of development.[13] The Communist government of 1957 to 1959 played an important role in strengthening the agenda of redistribution through land reforms and improvement in wages in the newly formed state of Kerala.

Another distinction of the state is the domination of progressive politics. Besides progressive political parties, Kerala is also characterized by a relatively high density of civic organizations.[14] In 1957 the people of the Indian state of Kerala elected a slim Communist Party of India (CPI) majority to their state assembly—in the first elections since the state had been formed—as part of a national Indian reorganization of states according to languages. The CPI-majority assembly formed a cabinet led by the Kerala CPI leader E. M. S. Namboodiripad, popularly called EMS. It led the state government for twenty-eight months until it was formally dismissed by the central government, which cited a breakdown of law and order consequent to violent anticommunist agitations on July 31, 1959. An important objective of this book is to unravel the dynamics of this agitation and the CIA's role in it.

The anticommunist agitators did not expect communism in Kerala to recover from this major setback. But the Communist influence did not wane, and Kerala continues to be a stronghold of the Communist Party. It recently came to international attention when the Communist-led left coalition won a second consecutive term in the state government, in contrast to the general tendency of declining left influence in India.[15]

The Existing Literature

There is a large body of existing literature dealing with the Communist government and its downfall.[16] There are doctoral theses that deal with related aspects, such as church and politics,[17] pressure group politics,[18] and media behavior.[19] The most surprising common feature of these studies is that there is no analysis of the possible involvement of an external agency like the CIA in the central government dismissal of the Kerala Communist ministry in 1959. The studies are all exclusively focused on domestic sociopolitical forces. The only exceptions are two publications by the historian Ajayan that attempt to link the CIA with the formation of the new anticommunist government in 1960.[20]

There have been numerous tracts and books critiquing the EMS ministry and supporting the anticommunist agitation[21] as well as writings by Communist leaders and sympathizers vigorously defending the government and denouncing the agitation.[22] It is understandable that the protagonists of the agitation would want to play down the role of outside agencies, but surprisingly, Communist leaders have also been silent on this aspect.

Finally, there are several popular books on the theme in Malayalam penned by journalist Rajeswari. His narrative, tinged with humor, has been popular but only casually touches on external finance for the agitations.[23] Similarly, well-known authors Gopalakrishnan (1994) and Sreekala (2010) have also ignored it.[24] The only exception is Thomas Isaac, who has broadly taken the stand adopted in this book.[25]

Source Materials in the United States

Policing an empire requires many resources and actions—financial resources, on-the-ground supporters, and dedicated and competent operations staff. A useful function is fulfilled by journalists attached to the empire's center. In the case of the U.S. project to topple the EMS ministry, an important role—whether consciously recognized or not—was played by the U.S. press, and especially by its newspaper of record, the *New York Times*. From 1952, when the first warning signs of exceptional Communist electoral strength in the areas that would become the state of Kerala appeared; to Kerala's official creation on November 1, 1956; to the election victory and installation of the EMS ministry on April 5, 1957—right through to the dismissal of the EMS ministry on July 31, 1959, the election of the anticommunist coalition on February 1, 1960, and the formation of an anticommunist government on February 22,1960—the *Times* provided its U.S. and international readers with a consistently anticommunist portrayal of the events.

For the year 1957 alone, a search of the *Times* archives gives forty-eight hits for Kerala, all but about five of them worriedly reporting on the CPI state assembly election victory, the formation of the EMS ministry, and some of the political events of that year. In 1958 the number of hits is forty-five. The year 1959—the year of the anticommunist campaign to oust the EMS ministry—sees 123 mentions of Kerala. In 1960, the year of the special election (February 1, 1960), thirty-six *Times* articles cemented in power an anti-CPI ministry. If we separate out the five years including and immediately surrounding the EMS ministry, plus the current year, the *Times* totals sixty-one years of Kerala coverage, with 1,332 mentions of Kerala, a yearly average of twenty-two.

Regarding original CIA sources, we have three major types of information:

- A set of five documents—out of dozens potentially available—including telegrams between the U.S. Embassy in New Delhi and the U.S. State Department in Washington, D.C., minutes of meetings held at either location, and editorial notes in some cases. The documents are maintained and made publicly available by "The Office of the Historian," and are usually referred to as FRUS, or "Foreign Relations of the United States." The documents are numbered and identified by date.
- Various materials from the Eisenhower Presidential Library in Abilene, Kansas, where we conducted research August 14 to 17, 2016. The most relevant materials are discussed in chapter 8.
- A trove of partially or wholly declassified ("sanitized") CIA reports—we have studied those dating from 1950, the earliest year of known coverage of India by the CIA—to 1960 when the EMS ministry was ousted by a special election. These documents are maintained in the CIA Reading Room, as required

by the U.S. Freedom of Information Act of 1966 and subsequent years.

On July 4, 1966, U.S. President Lyndon Johnson signed Public Law 89-487, the Freedom of Information Act (FOIA), that requires the full or partial disclosure of previously unreleased or uncirculated information and documents controlled by the U.S. government, state, or other public authority upon request. Over the fifty-five years since its passage, the FOIA has been altered at least ten times, and has been the subject of a plethora of court cases, including several that progressed to the U.S. Supreme Court. For our purposes, the most significant amendment to the FOIA was the 1984 "CIA Information Act," which clarifies and further specifies elements of the original FOIA as they apply to the purported special circumstances of the CIA's need for secrecy.[26] In fact, this question of how freedom of information can coexist with the need for secrecy was anticipated in the original act as Exemption One (of nine exemptions), which states that certain information can be held secret "if it is specifically authorized under criteria established by an Executive order to be kept secret in the interest of national defense or foreign policy."[27] What this all seems to mean in practice is that—after over five decades of the FOIA—the CIA director effectively has near total autonomy to grant or deny requests for CIA documents or materials.[28] We shall consider the impact of the CIA special exemption in chapter 8.

The CIA claims to have released over 30 million pages of declassified documents since the onset of the FOIA and some other disclosure orders.[29] Sifting through these documents to find information of interest has recently fostered the development of a new academic industry in the search for relevance within the mass of declassified materials.[30]

Despite significant shortcomings, the FOIA provides certain researcher-friendly features, such as the requirement that government agency compliance mandates the establishment of publicly accessible electronic reading rooms where citizens can relatively easily search and browse through documents.[31] The CIA has created its own reading room where interested citizens can search among hundreds or thousands of fully or partially declassified material, a vast collection of intelligence data.[32] Information or documents about clandestine or covert actions by the Agency are generally not included in the collection.

It should come as no surprise that the CIA reading room will not contain any specific details about the Agency's role in toppling the 1957 EMS ministry. It may, nonetheless, be useful to survey the contents of the many documents that are available from the time period and the events just before, during, and after the tenure of that ministry. This allows us to look in from the outside, to get an idea of how much information the CIA was able to gather, and to see how the plans for toppling the EMS ministry were woven together across several months.

At the time of our research, a CIA reading room search on the word *Kerala* brought up 393 hits. From this list, we were able to identify sixty-three separate documents covering the time period, from 1950 through February 1960 that show Kerala as part of the content. We also searched Travancore, Cochin, and Malabar, the three areas that became the state of Kerala on November 1, 1956.

The year 1950 is apparently the earliest for which any records exist in the CIA database. Two files from this year—June 12[33] and August 22[34]—deal with the arrest and interrogation of Communist Party activists or supporters. One concerns a certain T. C. Alexander, a Christian plantation owner reputed to be a sympathizer of and financial contributor to the Communist Party of India. According to the documents, he was released after promising to end his pro-CPI activities—and, it is noted, might also have benefited from his close friendship with a man named Chandrasekhara Nair, identified as "the present Inspector General of Police" in the pre-Kerala political units of Travancore and Cochin, princely states recently absorbed into the Indian union. Documentation of sources in this book is listed by dates in the text corresponding to links in the CIA section of the bibliography.

INTRODUCTION   19

On those links, the reader can directly access the CIA declassified documents discussed in the text.

One item of interest in these two documents is that the CIA was watching the CPI's activities at a micro level. It is also of interest that the CIA had begun watching the Kerala Communists early in its history. Furthermore, the document of August 22, 1950, states that the "Indian Central Intelligence Bureau" had apparently recruited another activist who,

> while working inside the CPI, was able to contribute the information which led to the arrest of several CPI members in the Edapally Police Station raid case. An effective raid on the Kalady headquarters of the KPC (Kerala Provincial Committee) was also attributed to the information this member supplied to the USTC (United State of Travancore-Cochin) police.[35]

That the CIA had such details in its records suggests a close coordination with the Indian Intelligence Bureau.

Source Materials in Kerala

Our greatest disappointment in our research was with the Kerala State Government Archives. There is no document whatsoever available in the archives on the anticommunist agitation of 1959. Except for a file on a judicial inquiry into police firing, a few files related to land reforms, and routine files of posting and transfer of officials, everything else has been systematically cleaned out. The attempts of one of the authors, who was the state finance minister, to search into police records also yielded no result. It was as if the year 1959 had been wiped clean of records. Therefore, our research in Kerala was limited to secondary materials like newspapers and pamphlets of the period and printed Legislative Assembly records.

We have carefully gone through the issues from 1957 to 1960 of four major newspapers: *Deepika*, *Mathrubhumi*, *Kerala Kaumudi*, and *Deshabhimani*. The back issues of *Deepika*, the mouthpiece of Catholics, were very useful in understanding the ideology and tactics of the Church. The newspaper clippings from *Malayala Manorama*, *Malayalarajyam*, and *Janayugam* collected by Dr. S. S. Sushamakumari and Dr. C. N. Somarajan were made available to us. The newspaper backfiles have been extensively used in documenting the chronology of the ministry and of the anticommunist agitation in *Beyond What the Eye Meets in Anticommunist Agitation*, an earlier Malayalam book on the subject by one of the authors. However, such descriptive chronological documentation has been avoided in the present book. The summarized statements we make on developments in Kerala are fully backed by voluminous records from newspapers. We have also made extensive use of nearly three-dozen autobiographies and memos of Communist leaders and leaders of the agitation, which are referred to in the discussions that follow.

The Pontifical Seminary Library at Aluva has one of the largest collections of anticommunist pamphlets published during the period. And many rural libraries in Kerala still have substantial pamphlets and other propaganda materials on the agitation. The records of the legislative debates are available at the Kerala Legislative Library.

Overview of the Chapters

Chapter 2, Policing the Empire: The U.S. Central Intelligence Agency. The CIA functions as the international police of the American Empire. Covert actions are essential to protect the interests of the empire. We present six case studies: British Guyana, Guatemala, Iran, Brazil, the Congo, and Indonesia/East Timor, where democratically elected left governments were overturned, or left electoral victories were subverted by CIA covert actions. The relatively longer treatment of Guyana and Guatemala is justified because of their similarities to Kerala and the fact that they were widely discussed from 1957 through1959 in Kerala. From these case studies, a template for CIA covert action is drawn. To what extent does the subversion of the EMS ministry in Kerala fit this framework?

Chapter 3, How the Communists Came to Power in Kerala in 1957. A historical survey of the region from ancient times brings out key features of a traditional caste-landlord-chiefdom society. The development of capitalism and the commercialization of agriculture and development of capitalism produced modern social classes. We discuss three social movements that emerged: caste reform movements, national movements, and peasant-worker-class movements. The Communists in Kerala creatively took part in these movements and, on the eve of independence, became the leadership of the national movement. Kerala Communists were the only political force that had a clear agenda for the development of the new state.

Chapter 4, Reform within the Constitution: The EMS Communist Ministry, Kerala 1957–1959. The new government proposed to implement land reforms, education reforms, administrative decentralization, industrialization, and welfare policies. All the proposals were within the constitutional limits, and most of them were in accordance with the policies of the Congress Party. The difference was that most of them were not being implemented by Congress governments. We will explain how the implementation of the new agenda would have accelerated growth, but at the same time ensured better distribution, and consequently improvement, in the standard of living of the people.

Chapter 5, Ousting the Communist Ministry: The Futile First Two Years and the New More Violent Opposition Strategy. Right from the beginning, the opposition approach to Kerala's Communist government was negative, and each of its programs was contested. We chronologically survey the major controversies and agitations during 1957 and 1958. We shall examine the aftermath of each of the agitations and demonstrate that they were losing steam. We shall also examine the outcomes of the by-elections to the assembly and the local governments to assess whether the popular support for the government was declining.

The opposition's failure to achieve its goals prompted it to move toward a new strategy to overthrow the government. The anticommunist agitation of 1959 was the outcome of this new strategy.

Chapter 6, The Fateful Months of June and July 1959: The Anticommunist "Liberation Struggle" and Dismissal of the Government. We analyze events during June and July 1959, that resulted in the dismissal of the ministry. There emerged an alliance among community organizations, and among opposition, strong political parties, with parallel but synchronized actions. How did this opposition unity emerge? How did the agitation gain momentum to create conditions making the normal working of the government impossible, so that central intervention for dismissal of the government became inevitable? We consider the role of violence and anticommunist propaganda by the Church, newspapers, and independent intellectuals in the creation of mass hysteria.

Chapter 7, Contributing to Anti-Communist Hysteria: The Christian Anticommunism Crusade and Moral Re-Armament. Many foreign groups were supporting the agitation financially and with propaganda materials. We examine the roles of two foreign groups that were visibly involved in the agitation. Notably, they were also active in the anticommunist campaigns in many other countries.

Chapter 8, Through CIA Eyes: Information and Instructions for Toppling the Ministry. After having surveyed the events in Kerala, we assess to what extent these events accorded with the CIA template described in chapter 2. How close and detailed was the CIA in monitoring the events in Kerala? Did the CIA possibly have anything to do with strategizing the events of 1959? Was the U.S. Information Service (USIS) involved in the anticommunist propaganda in Kerala? Did the CIA provide financial support to the agitation? Why has the CIA refused to claim credit for overthrowing the government in Kerala, as it has in other covert operations, even after seven decades? Why has the CIA been reluctant to declassify some of the key documents?

Chapter 9, Epilogue: The Aftermath of the Dismissal of the

Ministry. The first Communist ministry was dismissed halfway through its tenure. This disrupted the development agenda that it had started implementing. How did this disruption impact future development of Kerala, particularly the land reforms, decentralization, education reforms, and the overall development environment? We analyze the data for the 1960 election and draw current and future political implications. It was a major setback for progressive forces but surprisingly the movement recovered.

Chapter 10, Conclusions of the Study. We sum up the key conclusions that emerge, particularly regarding the nature of involvement of the CIA, in toppling the Communist ministry in Kerala.

CHAPTER 2

Policing the Empire: The U.S. Central Intelligence Agency

In 1975 Stonehill Publishing came out with one of the biggest whistleblower tell-alls in U.S. history. *Inside the Company: CIA Diary* chronicled the twelve-year career of a CIA covert operations officer, Philip Agee. His diary was "an attempt to open another small window to the kinds of secret activities that the U.S. government undertakes through the CIA in Third World countries in the name of US national security." As summarized by Agee:

> In the past 25 years [about 1947 to 1973], the CIA has been involved in plots to overthrow governments in Iran, the Sudan, Syria, Guatemala, Ecuador, Guyana, Zaire and Ghana. In Greece, the CIA participated in bringing in the repressive regime of the colonels. In Chile, The Company [a CIA self-name] spent millions to "destabilize" the Allende government and set up the military junta, which has since massacred tens of thousands of workers, students, liberals and leftists. In Indonesia in 1965 the Company was behind an even bloodier coup, the one that got rid of Sukarno, and led to the slaughter of at least 500,000 and possibly 1,000,000 people. In the Dominican Republic the

CIA arranged the assassination of the dictator Rafael Trujillo and later participated in the invasion that prevented the return to power of the liberal ex-president Juan Bosch. In Cuba, the Company paid for and directed the invasion that failed at the Bay of Pigs. Sometime later the CIA was involved in attempts to assassinate Fidel Castro. It is difficult to believe, or comprehend, that the CIA could be involved in all these subversive activities all over the world.[1]

As the curtains were drawn on the years of the Second World War, a new era of the Cold War opened. The war had had its own intelligence and covert operations, the inadequacies of which were revealed by the failure to anticipate or coordinate the many warning signs of the coming Pearl Harbor attack of December 7, 1941.[2] Further, President Harry Truman, who presided over the founding of the CIA, felt that the president required more detailed, yet easier to grasp and digest, material about overseas matters as U.S. foreign policy became increasingly central to overall government functioning. Today an important function of the CIA is to coordinate information for regular reports to the president. Daily reports started in 1961.[3]

The United States Central Intelligence Agency (CIA) was established by the National Security Act of 1947. The Agency rapidly expanded in numbers, budget, and covert activities in response to two challenges that arose in the postwar era, namely, emergence of powerful Soviet bloc and national liberation movements in the Third World.

Origins of the Empire

At the time the CIA was formed, the postwar world saw the rise, growth, or culmination of a vast array of social and political movements, many of them independence movements in Asia, Latin America, and Africa against traditional European colonial control. Many of these movements included substantial socialist or communist sympathizers—thus magnifying the fear in top U.S. circles that anticolonial independence movements could undermine American aspirations for world domination. The combination of factors helped lead to a situation where U.S. business interests saw an opening to push aside the traditional colonial powers and establish control by the United States. This put U.S. foreign policy more or less at odds with the independence movements, except when those movements could be infiltrated or taken over by pro-U.S. elements. This complex situation meant that the State Department—the locale of foreign policy and diplomatic undertakings—and the military would need the support of an intelligence agency able to gather relevant information and carry out local or multinational actions in furtherance of the newly developing U.S. domination over much of the postwar landscape. In short, as a by-product of the expansionist nature of its capitalist economy, the United States was putting together an empire.

Like David Burgess, who told the CIA to "go to hell," other critics of the U.S. empire have emerged. But unlike Burgess, Chalmers Johnson decided to write a book based in part on his disillusionment with U.S. foreign policy. Johnson served from 1967 to 1973 as a consultant to the Office of National Estimates of the CIA, joining a panel of experts to critique various internal Agency policies and practices in order to develop better estimates of opposition forces and practices. As Johnson puts it, "I slowly realized that at the CIA, the tail wagged the dog, that America's real business was covert activities, not intelligence collecting and analysis."[4] Much of the information about the nature of the U.S. empire that follows here is derived from his experiences and by his detailed and in-depth analysis of imperialism.

Perhaps the ultimate imperialist action is military invasion and occupation. This has been a common feature of U.S. relations with parts of Latin America in particular, where U.S. imperialist processes went on even before the Second World War. Chalmers Johnson notes:

Between 1898 and 1934, the United States sent marines to Cuba four times, Honduras seven times, the Dominican Republic four times, Haiti twice, Guatemala once, Panama twice, Mexico three times, Colombia four times, and Nicaragua five times (where they built bases and maintained an uninterrupted presence for twenty-one years except for a short period in 1925).[5]

Military Bases. One key component of any empire is its ability to maintain military supremacy anywhere in the empire on short notice. The basic structure of the U.S. empire has been a network of military bases like no other in world history. Across the Cold War period, from about 1945 through 1992, the United States maintained about 1,700 military installations in about one hundred countries around the world.[6]

Military and Civilian Personnel. As of September 2001, the United States was deploying 254,788 military personnel in 153 countries. With civilians and dependents included, the number doubles to 531,227.[7]

Training. In 1958 alone, in the midst of the EMS ministry, the United States trained 504,000 police officers in twenty-five nations. More recently, approximately seven thousand Special Forces were involved in the training of the military forces of ten countries.[8]

The CIA and Covert Actions

The most controversial of CIA activities are its covert actions. Over the eight years of the Eisenhower administration—during the period in which the CPI won the state assembly elections in Kerala (1957) and its Kerala ministry was dismissed by the central Indian government (1959)—the CIA carried out 170 major covert actions in forty-eight countries.[9] President Kennedy approved another 163 covert actions during his three years in office, from 1961 through 1963.[10] What are covert actions? According to the *Consumer's Guide to Intelligence,* they are operations "designed to influence governments, events, organizations, or persons in support of foreign policy in a manner that is not necessarily attributable to the sponsoring power. It may include political, economic, propaganda, or paramilitary activities."[11]

The Official View. The original five duties listed for the CIA in the 1947 National Security Act give little indication of the expansive roles the Agency could play on the world stage:

1. To advise the National Security Council in matters concerning such intelligence activities of the government departments and agencies as relate to national security;
2. To make recommendations to the National Security Council for the coordination of such intelligence activities;
3. To correlate and evaluate intelligence relating to the national security, and provide for the appropriate dissemination of such intelligence within the government . . . provided that the Agency shall have no police, subpoena, law-enforcement powers, or internal security functions;
4. To perform, for the benefit of the existing intelligence agencies, such additional services of common concern as the National Security Council determines can be more efficiently accomplished centrally;
5. To perform such other functions and duties related to intelligence affecting the national security as the National Security Council may from time to time direct.[12]

Function number 5, under the National Security Council, gave the CIA a green light to undertake covert actions. In the CIA's more recent mission statement, this authority is more clearly spelled out and is vested in the president.

The CIA, as of February 2023 lists its mission as:

- Collecting foreign intelligence that matters;
- Producing objective all-source analysis;
- Conducting effective covert action as directed by the president;
- Safeguarding the secrets that help keep our Nation safe.[13]

Controlling What's Covert

After several decades of (sometimes damaging) exposés, the Agency has presumably accepted that covert actions are a big part of its mission.

Concern over the possible side effects of covert actions emerged at the very beginning of the CIA. The earliest discussions within the Truman administration focused on how to manage the contradiction between the need for secrecy and the need for some form of control and accountability over the Agency's actions. At one point, a "Special Procedures Group" was established;[14] at another time, a "Special Group" was set up;[15] at yet another, an "Office of Policy Coordination" seems to have managed the covert actions.[16] Eventually the problem was solved by giving the CIA director near total power over Agency practices, budgets, and outcomes assessment. The CIA director was to be "guided," but not controlled, by the Joint Chiefs of Staff and, eventually, the National Security Council, made up of the president, secretary of state, secretary of defense, and a small group varying somewhat by administration and presidential preferences.

After its creation in 1947. the Agency grew quickly. Between 1949 and 1952, it went from 302 to 2,812 personnel (plus 3,342 overseas contract employees). Overseas CIA stations rose from seven to forty-seven.[17] The free rein of the director, however, led to questions about the limits to the Agency. The growing scale and unrestrained nature of covert actions led some to question the need for a large-scale, uncontrolled operation that was leading to countenancing "even the most unsavory of activities."[18]

An example of the concerns comes from the eminent U.S. diplomat George Kennan, who stated to the Church Committee in 1975, during its lengthy investigation and hearings into abuses committed by the U.S. intelligence services:

> Clearly, in recommending the development of a covert action capability in 1948, policy-makers intended to make available a

small contingency force that could mount operations on a limited basis. Senior officials did not plan to develop large scale continuing covert operations. Instead, they hoped to establish a small capability that could be activated at their discretion.[19]

COVERT ACTION PLAYBOOK: HOW THE CIA FUNCTIONS

Over the decades, several egregious cases of CIA covert action have been exposed. Based on a comparative analysis of many of these cases, authors Noam Chomsky and Edward Herman in their book, *The Washington Connection and Third World Fascism—The Politial Economy of Human Rights,* identified seven typical functions of a CIA operation:

1. Outright murder of political leaders like Lumumba [in the Congo] to be replaced by the more amenable Mobutu;[20]
2. Direct conspiracies with terrorists, mercenaries or military factions within a country, such as in Guatemala or Indonesia;
3. Political bribery—almost always a component of an operation;
4. Propaganda—sometimes through ownership or purchase of local newspapers or financing of fake opposition newspapers to discredit opponents such as in Brazil;
5. Organizing and/or funding of street demonstrations such as in Iran;[21]
6. Infiltrating of prodemocracy groups to sow confusion; and
7. Collecting information—always useful.

Expanding the details of the Chomsky and Herman analysis, historian Vijay Prashad[22] has developed a nine-step "manual" or playbook of actions typically followed by CIA operatives in carrying out covert actions—usually to topple a government and replace it with a more U.S.-friendly leadership, usually a dictatorship:
Step 1: "A coup has to be first prepared in public opinion."[23] This work may involve lobbying, placing articles in the press and other actions.

Step 2: Appoint the right person on the ground. This refers to the more high-level skilled operatives who should be put in charge of the planning and execution of the coup.

Step 3: Make sure the generals are ready. Most effective coups are carried out by top military leaders. These potential leaders are often trained and cultivated well in advance of their coup actions and indicate the connection between CIA operations and the many other features of the U.S. empire.

Step 4: Create economic chaos. A collapsing economy is a basic condition for regime change.

Step 5: Isolate the opposition/victims diplomatically. The wide network of U.S. allies and treaty partners makes this a logical step to take as economic instability sets in.

Step 6: Organize mass protests. Street protests can often lead to violence.

Step 7: The green light: plan for a moment when a signal can be given to move to the main goal of the action.

Step 8: Assassination: in a 19-page document from 1953, found among about 1,400 CIA documents that were released in 1997 under a Freedom of Information Act suit, there appeared a "manual" for assassinations, including lists of 58 Guatemalans to be subjected to "executive action"—that is, murdered—and 74 persons to be arrested or sent into exile (actual names deleted but the number and a blank space left in the released version). Most of the rest of the document lists and evaluates various means of killing such as gunshots, blunt instruments, etc., but also notes that "assassination can seldom be employed with a clear conscience. Persons who are morally squeamish should not attempt it," and "no assassination instructions should ever be written or recorded." Also: "The assassin needs the usual qualities of a clandestine agent."[24]

Step 9: Deny. An essential feature of covert actions is to keep them secret as long as possible. On conclusion of an operation, and in its aftermath denial should continue.

Along with a set of procedures as set forth by Prashad, the agents of the empire must recruit and train committed cadres. In keeping with the emotional and psychological needs of an empire, these cadres must hold their subjects in contempt, as David Burgess discovered during his five years at the U.S. Embassy in New Delhi.

Shortly after the 1959 dismissal of the EMS ministry, the CIA added a new office in Chennai (Madras), staffed by an agent named Duane "Dewey" Clarridge. In his book, *A Spy For All Seasons: My Life in the CIA*, Clarridge describes the Agency's "overarching objective . . . to keep India out of the Soviets' imperial clutches, whether the Indians liked it or not."[25] Most agents probably do not question their missions. They are self-selected not to. Yet a few became whistleblowers, speaking out against what they saw as immoral or counterproductive actions of the CIA and its parallel organizations in the U.S. military and foreign policy bodies.

The CIA and the Indian Intelligence Bureau: Covert Cooperation

The CIA was established pretty much in tandem with India's own Intelligence Bureau (IB). The CIA brought together a Second World War intelligence and sabotage unit, called the Office of Strategic Services (OSS) with various other U.S. civilian and military intelligence groups, theoretically to streamline and make more effective the use of intelligence and covert operations that had been developed as part of the U.S. contribution to the Allied war effort.

In South Asia, the OSS operated as part of the China-Burma-India (CBI) war theater, set up to undermine Imperial Japan's military expansion and to supply anti-Japanese forces in China to tie down Japanese troops and eventually launch invasions to recapture occupied territory in South and Southeast Asia. Up to 200,000 U.S. troops overall were deployed in the CBI theater between 1942 and 1946.[26] The first intelligence unit to be active came from the U.S. Army's G-2 unit. This unit had a rocky relationship with British intelligence. In April 1942, the famed OSS Detachment 101 was established; its headquarters in New Delhi was set up in 1943.[27]

Mahatma Gandhi had launched the "Quit India" campaign during this same period,[28] and OSS relations between the British MI6 and other British and non-British units were complicated by the sympathy of many U.S. personnel for the Indian Independence Movement. The OSS also had problems with Chiang Kai-shek, whose forces were ostensibly the main beneficiaries of the logistic work being done in India.[29] Gradually, the OSS began collecting intelligence not only on the British and the Chinese but on Indians as well.[30]

As the Second World War wound down, the alliance among the United States, Britain, and the Soviet Union frayed, and the Cold War began. The Chinese Communist Revolution of 1949, the establishment of Communist governments in Eastern Europe, and the success of several Western European Communist parties in mobilizing large-scale leftist political actions frightened the ruling classes of the capitalist nations. Anticommunist fears were pronounced in the United States, where they were further stoked by the media.

In 1947 India became independent and in that same year the OSS was superseded by the CIA as the chief international intelligence organization of the United States. Both the CIA and the British MI6 moved to establish relationships with the Indian Intelligence Bureau. In 1949 the Bureau's first Indian director, Tirupattur Gangadharam Sanjevi, a former district superintendent of police from Madras (Chennai today), traveled to the United States for three weeks of talks with representatives from the CIA, the Federal Bureau of Investigation (FBI), and the U.S. State Department.[31] One outcome of this visit was an agreement to establish "an official liaison on communist matters."[32] From this point on, the Indian IB appears to have worked as an effective partner with the CIA. In this capacity, the IB chose to look the other way when CIA aircraft flew through Indian airspace to support Tibetan resistance activities against Communist China. The IB also acquiesced in the CIA's setting up smaller stations at consulates in Bombay, Calcutta, and Madras.[33] By the 1960s, as summarized by diplomatic historian Paul McGarr:

One U.S. diplomat who served in the U.S. Embassy in New Delhi throughout the first half of the sixties, later attested that the Agency's presence in India at that time was "very large and very invasive . . . the CIA was deeply involved in the Indian Government."[34]

The IB probably looked the other way, too, while someone took over from David Burgess in 1959 and delivered the bribe money he had refused to touch.

Outline for Cold War Action: Document NSC-68 and the Doolittle Report

On April 7, 1950, the U. S. Department of State's Policy Planning Staff completed a TOP SECRET 58-page report titled "United States Objectives and Programs for National Security." The report was drafted under the leadership of Paul Nitze, a high-ranking State Department officer.[35] Nitze served as U.S. deputy secretary of defense, U.S. secretary of the navy, and director of policy planning for the U.S. State Department in the early years of the Cold War. According to the State Department's Office of the Historian, which provides declassified documents to the public about U.S. foreign policy, document NSC-68 "is among the most influential documents composed by the U. S. Government during the Cold War, and was not declassified until 1975."[36] The report argued that the Soviet Union was on track to equal U.S. military strength within a few years, and the authors proposed a massive buildup of U.S. weapons, both conventional and nuclear. The aggressive policies of the United States in the early Cold War period resulted in part from this report.

Concerned about the possibility that the CIA was operating beyond its boundaries, in June 1954 President Eisenhower commissioned General Jimmy Doolittle and the millionaire William Pawley to assess the CIA's capacity for covert action. Although the report was buried by then CIA director Allen Dulles, and wouldn't be fully declassified until 2001, its contents shocked some of the public when revealed around 1975. With a grim characterization of the Communist threat as a background, the authors set forth "principles" on which the Cold War would be fought by covert actions:

> It is now clear that we are facing an implacable enemy whose avowed objective is world domination by whatever means and at whatever cost. There are no rules in such a game. Hitherto acceptable norms of human conduct do not apply. If the United States is to survive, long-standing American concepts of "fair play" must be reconsidered. We must develop effective espionage and counterespionage services and must learn to subvert, sabotage and destroy our enemies by more clever, more sophisticated and more effective methods than those used against us. It may become necessary that the American people be made acquainted with, understand and support this fundamentally repugnant philosophy.[37]

Whether this was the best approach to protecting the United States can be debated, but it is likely the CIA had already absorbed Doolittle and Pawley's "repugnant philosophy." The 1950s and 1960s were a heyday for the CIA in expanding U.S. influence and control across the globe—that is, in maintaining and manipulating its empire. Through violence, trickery, and dictatorship—mixed with luck in some cases—the CIA blocked the efforts of reformers, nationalists, neutralists, and democrats, creating a world of intrigue and exploitation that lingers today. Six miniature case studies illustrate how this happened.

The CIA Versus Democracy: Six Brief Vignettes

Among dozens of CIA covert actions to topple existing governments, we have chosen six case studies of Guyana, Guatemala, Iran, Congo, Brazil, and Indonesia-East Timor. All these cases involve the undermining or destruction of democratically elected governments. They were contemporaneous with the CIA's Kerala intervention. All of them involved covert actions. All of them involved major acts of violence. All of them left behind scars that have yet to heal. And importantly, all of them have been points of reference in communist and anticommunist propaganda in Kerala. The Guyana and Guatemala coups were discussed with reference to the anticommunist agitation of 1957–1959 in Kerala. It is for this reason that we have chosen to discuss these two cases more elaborately.

GUYANA, 1951–1965
Cheddi and Janet Jagan and the People's Progressive Party

The nation of Guyana (formerly British Guiana, independent since 1966), on the northeast coast of South America, is a country of 89,500 square miles, with a population, in 2020, of 787,000. Only about 4 percent of the land, mostly along the coast, is arable, while the rest is dense forests and swamps.[38] Sugar and rice have been the main crops, along with mining of bauxite (for aluminum) and gold. Canadian firms control the sugar mills and the mines.

Historically, the population has consisted mostly of descendants of enslaved Africans or indentured laborers from India. The Chinese controlled the petty trade, while a small Portuguese-British white population owned factories and worked in senior bureaucracy and management. Native Americans lived in the forests. *A History of the Guyanese Working People 1881–1905*, by Walter Rodney, a Guyanese historian and revolutionary who was assassinated in 1980, is considered a classic in the chronicling of the working class in the Third World.

Cheddi Jagan was the son of an immigrant sugar plantation family from India who scraped their resources together to send their son to study in the United States. In 1943 Cheddi Jagan returned to British Guiana with his U.S. wife, Janet Rosenberg, a leftist activist whom he had met at dental school. While in the

U.S., Jagan had read progressive materials and became a strong supporter of British Guiana independence, as well as of progressive social reforms. In 1950 Cheddi Jagan, along with his wife and friends and contacts made on their initial stay in Georgetown, founded the People's Progressive Party. The PPP quickly absorbed other groups, such as the League of Colored People, led by Afro-Guyanese activist Forbes Burnham. With a Chinese vice president and Jagan's American wife as the editor of the influential mouthpiece of the PPP, *Thunder,* the party was, from its birth, a multiracial rainbow coalition.[39]

The 1953 Election and Winston Churchill's Coup

In British Guiana's 1953 elections, the PPP won a majority of the vote and eighteen of the twenty-five constituencies. The campaign was peaceful, and 73 percent of the voting population turned out.

The PPP began its term in office by repealing the Undesirable Publications Act and by allowing West Indian labor and political leaders to visit British Guiana. The PPP amended the Rice Farmers Tenure Act to compel landlords to maintain the water infrastructure and shift responsibility from the tenant to the landlord. However, the Governor's State Council, an appointed body, nullified both PPP acts.[40]

The first PPP ministry thus had to deal with the fact that it held little real political power. Even so, according to Cheddi Jagan's account of his career in *The West on Trial: The Fight for Guyana's Freedom,*[41] the first Jagan PPP ministry, which held office for 133 days, managed to set or propose policies to

> bring all schools under the supervision of government and local education committees; to reform local government so that on this level, too, there would be universal adult suffrage without property limitations; to appoint working people to government boards and committees; to revise the fees of government medical officers in order to make medical care possible for the poor;

to curtail unnecessary expenditure of public funds; to provide more scholarships, to bring about social security and workmen's compensation; to improve drainage and irrigation; to make available and usable large tracts of land then uncultivated; and to review and act on the recommendations of the Central Housing and Planning Authority. Increased [pay] rates were prescribed for certain categories of workers, primarily the sawmill workers, employees in cinemas and hire-car chauffeurs. An eight-hour day was approved for factory watchmen. And the Minister of Labour prescribed a $13 weekly minimum wage for employees at drug, hardware, grocery and dry goods stores.[42]

These modest reforms and initiatives are reminiscent of the actions of the EMS ministry in Kerala and those of Jacobo Arbenz in Guatemala. But, as in those places, even modest reforms were seen by the imperial rulers and the most hysterical of the local right-wing forces as flooding the country with communism.

A particular parallel presented itself with school policy. Despite the multicultural and multireligious nature of the British Guianan population, most British Guianan schools were run by Anglican, Catholic, and other Christian churches—even though the government paid their salaries. The churches opposed the secularization of education and the progressive agenda overall.

In another parallel with Kerala and with Guatemala, a key element of the PPP program was tenancy and land reform. In 1953 the PPP put forth the Rice Farmers Security of Tenure Ordinance, which would authorize the District Commissioner to announce particular times for weed removal and other irrigation canal maintenance. If the landlord failed to carry out these responsibilities, the government would then assign the work to farmers and charge the landlord. The bill also fixed rents for tenancy. Another bill was designed to protect sugarcane workers by promoting union rights on the fields. According to historian Stephen Rabe:

> Winston Churchill, who became the British Prime Minister in

1953, did not like the outcome of the elections in British Guiana. "On 9 October 1953, upon instructions from London, Governor Savage suspended the Constitution and took full control of the colony. British troops who had been stationed on warships, had already landed in British Guiana. The PPP had held power for 133 days."[43]

CIA director Allen Dulles was in a congratulatory mood when he briefed President Eisenhower and the U.S. National Security Council on the British actions, noting the strategic importance of British Guiana's bauxite reserves. As with some in the British colonial office, Dulles pointed to the supposed dangers posed by Janet Jagan, "an American-born Communist," married to "the head of the People's Progressive Party."[44]

The 1957 Election and Overthrow through Agitation

Prime Minister Churchill overruled his own cabinet to order British troops to remain in the colony despite the lack of evidence of any security threat posed by the PPP, and even though the colony "remained calm after the suspension of the constitution."[45] Returning from a visit to India, Jagan and Forbes Burnham, another leader of the PPP, were both imprisoned for several months for breaking a local travel ban.[46]

More ominously, U.S. labor agents, connected with the CIA, began infiltrating Guiana's trade unions. AFL-CIO agent (and former Communist) Jay Lovestone and AFL-CIO Latin America representative Serafina Romualdi began supplying several Guiana union leaders with cash and equipment, bringing some leaders to the United States for training.[47] U.S. agents also began to support Forbes Burnham, who was of African ancestry, whose grandparents arrived in the country from India as indentured immigrants, when he broke with Cheddi Jagan. This set up a process by which political parties and labor unions became identified along racial and ethnic lines, a phenomenon that bedeviled the nation for decades.

In response to growing international pressure, the British announced new elections in British Guiana for August 1957. The PPP had split, with Forbes Burnham creating a separate party. Even so, the Jagan wing won nine of the fourteen seats available for election. Burnham's wing won only three seats. In a conciliatory mood, the British colonial governor invited Jagan to form a ministry.

Although the agenda of the new government was even more modest than an earlier one in 1951, the World Bank and Western powers were less than cooperative. Frustrated by the delays, Cheddi Jagan began to talk of approaching the socialist countries for aid.[48] In March 1961, the CIA issued its first "Special National Intelligence Estimate" on British Guiana.[49] Updated April 11, 1962, it claimed, "We believe . . . that Jagan is a Communist, though the degree of Moscow's control is not yet clear."

1961 Election and Another Victory for the PPP

The August 1961 election was won by Jagan and the PPP, but with a slightly lower majority than previously. Even so, the PPP won twenty out of thirty-five seats. Meanwhile, the CIA became extensively involved in toppling the new government and preventing Britain from transferring any power to it.

The United States openly promoted Burnham and financed him. Burnham's attempts to consolidate his position by appealing to racial identity fanned social tensions. In February 1962, a weeklong general strike against Jagan's government culminated in a riot and fire that destroyed much of downtown Georgetown.[50] Racial tensions rose across British Guiana.

From April to July 1963, an eighty-day general strike was organized.[51] This strike had major CIA involvement: The *New York Times* reported on CIA and U.S. labor union collusion to oust

Jagan. A strike support fund organized by the U.S. AFL-CIO union federation funneled $1 million to feed fifty thousand people. U.S. labor leader George Meany deposited the funds through the Royal Bank of Canada.[52]

Unlike in Kerala, where the Catholic Chrch was powerful, Protestant and evangelical churches were dominant in Guiana, and these churches were deeply involved in the creation of mass mobilizations and mass hysteria. The CIA financed Harvest Evangelism and the Christian Anti-Communist Crusade (CACC). Screening of anticommunist films was an important propaganda activity that the CACC claimed. The fact that Christian believers were mostly of African origin widened the racial rift. A new radio station broadcasting *Voice of Labor* was started. A newspaper, *Labor Advocate*, was launched. The Christian evangelists proved to be most effective propagandists.

The economy was in tatters. Following the direction of a UN-sponsored adviser, certain financial measures were adopted that triggered big protests. This was interpreted as a move against African Guyanese who constituted a majority of the government employees. The reforms had to be withdrawn.

Ninety percent of the police were of African origin, and the government's control over them steadily declined. Two hundred persons died in the riots, thirteen thousand became refugees. There were 265 cases of arson and 665 cases of police firing.

On May 23, 1963, during the strike, U.S. president Kennedy ordered the National Security Council-CIA "Special Group," normally used for covert actions, to consider action to remove Jagan.[53] And Jagan had to agree to an early election before Guiana would be given independence. Realizing the PPP would again win the majority if free and fair elections were held, the CIA decided to rig the election.

The 1964 Rigged Election and Defeat of the PPP

The British, under strong U.S. pressure, switched the voting system in British Guiana from geographical constituencies to proportional representation—specifically designed to engineer a PPP defeat. The plan to set up a voting system that would facilitate a PPP defeat had been broached as early as July 12, 1962, in a memo from Secretary of State Dean Rusk to President Kennedy, which included "a plan for the CIA to manipulate the election."[54] The minutes of this recorded meeting remain classified.[55] The list of voters—especially expatriate voters—was falsified.

On May 26, 1966, British Guiana, under Prime Minister Forbes Burnham, was given independence by Britain. There followed twenty-plus years of authoritarian control and rigged elections, along with major corruption and mismanagement of the economy. The next fair election was not until 1992, after Burnham's death and the fall of the Soviet Union. Cheddi Jagan and the PPP were voted into power once again.

Arthur Schlesinger, Harvard historian, public intellectual, and advisor to President Kennedy, not only witnessed but, to an extent, also supported CIA operations in Guyana. At a luncheon seminar in 1990 with editors at *The Nation* magazine, Schlesinger apologized to Cheddi Jagan. In the words of *The Nation* editor, Victor Navasky:

> [Schlesinger] had to leave but before he did, he had something he wanted to say. And he proceeded to apologize to Jagan for what he called "a great injustice he and his Kennedy colleagues had helped to perpetrate."[56] "I felt badly about my role thirty years ago . . . I think a great injustice was done to Cheddi Jagan."[57]

And to the people of Guyana, we might add.

GUATEMALA, 1953–1954
Transition to Democracy and the Arévalo Government

The 1954 overthrow of the democratic government of Guatemalan President Jacobo Arbenz became the model proposed by the Church in Kerala for anticommunist agitation. Although a military invasion from outside to oust a popular, elected president, as in Guatemala's case, was irrelevant in Kerala, anticommunist hysteria was still a major factor in the Guatemala operation, along with a large dose of psychological warfare. The communist "threat" in Guatemala consisted primarily of four parliamentary seats held by the Communist Party, out of fifty-one seats in Arbenz's coalition.[58]

The democratic turn in Guatemala had begun in 1944 when the cruel thirteen-year dictatorship of Jorge Ubico was ended by a popular pro-democracy movement led by university students and labor organizations. In 1945 the first democratic election was held and Juan José Arévalo became president. Arévalo had been an intellectual educationist and a political refugee for a few years in Argentina. He was a liberal democrat but believed in the strong intervention of government for economic development. He did not accept Marxism and class struggle and described himself as "a spiritual socialist."

A new constitution was promulgated, guaranteeing universal voting rights (except for illiterate women), freedom of opinion and the media, and an independent legislature, executive branch, and judiciary—all totally novel for Latin America. What annoyed the United States was Arévalo's foreign policy. He broke diplomatic relations with Franco's Spain, supported the Caribbean Legion, opposed Nicaragua's dictator Somoza, and resurrected Simón Bolívar's ideal of a confederation of Latin American countries.

The actual big issue in the country was land ownership

inequality, with 2.2 percent of owners holding 70 percent of the land.⁵⁹ Thousands of unplanted acres were also held by the United Fruit Company, which owned Guatemala's rail lines, telephone services, and most of the infrastructure. Five percent of wastelands or uncultivated latifundios were to be compulsorily leased to farmers. Arévalo's most revolutionary reform was the labor law passed in 1947. Bonded labor, which drastically reduced the power of employers to dismiss workers, was abolished and collective bargaining and minimum wages were guaranteed. But the biggest impact was in the health and education sectors. The health budget increased 155 percent between 1945 and 1955. New pedagogic methods were employed, literacy improved, and the death rate came down.

Then Arévalo did something that was never done in Latin America. He retired after six years and held a free and fair election, which was won by one of his trusted followers, Jacobo Arbenz. The thirty-seven-year-old Arbenz became the youngest of the Latin American presidents. He advanced every one of Arévalo's policies vigorously. An important departure was the emphasis on Guatemala's independent economic growth.

The Arbenz Government and the United Fruit Company

Arbenz signed a law distributing thousands of acres to 100,000 low-income peasants. He also improved union rights, built a hydroelectric plant to provide low-cost electricity, and carried out other social reforms in the period of 1953 to 1954. United Fruit demanded a payment of $16 million for the vast holdings that Arbenz had expropriated, but Arbenz offered only $525,000—the amount the company itself had valued its land for tax purposes.⁶⁰ Arbenz also attempted to raise state resources by taxing large companies and the rich.

A notable aspect of the Guatemalan case is the ties between CIA actors working to overthrow this Third World nation and the immediate benefits they accrued.⁶¹ At the time of the coup, Allen

Dulles was the CIA director and a past director and board member of the United Fruit Company. His brother, Secretary of State John Foster Dulles, had drafted the original agreements between Guatemala and United Fruit.⁶² Both brothers had been members of the Sullivan and Cromwell law firm that represented United Fruit, going all the way back to the First World War. The Assistant Secretary of State for Inter-American affairs was also a UFCO shareholder. Allen and his wife, Clover, loved to visit Guatemala and had decorated their Long Island home with many Guatemalan furnishings.⁶³ Moving down the chain, Ann Whitman, President Eisenhower's personal secretary, was the wife of United Fruit's public relations director.⁶⁴ Undersecretary of State and former CIA director Walter Bedell Smith was seeking an executive position with United Fruit at the same time he was helping to plan the coup. He was later named to the company's board of directors.⁶⁵

Stephen Schlesinger and Stephen Kinzer's book, *Bitter Fruit: The Untold Story of the American Coup in Guatemala*, focuses on the role of the United Fruit Company in overthrowing the Arbenz government. Richard H. Immerman's *The CIA in Guatemala: The Foreign Policy of Intervention* adopts a larger vision, locating the toppling of the Guatemalan government within the context of Truman's and Eisenhower's foreign policy.

Starting in 1953, the CIA set up an operations center in Opa-locka, Florida, on the outskirts of Miami. In Nicaragua, dictator Anastasio Somoza lent the United States a camp with an airstrip, where the CIA gathered a mercenary army. Guatemalan military officers were bribed. Arbenz himself was offered a large bribe but rejected it. United Fruit joined in producing propaganda materials from its publicity office.⁶⁶

On June 18, 1954, the CIA-formed military in Honduras opened an attack on Guatemala. After a rocky start, the combination of military force and disinformation pried loose enough of the Guatemalan military to switch sides, allowing the CIA to replace Arbenz and impose a puppet ruler. Arbenz went into exile in several countries and died in Mexico City in 1971.

Psychological Warfare and Mass Hysteria

It remains a puzzle how the popular government of Arbenz, with its people's development agenda, could have been so easily overthrown by a motley army put together outside Guatemala. Arbenz was experienced in putting down coup attempts—in 1953 he had suppressed a coup. In all, there had been twenty-five small and big coup attempts during Arévalo's presidency. Guatemala's new dictator, Carlos Castillo Armas, had in fact been a refugee in Honduras after his failed coup attempt against Arévalo. It is this background that makes the fall of Arbenz government without fierce resistance a puzzle.

The answer to the puzzle may be the CIA's adoption of psychological warfare tactics. Given the importance of government propaganda and psychology in the crusade against communism, a special board had been created under the U.S. National Security Council (NSC). Guatemala was one of its first experiments.

The U.S. government's most important propaganda instrument was the media. Previously, Arévalo's constitution had banned all political parties with foreign connections, which included the Communist Party. But Arbenz had removed the ban and, though Communists were a small minority, it became easy to brand Arbenz's coalition as Communist. So newspapers unleashed stories about Communist infiltration, Communists causing breakdown of the economy and cruelties of the police. Pamphlets were dropped from airplanes. Anti-Arbenz films were made and shown everywhere. The CIA also purchased space in newspapers across Latin America, ruthlessly attacking the Arbenz government as a Communist threat.

Since most of the Guatemalan people were illiterate, the CIA set up a radio station, the Voice of Liberation, in Miami, creating the impression that the station was operating from Guatemala. Effective propaganda, interspersed with music and humor, was characteristic of the CIA's radio station. Once the invasion started, other radio stations were jammed, and even Arbenz's soldiers were forced to listen to the CIA's station.

The Catholic Church was also a willing collaborator, preaching anti-Arbenz pastoral letters at services where Communist "devils" were denounced. Special anticommunist services were held and there were religious processions against the government. Rumors were spread that the Catholic bishop was going to be arrested, inciting the faithful to violent protest. Students were also mobilized.

Other novel propaganda techniques to create terror and fear were deployed. Number 32, the Arévalo constitutional clause that prohibited the Communist Party, was widely used in graffiti. Death threats were sent to Arbenz supporters. Empty coffins were hung in front of houses, with such messages as "Here Hides a Communist."

Once the U.S.-sponsored rebel army crossed into Guatemala, the radio broadcasts became hysterical, effectively announcing that American Marines would not hesitate to land in support of the insurrection. The capital, Guatemala City, was bombed, electricity was cut, and at night explosives were ignited. A section of the invading military then moved to neutrality, wanting to avoid bloodshed, which created an opening for Arbenz's abdication without a battle.

The new president, Carlos Castillo Armas, immediately launched a terror campaign against progressives of all stripes. Thousands were killed or arrested, and Guatemala entered a period of military rule and extreme repression that lasted for the next forty years. Implementation of the Arbenz land reform was reversed, and the banana workers' union was made illegal.[67] During these decades, 150,000 to 250,000 people were killed by military, police and vigilantes. The economy stagnated. By 2004 Guatemala ranked 120th out of 173 nations on the UN's Human Development Index.[68]

Meanwhile, in 1999, the UN Commission for Historical Clarification, known also as the Truth Commission, presented to the Guatemalan president its report on murders, torture, illegal imprisonment, and other atrocities since the 1954 coup. The report ran to 3,600 pages.[69] The Catholic Church undertook a project, "Recovery of Historical Memory," for giving evidence before the Truth Commission. It was a way for the Church to atone for a historical mistake it had made in 1953 and 1954.

IRAN, 1953

In the mid-twentieth century, Iran was a Middle Eastern country with relatively well functioning democratic traditions and a liberal intelligentsia. In 1951 Mohammad Mosaddegh became the prime minister after winning a majority in the parliament. He was a progressive nationalist and secular. In March 1951, with full support from the elected Iranian legislature (Majlis), Mosaddegh nationalized the Anglo-Iranian Oil Company, based on concerns that the British had been taking an unfair share for many years. In doing so, Mosaddegh offered to guarantee the safety and jobs of British oil workers and set aside 25 percent of profits for compensation; but it was not enough. In response, the British navy undertook a blockade of Iran. Mosaddegh then expelled the British from Iran.[70] Sanctions were imposed on Iran creating severe economic strains.

Cornered, Iran sought the support of the Soviet Union. Iran's Tudeh Party (Communist) extended support to the government. In November 1952, British prime minister Winston Churchill approached the United States for assistance in overthrowing Mosaddegh's democratic and popular ministry. For Allen Dulles, who, as a lawyer, had represented the Anglo-Iranian Oil Company for years, Iran's independent trajectory was a personal affront. Dulles's CIA decided to oust Mosaddegh and install a puppet government under General Shahidi.

As "Operation Ajax" started, numerous agents were sent to Iran and an intense propaganda campaign was launched against Mosaddegh. CIA agents attacked and offended religious leaders, putting the blame on the Tudeh Party. In August 1953, under the leadership of Kermit Roosevelt (a distant cousin of the famous four-term New Deal U.S. president), a fierce tank battle took place in front of Mosaddegh's home. Meanwhile, as a huge procession of the clowns, gymnasts, jugglers, singers, and dancers moved through Tehran, people thronged to have fun. Suddenly, the merriment turned into an anti-Mosaddegh demonstration and riots spread through the city. The combination of street mobs, with support of elements of the army, forced Mosaddegh to surrender, and the United States installed Shah Mohammad Reza Pahlavi as ruler.[71] One year later, Iran signed a new agreement giving back its nationalized oil company.

> Underdeveloped countries with rich resources now have an object lesson in the heavy cost that must be paid by one of their number which goes berserk with fanatical nationalism.[72]

So opined a *New York Times* editorial on the signing of the oil agreement recounted in its regular news pages. In keeping with Cold War hysteria about Communist takeovers, the *Times* went on to state triumphally that "Moscow . . . counted its chickens before they were hatched and thought that Iran would be the next 'People's Democracy.'" Yet little, if any, evidence has ever been produced over the decades to suggest that the Soviet Union played any role in trying to capture the reigns of the Iranian state.[73] Instead, all available evidence indicates that Britain and the United States were behind the machinations that ousted the nationalist and democratically elected administration of Mohammed Mosaddegh. In particular, the CIA played a master role in the affair, as revealed by documents in the U.S. National Security Archive, declassified and published in 2013 by the National Security Archive research institute.[74]

The CIA overthrow of Mosaddegh and the installation of the pro-Western Shah was facilitated by one of the CIA's standard playbooks: Spread around a lot of money to buy a mob; use that mob to terrorize opponents; insert new dictator. In Teheran, local crime syndicates played this role.

In 1957, after consolidating control—with guidance from the CIA—the Shah's new administration organized an internal secret police force, the SAVAK, which created an Iranian regime, described in a 1976 Amnesty International report as having "the highest rate of death penalties in the world, no valid system of civilian courts, and a history of torture which is beyond belief. No country in the world has a worse record in human rights than Iran."[75]

In 1958 Kermit Roosevelt left the CIA and went to work for Gulf Oil, a member of the consortium that included the Anglo-Iranian Oil Company.[76]

INDONESIA, 1958–1965; EAST TIMOR, 1975–1978

With enormous natural wealth and the world's fourth-largest population, Indonesia was bound to claim the attention of the U.S. empire. The 1950s, however, witnessed a rapid rise in the democratic election results of the Indonesian Communist Party (PKI). Winning 16 percent of the popular vote in the 1955 national elections, the PKI increased its share in the 1957 local elections to gain first place in Central Java, in the provincial capital city of Jakarta, and with a significant majority in the historic Central Javanese city of Jogjakarta. Winning control of many regional councils, the PKI was also able to appoint Communists as mayors of several cities.

However, the CIA, with hardly a moment's hesitation, helped to organize a Guatemala-style military rebellion in Indonesia's "outer islands." A safe launching base was set up at Manado, on the island of Sulawesi (then known as Celebes), near the southernmost area of the Philippines, from which the rebels could garner supplies from the giant U.S. Clark Airfield.[77] The role of the CIA in the rebellion was revealed on May 18, 1958, when one of its pilots, Allen Pope, flying a U.S. B-26 bomber, was shot down by Indonesian forces on Ambon in the Moluccas (Spice Islands) and captured with incriminating documents. Pope had previously flown supplies for the French air force at Dien Bien Phu in Vietnam.[78]

At first, the U.S. ambassador publicly dismissed Pope as a "soldier of fortune." It might have been plausible that Pope was flying for an internal opposition government set up in Sumatra a couple of months before. But he had carried a diary listing his several bombing runs and other information establishing him as an employee of a CIA-owned airline. Against orders, he had smuggled these documents onto his plane to have bargaining power in case of capture.[79] After Pope's trial and conviction he was eventually freed on the personal request of Attorney General Robert Kennedy.[80] The outer island rebellion was crushed, but the United States was not finished interfering in Indonesian politics.

The Indonesian Coup and Massacre, 1965–1966

On October 1, 1965, then Colonel Suharto led a military coup against a supposed Communist takeover attempt that included the murder of six generals of the Indonesian high command. Although the coup was explained to people, both inside Indonesia and abroad, as a defense of the existing government, it soon became clear that a massive restructuring of Indonesian political life was occurring. Within weeks of the coup, Suharto had been promoted to general and took effective control of the armed forces. Even President Sukarno, still popular, became powerless to stop Suharto's plans.

Suharto's plans were simple and extreme. All left-wing newspapers were banned. Offices of left-wing political parties were sacked. Leaders of left-wing parties were arrested. Then army units began fanning out across the island of Java—and eventually the entire country—arresting, executing without trial or charges, arming right-wing organizations that joined in the executions of farmworkers, small farm owners, teachers, artists, students, ethnic Chinese, anyone associated with the left or with the PKI, even though membership in the PKI had been perfectly legal up to that point. By mid-1966 Suharto had consolidated his hold on the country's politics.

Labor unions were banned or brought under strict military

control, and elected union leaders either ousted or killed in the enormous bloodbath that the army leadership organized. Peasant organizations that had pressed for land reform were effectively destroyed, and virtually all organizations or individuals advocating social reform or control over U.S.-based multinational corporations were put out of action. In all, 150,000 to one million persons were murdered, and for decades the ensuing Indonesian military dictatorship held around a hundred thousand or more political prisoners at camps across the giant island chain.[81]

The U.S. Role

In high U.S. circles, the savagery of the Indonesian military massacres elicited celebration more than opprobrium. On June 19, 1966, the liberal *New York Times* columnist James Reston wrote a piece titled "A Gleam of Light in Asia" to characterize the "savage transformation of Indonesia from a pro-Chinese policy under Sukarno to a defiantly anti-Communist policy under General Suharto." Reston went on:

> Washington is being careful not to claim any credit for this change... but this does not mean that Washington had nothing to do with it... There was a great deal more contact between the anti-Communist forces in that country and at least one very high official in Washington before and during the Indonesian massacre than is generally realized.
>
> General Suharto's forces, at times severely short of food and munitions, have been getting aid from here through various third countries.[82]

Substantial additional information suggests that U.S. operatives—mostly CIA agents—assisted directly by providing lists of names of persons to be killed.[83] It also appears that "Managers of US-owned plantations furnished ... the names of 'troublesome' communists and union organizers who were then murdered."[84]

In 1981, Ralph McGehee,[85] a self-identified twenty-five-year CIA veteran, reported that in Indonesia, The Agency was extremely proud of its successful [one word deleted] and recommended it as a model for future operations [half sentence deleted]. In 1968 the CIA had "concocted a false account" of the Indonesian operation, under the title *Indonesia—1965: The Coup That Backfired*. This 356-page document is available to the public in the CIA online reading room (a link is in our Bibliography). An interesting side issue in the Indonesian case was the emergence of a new theory of economic development, emphasizing the direct role of the military in generating innovative investment and modernized practices within the economy. While one can doubt the actual success of this policy—for some it seemed like an invitation to higher levels of corruption and mismanagement—it has been labeled by at least one analyst as "Economists with Guns."[86]

East Timor, 1975–1978. One consequence of the Indonesian massacres was the international realignment of Indonesia from a nonaligned and somewhat anti-imperialist position to the position of a U.S. regional ally and subordinate enforcer. The massacres also consolidated a hysterical anticommunism that impacted the nation's entire foreign policy. This led General Suharto, in 1975, to use his powerful military against the tiny nation of East Timor in the eastern Sunda (Spice) Islands. Following the collapse of the Portuguese empire in 1974, East Timor, with a population of about 650,000, declared its independence.

But on December 7, 1975, Indonesian forces launched a massive attack on the tiny nation. In 1978, after three years of fighting, Indonesia received U.S. military aid sufficient to allow it to undertake airborne military attacks against guerilla bases held in the mountain areas by FRETILIN, the East Timor liberation movement.[87] Indonesia's ability to burn crops by aerial bombing led to a massive famine and the likely deaths of tens of thousands of East Timorese. Some estimates put the death toll at two hundred thousand to three hundred thousand.[88]

Finally, in 1998 General Suharto was forced to resign, and in 1999 the East Timorese voted overwhelmingly for independence and the removal of Indonesian troops. Today the independent nation struggles to develop its resources and build meaningful lives for its people. USAID provides assistance to farmers and has helped expand quarantine and intensive-care facilities in recent years.[89]

THE CONGO, 1961–1964

> But we who have been chosen to govern our beloved country by the vote of your elected representatives, we whose bodies and souls have suffered from colonialist oppression, loudly proclaim: All this is over and done with now.
>
> The Republic of the Congo has been proclaimed and our country is now in the hands of its own children.
>
> We are going to begin another struggle together, my brothers, my sisters, a sublime struggle that will bring our country peace, prosperity, and grandeur.[90]

So spoke Congo prime minister Patrice Lumumba on June 30, 1960, at the formal Independence Day ceremony at the Palais de la Nation in Léopoldville (modern-day Kinshasa). Lumumba's speech included a long denunciation of Congo's sufferings, discrimination, oppression, and looting under Belgian colonial rule. But his focus was on the future: that all Congolese people enjoy "to the fullest all the fundamental freedoms laid down in the Declaration of the Rights of Man . . . do away with any and every sort of discrimination . . . bring peace to the country."

Lumumba's brilliant and hopeful speech may have been premature. The Congo he and his fellow nationalists inherited was only tenuously "in the hands of its own children." Of Congo's one-million-plus inhabitants in 1960, about a hundred thousand, 10 percent, were European—mostly Belgian—associated with the rubber plantations, and especially the copper and rare minerals mines, that were generating fabulous fortunes. The main mining conglomeration, the Société Générale, generated about 70 percent of the entire economy of the new nation. In 1960 there were 1,600 American missionaries scattered across Congo's vast landscape.[91] U.S. investors held significant copper and rare earth mining interests in Congo, along with interests such as industrial diamonds in nearby white-ruled Rhodesia.[92]

Eighty years of Belgian colonial rule had left behind a fractured national political scene. In the most recent elections, Lumumba's party had won only a plurality, forty seats of a total of 137. The remaining seats were held by representatives of twenty-three different ethnic groups, not one of which had more than thirteen seats. In the executive branch, twenty-two ministries were spread across twelve different parties.[93] Lumumba and his party were the main forces holding this fragile democracy together. Only days after Lumumba's historic speech, that democracy became even more fragile in the aftermath of a mutiny within the military, followed a few weeks later by the secession of Katanga, a mineral-rich region. A struggle ensued when the CIA began covert actions against Lumumba, such as bribing Lumumba's supporters in the military not to help him hold on to power.

In the twenty years leading up to 2014, the CIA released a series of Freedom of Information Act documents described by Congo historian Stephen Weissman as "the most extensive set of CIA operational documents ever published."[94] Even so, four complete documents were kept secret and twenty-two were partially withheld. These and other, earlier documents reveal that CIA director Allen Dulles cabled Congo's capital of Léopoldville only one month after Lumumba's independence proclamation, saying: "We conclude that his [Lumumba's] removal must be an urgent and prime objective and that under existing conditions this should be a high priority of our covert action."[95]

The CIA had actually attempted to murder Lumumba with a vial of poison shipped in a diplomatic bag to Congo, where it was intended to be added to his food or toothpaste, but the plotters were not able to get close enough to him to carry this out.[96] Better to arrange for Congolese opponents to do the dirty work. The CIA then ceased any actions that might have protected Lumumba, who was subsequently arrested and assassinated by opposition forces.[97] Lumumba was then replaced, via CIA bribes to his opponents and other forms of assistance, by army chief of staff Mobutu Sese Seko.[98] The Agency even provided a public relations firm for one of Mobutu's allies to help him bolster his image. It also hired mercenary pilots from among anti-Castro Cubans and South Africans to bolster Mobutu's military strength.[99] Five years later, in 1965, Mobutu carried out a second coup to install himself as total dictator. He ruled viciously and corruptly until overthrown during a regional war in 1997.[100] Weissman estimates the deaths from Mobutu's rule and related wars at 3.5 million.[101]

Congo, once a source of rubber, copper, and palm oil, has recently become a new source of misery through low-paid artisanal mining of cobalt, an essential element in modern rechargeable batteries in smart phones, electric vehicles, and other electronic devices. Siddharth Kara has documented extensive child labor in some of the world's most dangerous mines in Congo. Digging by hand with limited safety conditions, thousands of children are paid too poorly to accumulate money for school. Medical care is almost nonexistent, and deaths or injuries from collapsing mine tunnels are frequent. As Kara summarizes:

> The inevitable outcome of a lawless scramble for cobalt in an impoverished and war-torn country can only be the complete dehumanization of the people at the bottom of the [supply] chain.[102]

BRAZIL, 1961–1964

According to the former U.S. ambassador to Brazil, Lincoln Gordon, the 1964 Brazilian coup was "the single most decisive victory for freedom in the mid-twentieth century."[103]

A fierce anticommunism had already grown up in earlier

decades in Brazilian business and church circles,[104] but various left forces had also emerged, particularly in the aftermath of the Cuban Revolution and the U.S. Bay of Pigs fiasco.[105] The United States intensified its penetration of Brazilian life and institutions under the influence of the Kennedy administration's Alliance for Progress. Much of this penetration was achieved via the Brazilian Institute for Democratic Action (IBAD), a particularly active CIA front, with its own radio station and ties to a wide range of academic and business organizations. CIA activities here were both public and covert. A growing polarization was pitting the emergent left of intellectuals and trade union activists against the powerful military, which was being trained in the United States via the U.S. Military Assistance Program, described by Ambassador Gordon as a "highly important factor in influencing the [Brazilian] military to be pro-U.S."[106]

Brazilian leaders chafed at U.S. preaching about the evils of communism and attempted to assert Brazil's independence and status as an incipient world power. The ascension to power of João Goulart in 1961 raised concern in the United States. Goulart had been elected vice president in 1956 and 1960, and was noted for his good relations with trade unions and support for improvement in minimum wages. When Brazil's president resigned in 1961, conservative circles opposed Goulart becoming president. After negotiations, a compromise was reached.

After João Goulart's accession to power on September 7, 1961, foreign policy differences were exacerbated by a growing list of left-supported internal reforms that further reflected the left-right divide. The new president nationalized oil companies; enacted new rent laws; supported revolutionary Cuba; honored Che Guevara; visited China, and established diplomatic relations with Soviet Union. The United States came to see Goulart as a Communist, who had to be removed.

The United States focused on Brazil's local and regional police forces, teaching anti-guerilla warfare, along with regular military development. To this end, it established the "Special Group" to expand counterinsurgency training,[107] by which four classic types of "internal aggression" were identified—particular to Czechoslovakia, China, North Vietnam, and Cuba—and then strategize the best methods to subdue or destroy.[108] Meanwhile, Alliance for Progress projects were to cut off social and political forces sustaining the aggression. Training of the police and military was apparently more successful than establishing work, shelter, and general social and economic reforms.

The period of 1961 to 1964 witnessed a slow-moving coup. Hysterical anticommunists formed new groups regularly. The CIA funneled large amounts of money and other resources to right-wing groups. Prayer meetings became an important instrument for mobilization against Communists. The Christian Anticommunism Crusade (CACC) claimed that it was the prayer conventions that ousted the Goulart government. The march of families in prayer on March 14 of 1964 turned into a mammoth demonstration against the government.

Everything came to a head on April 1,1964, when a group of military officers seized control of the Brazilian state and pushed it rapidly toward a dictatorship. A U.S. carrier fleet steaming toward Brazil—"Operation Brother Sam"—with weapons, oil, ammunition, and other supplies for the generals, turned around and headed back toward the Caribbean. The generals were not in need of immediate supplies.

A State Department document listing U.S. objectives in post-coup Brazil did not include any reference to land reform, which had been one of the big political issues for decades.[109] Brazil readjusted its foreign policy to be consistent with the United States by moving to support the blockade of Cuba and endorsing a U.S. intervention in the Dominican Republic.[110] Most political rights had been stripped from the Brazilian population under "Operation Clean-Up," the semi-official philosophy of "Security and Development."[111] Torture and vigilante murders, by means of "death squads," became regular methods of dealing with dissent.[112] U.S. advisors proliferated.

At least some of them participated in the torture and killing of prisoners.[113] The generals innovated new forms of terrorism and oppression—death squads, disappearances—for other Latin nations to emulate.[114] According to a 2004 Amnesty International Report,[115] children were sometimes forced to watch the torture of their parents, or the reverse. Electric shock was widely used.

> The end of a reed is placed in the anus of a naked man hanging suspended downwards on the *pau de arara* [parrot's perch] and a piece of cotton soaked in petrol is lit at the other end of the reed . . . wives have been hung naked next to their husbands and given electric shocks on the sexual parts of their body.[116]

The Brazilian military dictatorship lasted until 1985. In 2019 a national furor was awakened in Brazil when right-wing president Jair Bolsonaro and associates publicly praised the work of the past dictatorship, sparking statements of outrage by family members of some of the victims.

Overview of Selected Cases

The six accounts discussed above are all related to the overthrow of left and progressive governments that had been democratically elected. Sometimes, as in the case of Indonesia, overthrows occurred to prevent the ascension of Communists to power. These stories broadly fit the template of CIA covert action, listed in the beginning of this chapter. However, the case of Kerala is distinct from these countries' experiences in that Kerala was and is a state within federal India that was pursuing a policy of non-alignment and was unwilling to allow open cooperation with the United States, even in resisting Communism. Nevertheless, bear in mind the relevant commonalities of these six countries in order to understand the toppling of the Communist government in Kerala. These commonalities include 1) elaborate CIA collection of information so that appropriate counterstrategies could be devised; 2) influencing public opinion through the press and lobbyists; 3) organizing mass violent protests and anticommunist hysteria using religion and ethnic divides; 4) utilization of sections of government for repressing the Communists and, in the case of Guyana, deploying the power of the sovereign government to oust the Communists from government; and 5) financing anticommunist movements.

All of these elements are part of the story of the toppling of Kerala's EMS ministry. As in British Guiana, Iran, Guatemala, Indonesia, Congo, and Brazil, the power of covert action in Kerala led the way. In all these cases, the use of covert action developed as a response to popular, progressive, elected governments. These governments—as in Kerala—came about within the larger context of leftist and nationalist governments, and leftist movements that were popping up across the globe in the post–World War Two period.

How did these movements come about in Kerala? We shall take up the Kerala case in the next chapter. How did a progressive and democratic movement develop, and what were its particular characteristics? In particular, how did the Communists come to power as they unexpectedly did in 1957?

CHAPTER 3

How the Communists Came to Power in Kerala in 1957

"*LEFTIST COALITION DEFEATS CONGRESS PARTY IN TRAVANCORE-COCHIN, SOUTH INDIAN STATE.*"

So declared the call for a National Security Council briefing in Washington on March 9, 1954, with a follow-up meeting on March 10. Calling together the NSC would indicate a higher level than routine discussion. Presumably, the NSC would be required to approve a covert action. In any case, the draft agenda for the meeting included the warning that "Communists may enter [an] Indian state government." It also spoke to possible actions such as "Congress might invoke 'president's rule' by central government [in] New Delhi . . . this device [has been adopted] or threatened by Nehru in other cases to thwart Communists." The final summary note describes the underlying problem as "popular disillusionment on a local level with [the] Congress Party, which still appears to offer India [the] only chance for longer range stability."[1] These briefings were presented two out of twelve times the NSC was convened, from 1950 through 1960, to respond to events in Kerala—although the state was not brought into existence legally until 1956.

In 1954 the princely states of Travancore in India's south and Cochin in the center were merged to form Travancore-Cochin and in the first election the combined assemblies of the Communists and three other socialist parties captured a majority. The anxieties about this left coalition in U.S. intelligence circles proved to be premature, however, as the right-wing congress that ruled India's central government proved to be wily enough to split the left, supporting a minority government of the major socialist party, excluding the Communists from power. Only three years later, the Communists would win a more important election, gaining the right to form a ministry to govern the entire state of Kerala, which had been formed by merging the Malabar district of Madras Presidency with Travancore-Cochin, thus creating a single state for the Malayalam-speaking people.

Back at CIA headquarters in Langley, Virginia, operatives had been watching for leftist activity in India since at least 1950. Yet they knew little about the people or societies that had, by 1954, burst onto the scene with convincing electoral power. On the eve of the EMS ministry's 1957 ascension to power, Kerala had undergone a complex history with a number of events and processes that made the Communist ministry possible. To better understand the rise of the Communist movement in Southwest India and the 1954 election victory that called forth two meetings of the U.S. National Security Council, let us look back across a couple of centuries of historical developments.

Priests, Princes, and Landlords: A System Held in Place by Caste

For centuries, the territory of southwestern coastal India that eventually became Kerala State had been a collection of petty princedoms, often battling each other.[2] In a sense, medieval Kerala was more akin to the European feudal system, rather than overarching Asiatic empires that characterized most parts of India. Kerala, with two monsoons, numerous rivers, and natural water storage facilities, did not require artificial irrigation systems maintained by a large, centralized state power.

Under the caste system, those bound by occupational and kinship ties were arranged in hierarchical order, each separate from its upper and lower caste by taboos on intermingling. Kerala carried caste separation to the extreme, not only by prohibiting interdining and intermarriage, but also by prescribing the physical distance that members of one caste had to keep from one another.[3] Thus, the Brahmins, the highest priestly caste, had to keep a pollution distance of sixteen feet from the Nairs, the next highest caste; thirty-two feet from Ezhavas; and sixty-four feet from the Dalit (former untouchable) castes. The tribal peoples even had to keep out of eyesight. It was a social stratification system that denied civil rights, the right to an education, and the right to property to a majority of the population.

Land, the key means of production, was monopolized by the Brahmins as temple property (*dewaswom*), joint property (*brahmaswom*), or personal private property (*janmaswom*).[4] Brahmins leased the land to superior tenants, mostly upper-caste Nairs, some of whom were landlords themselves. The superior tenants in turn leased the land to tenants at will, whose leases could be terminated at any time, and who were mostly lower-caste Ezhavas or non-Hindu communities of Christians and Muslims. At the bottom came the agricultural-worker castes such as the Parayas and Pulayas who could own no property and were tied to the land of the Brahmin lords. One can perceive a close correspondence between the social structures of governance and land relations to the caste hierarchy. All reinforced each other.

European Traders, Armies, and Colonialism

Historically, Kerala ports were key inter-ports, where Chinese, Arab, and other traders met.[5] The arrival in Calicut (now Kozhikode) by the Portuguese sailor Vasco da Gama in 1498 ushered in a new factor: direct trade with European countries. Fantastic fortunes could be made in Europe by following da Gama's route around the southern tip of Africa to compete with the Muslim control of the Western Asia trade routes connecting Europe to South and East Asia and on to the Indonesian Spice Islands, rich with cloves, peppers, and other sought-after foods and medicines. The Portuguese were followed by the Dutch in 1604, and, in quick succession, the French in 1615. The British had already appeared in 1583.[6] Each European power set up trading stations and eventually aligned with one or more of the local princes.

Meanwhile, something else was churning inside Kerala's governance system. As rulers annexed the neighboring principalities, three principalities in the south, middle, and north emerged as centralized kingdoms.[7] The process of centralization that emerged abolished the chieftains and traditional landlords and created a stratum of rich farmers. The centralization process in the north was relatively weaker and was disrupted by the invasion by Sultan Hydarali and Tippu Sultan from Mysore. This invasion was a major disruption of the landlord system in the north.

By the 1790s, the British had begun to drive out competitive European traders and armies. Emboldened by their military successes, British forces added the conquest of local princedoms to their undertakings. In 1792 the British defeated Mysore under the military leadership of Lord Cornwallis (who had negotiated the surrender of British forces in North America at Yorktown in 1781, establishing the United States). The Malabar district also came under direct rule of the British, who reinstated the old landlord system. The princely states of Travancore and Cochin were under indirect rule of the British, paying heavy indemnities.[8]

As local princedoms resisted the expansion of British power in the region, several movements and violent uprisings occurred, but by 1820, through harsh military tactics, most local forces had been disarmed.[9] Those who held out were arrested and could face hanging or were pensioned off to disarm them politically.

Tea, Coffee, Cardamom, Rubber, and Coconuts

An outstanding feature of Kerala's economy was its early and rapid integration into the world commodity boom and rapid spread of a variety of commercial crops. The first plantation in the region was established in 1798. By 1945 the number had risen to eighty-nine. The number of plantation workers rose from 5,400 in 1901 to 71,300 in 1931. Tea, coffee, and cardamom were the principal plantings. Tea, in particular, generated enormous profits for investors, many of whom were British and some of whom were Christian missionaries.[10] Rubber, which was introduced in the twentieth century, was processed by big plantations and attracted a large number of smallholders.[11]

The colonial governments heavily subsidized the plantation sector of the economy by constructing roads and bridges, which also increased employment opportunities. The workers on the plantations, particularly where tea and coffee were grown, were drawn mainly from villages in Tamil Nadu, a nearby region of South India. The setting up of tea factories and primary processing of plantation products became an important industrial activity.

The spread of coconut cultivation to coastal and midland areas had a profound impact on society. It raised agricultural productivity and gave rise to industrial units for processing coconut products, such as oil and coir (coconut fiber). The coconut fiber industry included the manufacture of ropes and yarn, which could be woven into mats and other necessities. Defibering and spinning, once a cottage industry, spread throughout the coastal belt backwaters, and now became localized in the port town of Alleppey in Travancore princely state. Around forty thousand workers were concentrated in this town at the end of the 1930s. Around 200,000 workers were employed in the cottage sector.[12]

The coconut industry necessitated a large number of merchant intermediaries and petty capitalists. Exports were controlled by half a dozen European coastal trading firms that also monopolized trade in plantation products. The workers and, to a lesser extent, the petty capitalists and traders, were drawn from the lower-caste Ezhavas.

From Basel, Switzerland, missionaries introduced the tile-making process to northern Kerala in 1834. By 1911 there were 113 factories employing nearly two thousand workers.[13] In 1921 fourteen establishments employed 373 workers who made *beedis*—hand-rolled cigarettes; by 1937 there were around a thousand beedi rollers in Kannur town alone.[14] Coconut oil mills and rice mills, sawmills, railways, and ports also arose during this period, creating new labor opportunities. Establishments employing more than twenty workers had over twenty thousand by 1911.[15] Cashew nut processing was another major source of factory employment, localized in the town of Quilon, south of Alleppey.[16] Additional use of the coconut was made by "toddy tapping," processing then fermenting the juice into a mildly alcoholic drink.[17]

New Jobs, New Taxes: Undermining Traditions

The integration of Kerala into global trade, commercialization of agriculture, and the emergence of capitalist firms disturbed the traditional society significantly. A directive of 1812, for example, compelled the princely state of Travancore to collect a portion of the land tax in cash, something that had previously been done entirely with paddy (uncooked rice) or other produce. This forced farmers to sell at least part of their harvests for cash to be able to pay the new taxes.[18] Because of changes in the cropping pattern, Kerala became a food-deficit region, which compelled laborers and small tenants to seek wage work.

These complex processes resulted in the formation of new social strata in the traditional caste society, such as an industrial working class, capitalists, traders, and a middle class. More important, the new social strata emerged more from lower social castes and communities such as Ezhavas and Christians rather than the traditional elite castes. The traditional caste-class identity was disrupted. The newly rich realized that they were being denied the social status warranted by their economic status. Domination by the upper castes became a hindrance to upward mobility of the new classes. Even for the upper castes, customs and rituals became anachronisms in the age of an acquisitive economy that was rapidly expanding. This set the stage for social reform movements among all castes and communities.[19]

The School Entry Strike of 1907 and the Temple Entry Struggle of 1924

The most significant feature of the Kerala reforms was that they engulfed all castes, even the lowest untouchable caste. A memorable event was the months-long agricultural workers' strike for the right to an education, organized by Ayyankali, a low-caste Pulaya laborer, near Thiruvananthapuram in southern Kerala. The move was resisted by the upper castes but finally the government had to open the public schools to all castes.[20]

The reform movement among the Ezhava castes started with religious reforms by a charismatic reformer, Sree Narayana Guru. It soon developed into a campaign for inter-dining, public education, and civic rights. Narayana Guru became a source of legitimacy for reformers and radicals of all stripes, including those involved with rationalism, atheism, and organizing labor.[21]

The struggle to overcome caste/untouchable/unseeable indignities came to focus on overcoming temple-entry prohibitions. The most dramatic of these efforts was the Vaikom Satyagraha campaign, begun in 1924, to open the great Siva Temple at Vaikom in north Travancore. As with other temples, Vaikom's approach roads were closed to low-caste people. The campaign's first act was an attempt to use one of the roads by three leaders, a high-caste Nair, a low-caste Ezhava, and a former untouchable Pulaya farm laborer.[22] The three nonviolent disobeyers of the law were arrested before thousands of assembled onlookers. Similar arrests occurred for eleven days. Then the government set up barricades before which thousands of people sat, fasted, and sang patriotic songs. The struggle attracted activists from all around, even from outside Kerala. Eleven months later, the regional legislature failed by a single vote to pass a law opening the roads to all.

The following year, the Indian nationalist leader Mohandas K. Gandhi visited the protest but was able to negotiate only a temporary standoff agreement that left the demonstrators unsatisfied. Finally, in November 1925, twenty months after it began, the Vaikom Satyagraha campaign ended when the government threw open three of the four temple roads so that low-caste people could approach the temple, while high-caste people, using the still-restricted road on the eastern gate, kept a vestige of their old privileges. It was only in 1936 that the temple was finally and fully opened to all castes.[23]

Although the Vaikom struggle ended in somewhat of a mixed outcome, it stimulated great excitement and political ferment throughout Kerala. The spectacle of the police barricading the roads to the temple and facing off against crowds in the thousands fostered greater passions and more radical ideas among the lower-caste activists, along with some of their higher-caste allies. In particular, the vacillating role of Gandhi seems to have aided in the growth of more left-wing sentiment among many of the nationalist organizers.

The National Movement for Freedom and the Emergence of the Left

Political life had remained in deep slumber in northern Kerala after the anti-British feudal and peasant revolts of the nineteenth century until the rise of Gandhi to the national leadership. His call for the non-cooperation with the Indian government created a national upheaval in 1920. The national movement also collaborated with the Khilafath agitation against British policy toward Turkey by nationalist Muslims. However, the agitation came to grief in south Malabar where it grew into a peasant revolt that unfortunately slipped into communal overtones and was brutally suppressed by the British. After this setback, it was only in 1930 with the civil disobedience movement that the national movement in the state surged ahead. The surge brought forth a new generation of young leaders, many of whom were soon disillusioned by Gandhian passive tactics and compromise. This led them to the Congress Socialist Party (CSP, or the Congress) platform that was emerging at the national level as a left pressure group within the Congress.[24]

The growth of influence of the Congress Socialists roused resistance from the Gandhian right within the Congress. Yet in 1934 and 1938, the CSP gained leadership of the Congress Committee in Kerala.[25] The socialists used their office to build up peasant organizations, trade unions, and other mass organizations. They were the main force behind the network of village libraries and effectively propagated socialist ideology.[26]

The Communist Party of India had been formed in 1920 in Tashkent, and various groups came together for its first congress at Kanpur in 1925. These early decades of the CPI had been characterized by a sectarian attitude toward the national movement. However, the Communists in Kerala escaped this phase because they reached communism through Congress Socialism. In 1938 EMS, who was the secretary of the CSP at the national level, along with P. Krishna Pillai, K. Damodaran, and N. C. Sekhar, secretly formed a Kerala unit of the Communist Party of India. On January 26, 1940—the tenth anniversary of the declaration of the goal of independence by the Congress Socialist Party—the Communists announced their existence with a massive wall-writing campaign. The entire rank and file of the CSP in Kerala joined the Communist Party.[27]

Meanwhile, the political movement in southern Kerala took a different route because of Gandhi's policy of not mobilizing the national movement under the banner of the Congress in the princely states. Thus, in Travancore the national movement was organized under the Travancore State Congress, which effectively was a confederation of community organizations.[28] The key slogan of the state congress was to set up an elected government under the king. Similar organizations, called Praja Mandalams, came up in Cochin. Many younger nationalist workers moved toward secular and radical thinking in the southern region also.[29]

Organizing the Peasants and Industrial Workers

A major focus of CSP activities was mobilizing the peasants in Malabar. Administratively, Malabar was under what was called Ryotwari settlement, in which revenue settlements (taxes) were directly established with the peasants, unlike the Zamindari settlement in other parts of India, where the settlement was made with the landlords. EMS pointed out that the tenurial system in Malabar was more like the latter system. The rents were so high that the living conditions of the actual cultivators and agricultural workers were deplorable. The tenancy movement was initially led by the superior and better-protected tenants. The CSP built up a militant agrarian movement focusing on the agricultural workers and poor peasants. The key goals were the reduction of rent, implementation of tenurial reforms, and removal of regressive feudal exactions. The movement was growing into a no-rent campaign.[30]

The CSP was instrumental in transforming the existing philanthropic workers' associations into militant trade unions and setting up new trade unions in most of the industrial centers. During the strike wave of 1935, CSP members organized the first All Kerala Trade Union Conference at Calicut. Similar conferences were held periodically and attended by trade union representatives from all three geographical segments of Kerala.[31]

Because tenancy was much lower in Travancore and Cochin, the development of militant peasant movements in those regions was muted. But the militant trade union movement developed here, particularly in the industrial port town of Alleppey.[32] The Travancore Labor Association (TLA), formed in 1922, slowly transformed itself into a militant trade union under pressure from the ranks living in deteriorating labor conditions and wages due to the Depression. The major contribution of the CSP was the role it played in the spread of socialist ideology among the workers, who united in factory trade unions to agitate against economic grievances. Outside the factory, workers became activists in the anti-caste movements in the struggle for social justice. The general strike of 1938, under the leadership of CSP cadres, was a major turning point when the workers began to view political and social problems from the point of view of the working class.

The General Strike of 1938

After numerous strikes in individual factories against wage reductions, the TLA in 1938 called for an indefinite general strike in the coir industry, seeking a charter of demands. The most important demand was ending wage reductions. The strike also coincided with the agitation for "responsible government," that is, government responsible to the elected legislature, launched by the state congress.[33] The strike, in solidarity with the struggle for "responsible government," threw the region into unprecedented mass mobilization and confrontations with the repressive state machinery. To the great disappointment of the workers and many agitators, the state congress members surrendered to the administration and withdrew their agitation. Though a section of the trade union movement wavered, the CSP cadres, led by the legendary organizer P. Krishna Pillai, persuaded the strike committee not to end the strike until some of the economic demands of the workers had been met. Despite vicious repression let loose by the police and military, the workers continued the struggle for twenty-five days. The employers agreed to a token increase in wages and the government agreed to an inquiry committee to thoroughly examine the workers' grievances. A new crop of class-conscious cadres, toughened in the struggle, rose to the movement's leadership, replacing the moderate leaders.[34]

The heroic struggle of the coir workers of Alleppey against

all odds won the admiration of the young leaders who styled themselves as "Youth Leaguers" and the radical elements within the state congress who were disillusioned by the vacillations of the leadership. Many of them traveled to Alleppey in solidarity with the strikers.[35] This collaboration led to the formation of the Radical Group in May 1939, with M. N. Govindan Nair as the secretary. The Radical Group was to function as an organized socialist faction within the state congress, along the lines of the CSP in Malabar. Most of its members later joined the Communist Party.

The Left Turn of the Social Reform Activists

Though the CSP gave primacy to the mobilization of workers and peasants, cutting across caste distinctions, they were also active in the social reform movements. Unlike the right-wing leadership in the national movement in Malabar, the CSP offered support to the struggle with a coalition of caste and community groups in Travancore for "reservation," a job program similar to what is now called *affirmative action* in government employment in the United States. During the Vaikom Satyagraha of 1924, the left had not emerged on Kerala's political horizon. A decade later, in 1931–1932, when a similar temple entry agitation was organized at Guruvayur Temple in northern Kerala, the leaders of the CSP, A. K. Gopalan and P. Krishna Pillai, were in the thick of the struggle.[36] Yet another decade later, in 1947–1948, the temple entry movement at Paliyam Temple in Cochin was organized under the red flag.[37] The class and mass organizations actively undertook anti-caste and social reform slogans from their own class and mass platforms.

During the independence movement, all the Communist cadres were active in their own caste and community movements. This active involvement attracted the radical elements in the social reform movements to the Communists' fold. This was particularly true of Ezhavas and the agricultural labor castes.[38]

One feature of this process was the role of high-caste radicals

HOW THE COMMUNISTS CAME TO POWER 73

in helping to organize unions among the poorest and lowest-caste workers. This meant going to their houses, sitting next to them at meetings, and—when police repression struck, as it often did—hiding with them, working at close quarters with them, and breaking the dining segregation that was a major symbol holding the concept of social pollution in place. As noted by anthropologist Kathleen Gough, who conducted many years of research in Kerala:

> It is the Communists who eat in the homes and tea shops of Harijans [former untouchables], organize drama clubs among them, file suits on their behalf, and agitate for fixed tenures, higher wages, and a share in the land.[39]

Anthropologist Joan Mencher, who also spent many years studying in Kerala, cited a Harijan villager who recalled in 1971:

> Twenty years ago, the influence of Communism brought a new shape to the life of my village. Some of the high-caste Nairs became the spokesmen of this new ideology. My father and uncles also joined them. They, the leaders of all castes, conducted meetings in Pulaya houses, slept in Paraya houses, etc. This phenomenon actually swept away the caste feeling in my village, especially untouchability. I have gone to the homes of my high-caste friends, and they come to my house also and accept food. We have many Nair friends who come to my family house, take food and sleep overnight.[40]

Along with the real and important role of union and Communist organizers in helping to win economic benefits such as the land reform and higher wages, great importance was attached to simple acts, such as breaking the eating taboos and crossing the thresholds of each other's houses. These acts cemented the anti-discrimination struggle by making its principles real in people's immediate lives.

How Communists in Kerala Weathered the Second World War

During the initial phase of the Second World War, the CPI adopted a line of unconditional resistance to what it considered an imperialist war. The consequent police repression and preventive detention of cadres forced the young Communists to adopt underground organizational forms and new styles of mass work. Thus, the first phase of the war rapidly transformed the loose and open organizational structure of the CSP into a Communist Party of *steel discipline*—a phrase that gained wide currency in Malayalam.

The CPI changed its characterization of the war because of the German aggression against the Soviet Union. While there was no doubt in the mind of any Communist on the need to rally to the defense of socialism around the world, there was much confusion as to how to link this international task with the struggle for national liberation. The patriotism of the Communists was challenged by congressional activists who launched the "Quit India" agitation in 1942. A faction of socialists moved to an anticommunist platform.

A good section of the nationalist masses also became isolated, temporarily, which was indeed a matter of deep concern and frustration among the Party cadres who had just emerged from the ranks of Congress socialism. However, the wild accusations of Congress leaders about the Communists being the agents of the British were never taken seriously. Kerala Communists possessed one great asset: they were the leaders of the national independence movement in Kerala.

Despite the generally adverse situation, the period during the war proved to be one of organizational consolidation for the CPI. Party membership and membership of the mass organizations increased. The sales of Party literature and the Party journal *Deshabhimani* vastly improved. Though cooperation with the war effort through increasing production was adhered to, the cadres exhibited extraordinary skill, especially in working-class centers like Alleppey, in adopting tactics that ensured the fulfillment of day-to-day demands of the masses without recourse to forms of struggle that would have disrupted production.[41]

The Communists were at the forefront of every effort to relieve the distress caused by the war, such as famine, scarcity of such necessities as cloth and kerosene, the outbreak of epidemics, and natural calamities. Since Kerala was a chronically grain-deficient region, the disruption of supply routes created famine conditions. The CPI worked out concrete proposals for the procurement of grain stocks and statutory rationing, and organized mass campaigns for their implementation.[42] When rationing was introduced, the Party again came to the forefront to expose its inefficiencies and to agitate for remedial measures. The Party's relief work won it widespread admiration.

The Punnapra-Vayalar Uprising of 1946

After the war, many militant struggles, such as Tebhaga, Telangana, and the Royal Indian Navy Mutiny, broke out in parts of India. Encouraged by this, the CPI put forward the slogan of power by the people. In August 1946, the Central Committee of the CPI called on the Party to develop these struggles into "local battles" and to "raise the question of state power."[43]

The new line was reflected in the upsurge of struggles in Kerala. In Malabar, the CPI's main thrust was in the agrarian sector—a campaign against hoarders and forcible occupation of wastelands—which led to violent confrontations with the police in many centers, such as those at Karivallur and Kavumbai. However, the major battle was the Punnapra-Vayalar struggle, named after the two main centers of confrontation near Alleppey in Travancore.[44]

The prevalence of landlordism and feudal vestiges was higher in the area around Alleppey compared to the other parts of Travancore, resulting in serious agrarian tensions and the spread of agricultural workers' unions. Fisherfolk agitated against the tyrannical overlordship of the traditional elite over the poor fishermen of the Catholic community. Along with the near famine conditions pervading the countryside after the Second World War, these factors provided fertile soil for the fast development of a revolutionary movement in the countryside.

Threatened by the unrest, the rural reactionaries attempted to terrorize the workers into submission. The workers at first retaliated sporadically, and later in a more organized manner. By the first week of September 1946, the military entered the area to confront the "Communist menace." With the approach of the harvest season, tensions and repression escalated, forcing the terror-stricken workers in many localities to flee from their homesteads to areas where the movement was more robust and they could set up camps for self-protection.

The American Model

Meanwhile, the political scene in Travancore was rapidly changing. The royal family of the princely state of Travancore appears to have supported a plan by its chief advisor, Dewan Sir C. P. Ramaswami Aiyar, to make Travancore into a separate nation.[45] According to a January 1946 proposal, called "The American Model," this would involve an elected legislature, and an executive with wide powers would serve exclusively by appointment of the Maharaja. While the Congress Party opposed this plan, some of its leaders were willing to negotiate with the Maharaja and his family; thus there were fears of a backroom deal. As part of the opposition, the CPI coined the slogan "American Model into the Arabian Sea."

The party leadership in Travancore, closely following the CPI's new tactical line of raising the issue of state power, tried to link the fierce partial struggles in the Alleppey countryside with the general political struggles for a final onslaught on the feudal monarchy. A section of the State Congress leadership agreed to launch a mass agitation on the scale of 1938's general strike. However, unlike in 1938, the organized working class, through a general strike across Travancore, was to spearhead the struggle. The self-defense camps developed in the Alleppey countryside were to be transformed into volunteer camps where the workers would be trained in close physical combat and military maneuvers.

The general strike began on October 22. It was evident from the beginning that the strategy had failed. Not only did the State Congress not support the agitation, as the liberal national leaders had promised, but a section of the Congress came out openly against the uprising. Thus, the statewide mass agitation never materialized. The general strike was a success only in Alleppey, as the non-Communist left developed cold feet at the last moment.

The Alleppey workers were isolated. Martial law was declared in the region, and military reinforcements were moved in. In large-scale military operations mounted against the volunteer camps, around five hundred workers were gunned down or tortured to death. Despite the self-sacrificing heroism and political determination of the workers, resistance was ruthlessly suppressed in less than a week.

The crucial flaw had been the failure to ensure a statewide agitation, as in 1938. The Party also overestimated its preparedness to organize such a movement. The tactics adopted in the struggle closely corresponded with the "general strike and mass insurrection model" and ignored the need for mobility and guerrilla warfare actions.

The Punnapra-Vayalar uprising in Travancore was the peak of the national movement in Kerala. It sealed the fate of the monarchy in Travancore.[46] More important, it signified the maturation of the working class, which had emerged as an independent political force in 1938 to become in 1946 the leadership of the national independence movement. This status and prestige that the Communists had gained through militant struggles, particularly in North Malabar and Punnapra-Vayalar on the eve of independence, was an important factor that facilitated the rapid spread of support for the CPI in the 1950s.

The Movement for a United Kerala

In a sense, the Punnapra-Vayalar uprising was a blow against separatism and a vote for national unity. A united Kerala of the Malayalam-speaking population within the Indian Union was the CPI's answer to the national question. The CPI, which had already brought the three regions of Malabar, Cochin, and Travancore under a unified regional political leadership and an all-Kerala trade union movement, put forward as an imperative the formation of a "United Kerala." The struggle for a United Kerala was to be an inseparable part of the struggle of all Indian people for national freedom and the liquidation of feudal monarchies.

The perspective of the CPI enabled it to ride the crest of the wave of Malayali subnational feeling as well as a cultural movement in the postwar years. *Kerala: The Motherland of the Malayalees*, a book by EMS, published in 1948, played a role as an important text of the evolution of the culture, society, economy and politics of the Malayalam-speaking people and a progressive manifesto for its future.[47] The CPI also skillfully used various performing arts for propaganda. It continuously intervened in literary debates and drew the younger generation of writers to progressive platforms. One of its greatest victories was in theater, where it came to have near complete domination. Almost every well-known literary figure or artist was either a Communist activist or sympathizer at one time or another. Libraries and reading rooms mushroomed. Cultural transformation played a vital role in the making of a progressive Kerala.[48]

Toward the Electoral Victory of 1957

The Communist Party was banned and remained so, even during the 1952 parliamentary elections in Travancore-Cochin. Nevertheless, it gained control of the municipality of Alleppey, where the most brutal anticommunist repression had taken place. In the north, it won a majority with support of independents and post-election support in the local government in Malabar. The writing was on the wall. But interestingly, the Communists pretended to ignore their growing popularity in the run-up to the 1957 election, and the anticommunists were too confident to carefully read the signs.

It was in nearby Andhra State that the Communists had expected their first electoral victory in India, helped by tailwinds of the Telangana armed struggle. However, the Congress Party, sensing a possible election setback, succeeded in forging a broad united front with other political parties. The imminent threat of a Communist victory polarized the voters in favor of the Congress Party. Though the CPI won 40 percent of the votes in Andhra, it could gain only 8 percent of the seats in the State Congress.

Learning the lessons from the Andhra debacle, the CPI in Kerala did not make any tall claims and announced as its aim the formation of a united front government with the other left parties. However, the other left parties decided to fight on their own, and the CPI had to be content with supporting several prominent independents. Even CPI General Secretary Ajay Ghosh publicly refused to claim victory in Kerala. The Congress, overwhelmed with self-confidence, let its guard down and did not heed the advice of the Church to forge an anticommunist united front.

But one group was clearly aware of the united front potential: the Central Intelligence Agency (CIA). We have referred to its alarms after the 1954 Travancore-Cochin election at the beginning of this chapter. The new Kerala state was branded by the CIA just after its birth as "the most likely of all Indian states to escape from Congress [Party] control as a result of the [upcoming February 1957] elections."[49] In Kerala's first State Assembly elections, the Communist Party secured 40 percent of the votes, winning sixty seats so that—along with its five independents—it won a narrow parliamentary majority.

Why did Kerala emerge as a much more progressive region than the rest of India? Over the previous several decades, Kerala had produced a remarkable number of committed organizers and leaders. From the labor unions, caste improvement associations, peasant organizations, and the independence struggle, Kerala put forth men and women who devoted much of their lives to improving the lot of the poorest farmers and laborers.

Three factors seem to have propelled the Communists into a dominant position in the state. The first was that the Communists emerged as the rightful leaders of the national movement in Kerala. The second was the Party's success in creatively dealing with the caste question, which enabled the Communists to rally the best among the anti-caste movement into its fold. The third was the fact that the Communists symbolized the Malayali regional urges while maintaining support for the national independence movement and dominating the cultural scene of literature and the arts.

Whatever the causal factors that historians may agree on, a significant element of Kerala's success in promoting the interests of ordinary people was greatly expanded by the election victory of the EMS first ministry in 1957. In the next chapter we consider how the EMS ministry, in power for twenty-eight months, attempted to promote those very interests that had brought it to power.

CHAPTER 4

Reform within the Constitution: The Communist Ministry in Kerala, 1957–1959

"The government I am going to form is not for building a communist society. We will attempt to implement the immediate program outlined in the election manifesto of the Communist Party."

Thus E. M. S. Namboodiripad, the Chief Minister-elect, assured the Kerala governor, the formal head of the state government appointed by the central government under India's federal system. His cautious approach was reflected in the statement of the secretary of the Kerala State Committee of the Communist Party, M. N. Govindan Nair,[1] who said, "We are not going to do anything wonderful"—speaking to *New York Times* India correspondent A. M. Rosenthal on March 20, 1957, just after it was announced that the CPI had won the Kerala State Assembly elections and was in position to be asked by the state's governor to form a ministry.

Of 126 assembly seats, the CPI had won sixty, plus five seats won by independents supported by the Party. To carry out the Party's election manifesto the winners would have to remain united and hold on to nearly every seat. The entire project could be vulnerable in the case of a loss in any by-elections.

While possibly putting somewhat of a damper on the celebrations and the spontaneous unleashing of optimism and hope spreading across Kerala, Nair's measured remarks to the *Times* were undoubtedly in keeping with the cautious approach the CPI leaders were taking with regard to the Indian federal government which, the *Times* assured its readers, had a stronger hold on its state ministries than did the states and their governors of the United States. And just to make sure, *Times* correspondent Rosenthal reminded his readers that "the Communist victory in Kerala is not an indication of a national swing. The Congress Party is still in firm control of most parts of the country."[2] Despite that assurance, U.S. officials would fret about the possible national consequences of the CPI victory up until the ministry it produced was finally removed from office twenty-eight months later, by an action of the central government in New Delhi.

In the meantime, ordinary people on the streets and in the villages of Kerala were not feeling so cautious. Their election victory had not come merely as the result of a vote. It was instead the outcome of decades of sacrifice, of organizing, petition signing, marching by the thousands in long *jathas* (processions or parades), rallies, strikes, battles with police and with landlord goon squads, living and working underground, overcoming caste privileges, running election campaigns, and engaging in parliamentary debates.

On March 30, 1957, the ministry was officially formed at Ernakulam, the state's largest city, with the election of Communist leader EMS Namboodiripad as the first Chief Minister in the history of Kerala. The proposed other new ministers made up a galaxy of the best thinkers and veteran political leaders like Professor Joseph Mundassery, a celebrated Malayalam literary critic, V. R. Krishna Iyer, a jurist who would later go on to become judge of the supreme court, Dr. A. R. Menon, a well-known medical doctor, and leaders like C. Achutha Menon, a future chief minister of Kerala, and Communist veterans like K. C. George, E. P. Gopalan, T. V. Thomas, and Chathan Master. K. R. Gouri was the lone woman member. She continued to be a powerful presence in Kerala politics for the next five decades.[3]

As described by H. D. Malaviya, leftist journalist and press attaché for the new ministry, as well as a Congress Party member:

> It was a festive day in Ernakulam. Huge masses of people poured into the city from all neighboring areas. The enthusiasm of the people was unprecedented. They went round the city shouting, singing, and dancing. A three-mile-long procession moved from one end of the city to the other. And in the mammoth mass rally which followed, nothing could be seen except red flags, festoons, and banners. Nothing could be heard except drumbeats, slogans and bursting crackers. And the mass singing and dancing, drum-beating and cracker-bursting continued till a late hour after the rally was over.... The people of Kerala were celebrating their victory . . . the triumph of the common man in Kerala.[4]

On April 5, when EMS took the oath of office, further massive celebrations occurred across Kerala. For the next twenty-eight months, Kerala's common man and common woman would ride a roller coaster of triumphs and tragedies. This chapter presents an overview of the main achievements and events of Kerala's first ministry—the EMS ministry.

The First Act: Ending the Eviction of Tenants

The roller coaster began in the very first week of the ministry when Chief Minister EMS Namboodiripad promulgated a comprehensive and unconditional "Stay of Eviction Proceedings" to protect the interests of tenants across Kerala.[5] The stay prohibited "all evictions of tenants, subtenants and occupants of homestead land on any ground including failure to pay rent." Furthermore, all court proceedings initiated by landlords against tenants, subtenants, or occupants of homesteads were stayed.[6] The CPI election manifesto had promised a "Land-to-the-Tiller" reform of Kerala's arcane and exploitative land ownership patterns. The landlord beneficiaries of the traditional exploitative system were organized to stifle any system that would result in tenants receiving title to the lands they worked. One of their typical practices was to evict tenants from the land in advance of any reforms that might benefit them. This threat of eviction was one of the components of the traditional system that rendered tenants vulnerable to landlord exploitation. The stay of eviction order would protect them from landlord machinations to evict them until the major reforms took place.

The stay was comprehensive and detailed. As summarized by land reform observer and analyst Ronald Herring, it covered "a wide variety of . . . tenancy-like rights in land, irrespective of the deed or document held by the landlord. . . . Certain deeds of surrender executed after the ministry took power were presumed to have been executed under duress and [were therefore] invalidated." Furthermore, based on the historical experience of the many ways landlords tricked both tenants and the government,

> cultivators were permitted to produce evidence that they were cultivating tenants even though described as agents or servants in documents.[7]

The new Revenue Minister, Mrs. K. R. Gouri, was already working with her staff and with the major peasant organizations and agricultural laborer unions to draft and fine-tune the bill. For the next twenty-eight months, Gouri and her office wrestled with the details of the Kerala Agrarian Relations Bill, developing a text that would bring justice and hope to thousands of tenants, while skirting the ever-hostile Kerala judiciary and New Dehli's central government that tended to side with landlords, despite the Congress Party's own supposed support of a land reform with similar content.

The Land Reform: Abolition of Tenancy

Along with the treacherous political landscape, drafting the bill was sometimes stymied by the complex existing relationships it would have to overrule. Ronald Herring described the pre-reform setup as "the most bewildering in India, a maze of intermediary rights, esoteric usufructuary mortgage tenures [and] complex subinfeudation."[8]

In simplified terms, Kerala had developed a three-tiered system for rice land. At the top was a class of landlords called *jenmies*, mostly Brahmins. Below them was a class of "superior" tenants called *kanamdar*, who leased land from the *jenmies* but then subleased all or part of the land to yet a third class of "inferior" tenants called *verumpattamdar*, who did the actual cultivation work. The cultivating tenants also hired low-caste former untouchables such as the Pulaya and other low-caste workers. A great deal of land was also owned by Hindu temples which was leased to tenants in some villages.[9]

A key element of the system was manipulation of the fear of eviction. The superior kanamdar tenants could often negotiate multiyear leases with their jenmies, giving them some protection against eviction, but the verumpattadar tenants were often stuck with only an annual promise of land to rent, a setup sometimes called "tenant-at-will." To get an idea of the levels of exploitation involved, we cite a CPI peasant association study from 1948 of twenty-four tenant households paying from 60 percent to 94 percent of their gross harvest to their landlords. All but five of these tenants had substantial debts.[10]

The Kerala Agricultural Relations Bill substantially reduced rent arrears (debts) for smallholders and proposed that current rents be limited to one-sixth to one-twelfth of gross produce on dry lands, and one-fourth to one-sixth on wet (irrigated) lands. According to EMS:

> Left to itself, the Communist Government would have

provided for the scaling down of old debts on a far vaster scale, but had to satisfy itself with much less, since it knew that Presidential assent would not be forthcoming if these were provided for.[11]

After fair rents and fixity of tenure had been established, there was to be a "peasant day," on which all cultivating tenants were deemed to have purchased their holdings, therefore removing ownership from the landlords. The government would then immediately purchase the lands, which would then be repurchased by the cultivating tenants at sixteen times the fair rent, which could be made in up to sixteen payments spread across sixteen years.[12] The importance of this procedure was to avoid a situation where the former landlords could attempt, through the legal system, to recover their lands, with the argument that the former tenants were not paying their installments. Landlords, however, were allowed to keep certain amounts of land, as long as they verified. They would cultivate it themselves or at least manage the agricultural labor force doing the physical labor.

Another prominent feature of the bill was the establishment of "land tribunals" to manage the transfer of rights, to fix fair rents and costs, and to handle disputes that were certain to arise in the complex implementation of the act. These tribunals were to have three members: one, an advocate nominated by the government, who would be the presiding officer; and two members elected by the local population.[13] It was thought that about three hundred such tribunals would be needed to administer the implementation of the act.[14] A key responsibility for the tribunals would be to fix fair rents on agricultural land.[15] Another responsibility was to manage the 50 percent of land that would be distributed to landless agricultural laborers. These beneficiaries, the Scheduled Castes and Tribes (former untouchables), would be required to pay only 55 percent of the market value, in sixteen installments.[16]

Land for Agricultural Workers

The surplus land was to be distributed to marginal peasants and landless agricultural workers. A relatively low fifteen acres of land was set for a family, and excess land would be taken over as surplus by the government for redistribution. It was estimated that, given the size of distribution of agricultural holdings, at least half a million acres of surplus land would be available, which would substantially address the land issue for marginal peasants and landless agricultural workers. Besides, the landless agricultural workers living in the garden lands of tenants and landlords would have the right to the hutment land (land up to ten cents, equal to one-tenth of an acre, in the immediate vicinity of their huts).[17]

Many of the landless workers were paying rent to the landlords on these small garden plots, where bananas, coconuts, cashews, areca nuts, mangoes, cassava, and other crops were grown. The hutment dwellers who lived on these plots, often in ramshackle huts, were called *kudikidappukaran*, from "kudi" or "hut." The EMS ministry land reform would give them ownership at no cost.[18] However, a large percentage of kudikidappukars, often being from former untouchable households, lived on rocky and steep plots. Nevertheless, the bill would have provided them with limited security.

Stalling the Land Reform

As part of its strategy to bring down the ministry, Congress and other opposition groups used up much time at every stage in considering the land reform bill. The ministry collaborated to a certain degree because of a desire to involve as much of the population as possible. The bill was publicly debated continuously for forty-eight days,[19] while the select committee discussing the bill received up to seven hundred statements of opinion. Numerous motions had to be considered. Outside the state assembly building, *jathas* were common. Conferences and demonstrations took place across the state as well.

Final passage occurred on June 10, 1959, but the dismissal of the ministry by the central government on July 31, 1959—less than two months later—led to several years of presidential rule, alternating with various state ministries that passed ineffective substitutes. This left the Kerala Agrarian Relations Bill in limbo until 1969, when a full enactment took place. But popular pressure had built up to such an extent that the reform was informally enacted sooner in many areas where the peasant movements were strongest.

Taxing the Plantations

An initial inquiry by the Kerala government to the central government as to whether the plantations could be nationalized (or taken over by Kerala State) led nowhere. A major block was that the prominent plantations were owned by foreign companies and that permission from the government of India would be required for any such move.

While stymied on nationalization, the EMS ministry found a partial workaround. They passed a new surtax of from 6.4 to 25 percent on high agricultural incomes of $5,250; to as much as 62.8 percent on annual incomes of $210,000 and above. As characterized by a *New York Times* correspondent on June 18, 1957:

> By levying a high tax on the plantation industry, the Communists apparently have tried to obtain the same results they had expected to get by nationalizing it.

The surtax also generated a small surplus in the state's operating budget.

While raising taxes on the rich and privileged, the EMS ministry increased benefits as much as they could for ordinary people. Initially, CPI member ministers took a pay cut from 500 rupees to 350, while independents supporting the ministry took the 500 rupees option. One goal of this voluntary pay cut, said EMS, was to show people that "here was a group of dedicated servants of the people, rather than self-seekers who use politics for their own personal and factional ends."[20]

Month Three: The Education Bill

In July 1957 the Assembly met to consider the EMS ministry's Education Bill along with the establishment of Kerala University. Like the land reform, the Education Bill became a flashpoint for opposition, both within and outside the Assembly halls.

Educational expenses made up about one-third of the entire Kerala state budget. Kerala was already known for its high levels of literacy, in part the result of decades of school construction totalling ten thousand schools in 1957. Of these, however, six to seven thousand were privately run and, of those, about 2,200 were controlled by the Catholic Church.[21] The Church's vehement, and eventually violent, opposition to the Education Bill led to its becoming a key factor in toppling the EMS ministry.

The problem with the private schools was that, owing in part to high levels of unemployment among educated Malayalis, management had a free hand and could manipulate and exploit teachers, who had essentially no say in running the schools. Teachers could be hired or fired at will, were poorly paid, and had no pensions or other traditional benefits. Getting hired often meant paying a substantial bribe. Getting fired could occur without advance notice. Because the government over the years had grown less able to intervene in school management at any level, its regulations did not apply to these private schools.[22] Yet most private schools received government "grants-in-aid" that constituted a substantial part of their income.

The Communist Party had promised in its election manifesto to reform the school management system and to establish benefits and protections for teachers. It had signaled a serious commitment on this issue by appointing Joseph Mundassery as minister for education in the EMS cabinet. Mundassery, a Christian, had worked for twenty-seven years at St. Thomas College in Trichur (Central Kerala). After witnessing the abuse of teachers by management during this time, Mundassery wrote a novel, *Professor*, that was widely read and influential in exposing the harsh lives of the teachers.[23] Originally a Congress supporter, he had gradually become disillusioned with the Congress Party's ineffectiveness, moved to the left, and, in 1957, had run as an independent candidate, supported by the CPI.[24]

Mundassery promoted an Education Bill that covered a range of school-related topics.[25] Discussion of this bill has been colored by controversial clauses regarding the appointment of teachers and regulation of managements. The central theme of this bill was the democratization and universalization of education. With widespread popular demand for education from below, the bill attempted to take these aspirations forward. It presented a program of universal and compulsory school education, in which parents were obliged to send their children to school until they completed a full course of primary education or reached the age of fourteen. It also provided that "where the guardians are too poor to provide meals or to buy books, and writing materials, the government, on the recommendation of the local education committee, may provide children with midday meals and necessary books and materials free of cost."[26]

Never before had a state government taken such a forthright stand to implement a constitutional mandate of universal education. Though the bill became moot with the fall of the government, steps were taken to expand the education facilities, particularly in the Malabar region. The bill also contained several provisions to improve the conditions of teachers:

- Teacher salaries will be paid directly by the state government or an agency approved by it;
- Government will establish pension funds and other related benefits for teachers;

- Pay scale of teachers will be raised significantly;
- If deemed in the public interest, government may take over management of a school for a certain period of time not to exceed five years;
- In cases of retrenchment, laid-off teachers will be given priority for rehiring.

Major clauses that were regulatory in nature included:

- The government will maintain a state registry of qualified teachers—all teachers to be hired must be on this registry—current teachers are grandfathered in and therefore considered to be on the registry;
- Communities will set up advisory boards to deal with educational matters including verifying that "employment of children does not interfere with their attendance in government or private schools";
- Private schools can opt out of these conditions but, in that case, cannot receive grant-in-aid from the state government.

These provisions mostly impacted primary education, so the University Act was amended and, in October 1957, the Oxford-educated economist Dr. John Matthai was appointed as vice-chancellor of Kerala University. Plans were laid for establishing an engineering college in Trichur along with ten polytechnics across the state.[27]

In the meantime, the Education Bill progressed slowly, hampered by anticommunist hysteria fanned especially by the Church, which led to a presidential review and later a national supreme court review that altered somewhat the language concerning minority group rights.[28] Lengthy delays also occurred, owing to numerous amendments and prolonged debate in the Assembly. The bill passed on November 29, 1958, and was due for implementation on June 1, 1959. But by then, the state was in the grips of agitation to oust the ministry.

Improving Labor Conditions

Kerala's industrialization was characterized by export-oriented agro-processing industries of such materials as coir, cashew, handloom textiles, bamboo, along with handicraft technology, often produced in small-scale, self-employed units. Cheap labor was the basis for the viability of these traditional industries—and the labor conditions were abominable. Trade unions were present mostly in the factory sector of these industries, where workers demanded improved wages and labor conditions. But because unions were resisted by employers and repressed by police, labor protection laws would have to be promulgated.

State intervention was also necessary for the revival of these industries. The expansion of cooperatives was the CPI ministry's solution for eliminating the middlemen and ensuring better returns to the self-employed and wage workers in petty production. The most significant measure was taken in the coir industry, where, based on a commission report, the existing cooperatives were revamped.[29] The attempt to reorganize the toddy (sap fermented into an alcoholic beverage) tapping industry, which was a stronghold of the Communists, on cooperative lines was resisted by the liquor contractors and the anticommunist opposition. Similarly, an attempt was made to organize labor contract societies to undertake public works.[30] These attempts were criticized by the opposition as political nepotism and corruption because Communists dominated these cooperatives. Nevertheless, the traditional industries, which accommodated a large part of the surplus labor in Kerala, received policy attention for the first time.

Defanging the Police

Early in the first Kerala ministry, a unique innovation was promulgated by the chief minister, EMS:

> It is not the job of the police to suppress the trade union peasant

and other mass activities of any mass organization, or a political struggle waged by any political party; it is the job of the police to track down and punish those who commit ordinary crimes.[31]

The chief minister continued that, traditionally, "The police have been using security proceedings under section 107, prohibitory orders under section 144, detention without trial, lathi [nightstick] charges and firings to suppress all popular agitations."[32] Or, as stated by EMS:

> This use of the police for suppressing people's movements has become so normal a feature of our public life that they have come to be considered as part of the "rule of law."[33]

Instead of the traditional use of the police, EMS proposed:

> The settlement of the labor or other disputes is to be left to the labor or other departments of the Government and not to be taken over by the police; the police should arrive at the scene of any labor, agrarian or other mass or political struggle only in case these struggles lead to an actual, or imminently threatened, breach of the peace or violent action.[34]

This policy of police neutrality in labor, property, and political disputes was immediately attacked by the opposition, which claimed that the practical outcome of the policy was to demoralize the police. Further, they argued that it fostered a spread of criminal behavior, especially by the oppressed classes, many of whom would feel that having "their" government in power would mean they could take laws into their own hands and interpret as they wanted.[35] In response, EMS pledged that the CPI ministry would establish clear limits in mass actions and in collective bargaining. He added, "The personal life and property of the employer or landowners was inviolable" and that "revolutionary justice" was not a policy of the Ministry or of the Communist Party of India.[36]

Conversely, the privileged groups were used to depending on "the coercive power of the police" in any disputes, and the CPI ministry would have to tread carefully in applying the new policy.[37]

Labor and Welfare Policies

One way to enhance police neutrality is to reduce the amount of conflict in labor disputes. The first ministry approached this problem in a number of ways. First, the chief minister publicly assured industrialists that their right to earn a profit would be honored.[38] Second, the labor minister, T. V. Thomas, attempted to engage organized labor on an industry-by-industry basis, rather than by individual employers or companies. This led to the establishment of industrial relations committees in several industries and the development of long-term contracts. Workers, employers, and the state worked jointly on issues such as rates for minimum wages, pensions, and other traditional benefits, as well as for working conditions.[39]

Minimum wage committees were appointed for some of the industries. Among the typically conflict-ridden rubber, tea, coconut, and cardamom plantations, wages were slightly increased, and amendments to the Plantation Labor Act now required schools and hospitals with certain minimum facilities to be established at the plantations.[40]

In June 1958 a Pay Commission for government employees released its findings, leading to pay increases for low-level government employees of 15 to 100 percent. In the private sector, a number of new industries were brought under the minimum wages acts, including cashew, tile manufacturing, toddy tapping, and agricultural labor.[41]

The ministry also helped facilitate broader access to private sector benefits. A remarkable feature of the EMS first ministry was its actions to inform women of their maternity benefits and to support them in making applications to their private-sector employers for these benefits. During the ministry, applications increased by almost 100 percent.[42]

Fighting Inequality, Undermining Caste

Kerala was long known for the depth, scope, and oppressiveness of its caste system, one of the strongest and most elaborate in India. The EMS first ministry worked to undermine it. EMS summarized the CPI position as follows:

> Caste... has existed for centuries.... The solution for the problem of caste and communal politics is, therefore, the abolition of caste and communal distinctions in daily social life.[43]

The CPI had developed a reputation for being against caste in daily social life. As summarized by G. K. Lieten, regarding the Kerala caste system:

> The first Namboodiripad ministry formed a kind of watershed. Wherever the Communist Party was active, caste barriers declined. Intimate social contacts between [different castes] became a feature of those rural areas where Communist activists had been making revolutionary changes. Punitive actions were organized against caste Hindus for misbehavior towards lower castes.[44]

Numerous scholars and observers have verified these conclusions.

As a seasoned anti-caste—formerly high-caste—activist himself, EMS noted that it would be

> idle to just preach the unity of the common people belonging to all castes and communities without taking steps so that the common people themselves begin to see their unity. This will not happen so long as social oppression of certain communities continues. That is why the Communist Party supports the demands of these backward communities and scheduled castes [former untouchables] for certain concessions for a temporary period to enable them to catch up with ... the rest of society.[45]

As noted in the previous chapter, this policy, sometimes called "reservation," resembles what is known in North America as "affirmative action." To EMS and the first ministry, it included "educational concessions of facilities for entering Government services and of other means of helping the members of the backward communities." EMS—who had taken the lead in supporting the Malabar nationalists in the struggle launched by non-Hindu communities and lower castes for reservation in public employment during the 1930s in Travancore—was now of the opinion that the elite among them, other than scheduled castes and tribes, could be left out. This position became problematic, and the Communist Party decided to maintain the status quo with respect to reservation.

Democratic Decentralization and People's Participation

In recent years international development theorists and practitioners have undertaken much thought and action in support of decentralization. A great deal of investment and experimentation has led to a near consensus that only a few cases of successful decentralization (consequences favorable to greater democracy and better general results) have ensued.[46] One well-known establishment expert has even asked: "Only in Kerala?"[47]

Kerala's broad success in achieving meaningful decentralization with positive spillover effects is widely known. The Kerala decentralization model was launched with much fanfare in 1996 and has continued to the present. But few are aware that a comprehensive decentralization program like the much-acclaimed 1996 mass campaign to introduce a third tier into the formal governance structure had been launched in 1957 in Kerala.

Indeed, on August 15, 1957, Chief Minister EMS convened an Administrative Reforms Committee (ARC) of eight members to:

> review the working of the administrative machinery as at

present organized and the systems, procedures and precedents under which it functions with a view to assessing their adequacy for a democratic Government in a welfare State.[48]

EMS listed six areas for consideration, including:

> measures for decentralization of powers at various levels [and] to suggest methods for democratization of the organs of Government at the various levels with a view to effective participation of local self-governing institutions or other representative bodies in the administration of Kerala.[49]

The Administrative Reforms Committee began by issuing an appeal for comments and ideas from a broad array of groups, including all that might hold an interest in public administration. They received 114 replies. This was followed in November 1957 by a questionnaire distributed among about one thousand officials, service associations, and "important persons in this State and outside." As the process unfolded, the Committee eventually held hearings of witnesses and discussions on sixty-two different days. Committee members heard formally from 158 witnesses. Additionally, informal discussions were held with several other participants.

The ARC's 221-page report begins with a history of various administrative structures that had grown up in Travancore, Cochin, and Malabar, the three contiguous Malayalam-speaking areas that formed the eventual state of Kerala in 1956. From a survey of this history, the committee concluded:

> An essential requisite for efficient administration is a wide delegation of powers to the officers at the lower levels of the hierarchy. ... Kerala has a major defect in that the effective participation of the people in general administration does not extend below the Central and the State levels. Democracy has not reached down to the village.[50]

The connection between democracy, self-government, and efficiency of administration is highlighted throughout the report. In assessing the consequences of more than a century of foreign domination, the report notes that the "pre-independence administration in India was . . . over-centralized." This is viewed as an expected consequence of a regime in which some hold power over a foreign population.[51] A further consequence of that situation is that "executive mindedness" comes to the fore, rather than initiative and creativity.[52]

The next section of the report considers the historical development of the Panchayats (village boards) in Kerala, concluding that the state needs

> full devolution of powers to the Panchayats and that they should not include any of the agency functions or functions which are to be vested in a higher body.[53]

Finally, the report notes:

> As Panchayats gain experience in the exercise of these functions and gather vitality and strength, the scope of the activities of the Panchayats will increase. We would urge a continuous search to effect greater and greater delegation.[54]

The report also considers the roles of the district-level institutions with elected councils, and the various line departments, such as education, health, and public works, and provides a list of 143 recommendations.

The first is that "Panchayats should be made the basic units of administration at the village level."[55] A sampling of other recommendations includes the following:

- Direct election of Panchayat members by adult franchise, with at least one woman;
- Functional committees for different subjects;

- Ward committees for each ward;
- Panchayats should be assigned to maintain government-owned primary schools;
- Panchayats will have to employ their own staff for performing mandatory functions;;
- The powers of the Panchayats and the departmental officers over the staff should be clearly defined and there should be no room for conflict between the two;
- Non-official bodies at the district level but direct election of members.

Numerous additional details create the structure of a decentralized, Panchayat-based rural village society.[56]

The Administrative Reforms Committee submitted its report on July 26, 1958. A comprehensive Kerala Panchayat Bill was introduced in December 1958, and later the Kerala District Councils Bill was introduced. However, the dismissal of the EMS first ministry by the central government in New Delhi on July 31, 1959, meant that the legislative process for decentralization could not be completed.

EMS considered decentralization as a process of deepening and strengthening the parliamentary democracy, from the existing central and provincial level to the local level. Such a step would create greater democratic space for people's political mobilization and open up possibilities of their participation in the development process. Notable achievements in this direction were the voluntary participation of people in strengthening local irrigation works and constructing rural roads.

Sheemakonna: A Gift from 1957

Another instance of large-scale people's participation promotion was the massive planting of Sheemakonna (gliricidia) shrubs in the state. Native to Central America and the Caribbean, gliricidia is a medium-height tree, grown to provide intermittent shade for coffee trees and live fencing for groves. But a major use of gliricidia is as a green manure, with the trees' leaf droppings providing substantial nitrogen, phosphorous, and potassium, three of the most critical components of fertilizers. Beginning from the time of the EMS first Communist ministry, Gliricidia Week and Gliricidia Month celebrations have become a fairly common practice in Kerala.[57]

Besides propagation of Sheemakonna, a participatory approach was promoted in agriculture—although its full realization could only have been achieved after implementation of land reforms. Mass volunteer labor was mobilized for repairing and constructing irrigation works and roads.

Fiscal Policy

The EMS ministry attracted some of the best young minds in Indian economics to advise it. A group of fresh young economists, such as Asok Mitra, I. S. Gulati, Asok Rudra, and Satyabrata Sen, all of whom later would be leading lights in academics, had volunteered to come to Kerala to prepare the budget and advise the government. By the time the state government came into being, the Second Five-Year Plan was already finalized, and it came to light that the state had one of the lowest per-capita plan allocations. While highlighting the central government's discrimination against the region, the EMS ministry adopted a positive approach to additional resource mobilization and expanding public investment.

Professor I. S. Gulati, who would later become the two-term vice chairman of the Kerala State Planning Board, wrote a series of four articles in the *Economic Weekly*, explaining the policies of the Communist government. This is what he had to say about the first budget:

> Those who prophesied that the objective of the Kerala Reds was only to expose the "high handedness" of the Centre dominated

by the Congress Party have been proved wrong. On the contrary, the Kerala Reds seem to be keen on avoiding a clash with Centre even on questions on which they hold very strong opinions . . . . Kerala's Finance Minister deserves to be complimented because he has refused to yield to the tempting precedent set by Congress Government in other States . . . of not making the required tax efforts . . . . On the contrary, he has introduced new taxes to the tune of ₹2.32 crores and converted his deficit into a small surplus. This additional taxation should fetch nearly ₹9 crores over the Plan Period. This exceeds the target set for the State.[58]

The budget significantly increased the outlay on education and health, but could still generate a surplus for capital investment because of additional resource mobilization. The rationalization of the sales tax into a single-point system would have imposed an additional burden on all people. Most of the other proposals, such as a supertax on agricultural companies, were progressive in character.

Private Industrial Investment

For various reasons, including the political instability in the region during the first decades of independence, the region failed to get an equitable share in the national plan outlay. A cycle rim factory and a DDT factory were the sole industrial proposals in the plan for the state approved by the central government.

Given this situation, the state government did not hesitate to seek private corporate investment to develop industry in the state. In one of his first statements, Chief Minister EMS had made it clear that the new government

> would encourage the capitalists to invest in industries, trade, and other economic activities. Our party welcomes capital from anywhere—even American capital. The only condition is that they should be on fair terms.[59]

The agreement reached with one of the largest corporate houses of Birla to establish a rayon factory generated a lot of controversy, even certain criticism from the Party.[60] But the factory was established. Besides the rayon factory, discussions were also held with other private industrialists to establish a paper factory and an insulated cable factory, as a joint venture with a Japanese company.[61]

Redistributive Development Strategy

The development strategy of the 1957–1959 government, though it accepted the importance of industrialization, was clearly focused on redistribution. The public provision of education and health care had been a tradition in southern Kerala as a result of pressure from mass movements, even before the formation of the state. The EMS ministry took this legacy forward in a more comprehensive manner. There was a significant increase in public expenditure in education and health care, particularly in the northern (Malabar) districts that had lagged behind historically.

Another important redistributive measure was the expansion of fair-price shops from about one thousand across the state up to about six thousand. These shops were supplemented by People's Food Committees that were intended to monitor the program so that the neediest received the fairest-priced goods, while those able to feed themselves would not enroll in the program, and ration "ghost" cards could be avoided.[62] Universal rationing in Kerala would play a vital role in providing nutrition and keeping hunger at bay in a state where cropping was dominated by commercial crops that created a chronic food deficit.

The EMS ministry's main contribution to a redistributive development strategy was land reform, which dramatically changed the asset distribution in favor of the lower strata, and created conditions for the improvement of wages and working conditions of the poor. The ministry thus contributed significantly to the acceleration of Kerala's social indicators of development, and thereby to the people's standard of living.

CHAPTER 5

Ousting the Communist Government: A Fruitless Two Years and a New, More Violent Strategy for the Anticommunist Opposition

> On April 5th afternoon 12 o'clock of Nineteen Fifty-Seven, a sense of insecurity descended into my village.
> — O. V. VIJAYAN

This is the opening sentence of a satirical short story on the theme of breakdown of law and order in the state, even as the Communist ministry was being sworn in. O. V. Vijayan, who penned it, would later be acclaimed as the greatest novelist writing in Malayalam, noted for his postmodern stances and irreverence for authority.[1] At one level, the feeling of insecurity was laughable but, at another, it was a deadly serious political allegation.

Despite the many positive achievements of the Communist ministry, not everyone in Kerala was happy. Attacks began and continued throughout the first two years of the ministry. On the third day after the ministry assumed power, the All-India Congress Committee (AICC) General Secretary, Shriman Narayanan, announced in New Delhi that law and order had collapsed in Kerala.² The provocation was the order of the new government setting free dozens of political prisoners, and, as it was the anniversary of the 1857 national rebellion against British rule, reducing sentences, including death penalties for some prisoners.³

K. B. Menon from Kerala alleged in the national Parliament that the Communists were setting up parallel "cell rule" in the state—the cell being the lowest organizational unit of the CPI at the grassroots level. The allegation was that these local units had become extra-constitutional authorities, interfering in local administration and even adjudicating judicial matters. Menon even presented a dozen examples of cell courts of the Party. The state government responded, case by case.⁴

But in Kerala these allegations landed in a context where public mediation of social disputes by caste organizations and community leaders was a long widespread tradition. In the 1940s powerful laborers and peasant organizations began to take over the mediation task of the caste organizations, which was misinterpreted as "cell courts." And generally the opposition, primarily the supporters of the Congress Party, took it for granted that it was the Communist Party leadership, not the elected ministers, who made the decisions.

In his first statement after meeting the governor, Chief Minister-elect EMS had made it clear that the politburo and Party state committee would decide only broad policies and would not interfere in the day-to-day running of the government.⁵ Many of the key appointments by the new ministry were remarkable for their openness and nonpartisanship. Dr. John Matthai, who was selected as vice chancellor of Kerala University, was a former member of the Nehru cabinet, and pro-business in his views. He had been a key architect of the Bombay Plan, which reflected the perspective of major business houses regarding post-independent India's economic development. So were the members of the Administrative Reforms Commission who, except for EMS, were well-known professionals with long administrative experience.

Nepotism in public appointments was another charge against the government. Until the EMS ministry came to power, the Communists were virtually denied government employment. Every job aspirant had to undergo police verification to ascertain his or her past activities—most important among them being connected with the Communist Party. The new government ended this practice, much to the consternation of the anticommunists.

Crimes and an Escalation of Violence?

The incidence of crime in Kerala was hotly debated. The opposition alleged that a sharp increase in crime had been registered. In response, the government published the crime trends in Kerala, including the reported crimes in the three former regions that were integrated in 1956 to form Kerala State. There were 21,063 registered crimes in 1956; 22,624 in 1957, an increase of 7.4 percent. But the increase in crimes during the previous years was at much higher rates and, in ratio to population, the incidents of crime were now lower in Kerala than in most other states.[6] Our searches, in 1957 and 1959, of government of India crime data revealed the number of crimes is lower than the official figures of the government of Kerala: 12,103 in 1957 but 8,718 in 1956, which would indicate sharp increase in crime in 1957. But given that Kerala was formed only in November 1956, it is not possible to ascertain how the figure for 1956 was derived.

Though we cannot clear up the confusion regarding crime data, it is plausible that a significant increase in crimes registered did take place. With the Communist government in the saddle, the poor and lower castes would have become more assertive, which would have been strongly resisted by the dominant castes and classes. A number of violent social confrontations did take place. The most notorious case among them was an incident at Varantharapally in Thrissur district, when six persons were killed by Communists. The following description of the incident is by Fr.

Vadakkan, a Catholic priest, and one of the prominent leaders of the 1959 anticommunist agitation:

> It was the drunken anti-Communists goons who attacked the communist jatha. Pushed to the wall, some of the marchers retaliated with knives. That is how six persons were murdered in Varantharapally. The local chiefs could not bear the sight of the agricultural workers and rural poor, who had been for centuries repressed, raising their heads high in defiance and arguing back.[7]

The Anticommunist Militias

A factor that played into the escalation of violence was the formation of trained volunteer groups by the Church and landed gentry. The earliest of such groups was the Social Scout Movement (SSM) established by Fr. Vadakkan in 1957. Though they were not exclusively Christian volunteers, they, in effect, remained a Christian strike force, trained on Church premises.[8] After the Varantharapally violence, Fr. Vadakkan went on a hunger strike, demanding that community organizations and political parties raise a Peace Army. According to police estimates, there were nearly a *lakh* (one hundred thousand) volunteers in the Peace Army.[9]

For reasons we have not been able to decipher, the volunteer force raised by the Church after the CPI victory was named the Christophers. Maryknoll priests in 1945 had founded the Christophers as an inspirational group of volunteers who undertook evangelical activities and provided a variety of social services. But the Christophers in Kerala had very little to do with the original intentions, organization, and activities of the Maryknoll priests. The Church in Kerala had raised this volunteer force ostensibly for self-defense in response to a Communist victory in the state.

An organizing committee was set up in every parish to mobilize volunteers, one volunteer from every house being the goal. Retired police and military personnel trained this khaki-and-blue-shirt force for marches, and in the use of weapons like clubs and knives. Volunteers were paid allowances when they were deployed in service or action.

The Christophers came to public attention when they marched at the head of the Anti-Education Bill demonstration in Thiruvananthapuram in August 1957. The following is the answer given by Home Minister V. R. Krishna Aiyar to a question about their activities raised in the Assembly in December 1957:

> They are being trained to march with flags on sticks three feet long and one and a half inches in diameter used to tie the flags. The reason given is for carrying flags in the marches. But sticks can be used as weapons . . . training takes place in the church premises . . . financed by Bishops.[10]

They were in the forefront of almost all the antigovernment agitations.[11]

The piety organization called the Legion of Mary was converted into another support organization for the agitations. Adopting the organizational structure of the Roman Catholic army made it amenable to such a transformation. It played an important role in mobilizing Christian women for antigovernment agitation.

In addition, there were many armed volunteer groups organized by landlords. The most notorious among these was the Niranam Army (Niranam Pada), whose main objective was to confront the rising militancy of agricultural workers in Kuttanadu.[12] With such a large-scale private mobilization of trained volunteers, it would have been surprising if the state's crime rate had not increased.

The Food Agitation

Kerala was a chronically food-deficit state, with domestic production hardly meeting half the normal calorie daily requirement.[13] In 1957 the government of India created food zones, reasoning that surplus production from other southern states was sufficient to meet Kerala's requirements. Thus, the government reduced the central supply to the state. The expected free movement of rice from the surplus states did not materialize, and a situation of severe scarcity and price-rise resulted. The price controls that the central government promised were also not effectively enforced.

The reduced central supply was insufficient to meet the requirements of the fair price shops opened by the new government.[14] The opposition launched a food agitation campaign by organizing hunger jathas (processions). In the Assembly, all political parties demanded that the government directly procure rice from outside of Kerala.

A contract with a wholesale dealer for procuring rice from the nearby state of Andhra Pradesh was drawn up by the government. Soon the allegation was raised that the CPI received a commission of ₹0.16 million in the deal. The "Rice Deal Scam" became the biggest political controversy and shadowed the government till its end. The government appointed a judicial inquiry into the rice deal. Its report did not exonerate the government completely.

Though this "Enquiry Report" did not suggest that the Party had benefited from the transaction, it held that there was an "avoidable loss" of ₹0.12 million. The report qualified this finding with a statement: "Had any other mode of purchase been adopted, in the peculiar circumstances, there would still have been this uncertainty about the prevailing Freight On Road Price (FOR) prices."[15] Decades later, the food secretary, in his autobiography, wrote that there was not even a paisa's worth of corruption in the deal.[16] All in all, however, the Rice Deal Scam was the only serious allegation of corruption that the opposition could raise against the government.

The Enquiry Report was submitted in 1959 and provided ideal leverage for opposition parties to launch a joint agitation parallel to that launched by an alliance of community organizations. There was also a humorous fallout from the rice deal controversy.

The government, besides establishing a network of fair price shops, had also begun to promote substitutes for rice, its favorite being macaroni made from cassava, which was abundant in Kerala. This proxy macaroni prompted the creation of a hilarious and popular musical story-telling performance, Lord Macaroni (Bhagavan Macaroni), lampooning the government, vilifying the ministers, and raising the rice deal corruption accusation. It did not take long for cassava macaroni to exit the scene.

The Kattampally Land Agitation

A major challenge to the ministry in the opening year was the land struggle at Kattampally. Government land in this area had been encroached on at the initiative of Congress Party activists who had connived to get some landless Scheduled Caste families, most of whom were hutment (shack) dwellers, onto the lands of the main encroachers. The government's promise that priority would be given to landless worker families in the distribution of land could not pacify the agitators, dragging on for four months. Finally, a compromise was reached on much the same terms as the government had offered at the beginning of the agitation.

The Anti-Agrarian Bill Agitation

The Agrarian Bill, which at one stroke would have disempowered the traditional landlords and undermined the economic base of the upper castes, provoked a bitter backlash. But surprisingly, the political opposition to the reforms was relatively muted. The main opposition of the Congress Party, let alone the socialist opposition, the Praja Socialist Party (PSP) and Revolutionary Socialist Party (RSP), could not outright oppose land reforms as a policy. The stand of the chief minister was that his government was trying to implement a program that had been "put forward by Congress but which their state governments were not yet able to implement."

In the prolonged legislative process through which an agrarian bill was finally enacted (discussed in chapter 4), the most serious opposition came from the Nair Service Society (NSS), the caste organization of the upper-caste Nairs, who stood to lose heavily from the reforms. They were aggrieved not only by the agrarian bill but also by the refusal of the government to concede to their demand for a new engineering college. As a result, there was a shift away from upper-caste support for the Communist government. Many political observers felt that the extreme bitterness of NSS could have been reduced substantially if the government had adopted a more flexible stand with respect to their plea for the engineering college.

The Agitation Against the Education Bill

The Education Bill became a subject of controversy even before it was released to the public on July 7, 1957. Christian newspapers started publishing shocking revelations about motives of the government. They alleged that the government was trying to destroy Christian educational institutions and nationalize education. Though the Congress as an organization did not denounce the bill, individual Christian Congress opposition leaders like P. T. Chacko came out strongly against it.

The dilemma for the Congress was that many of the clauses against which the Church was protesting, including public recruitment and payment of teachers and regulation of management, were also prevalent in some of the educational laws passed in Congress-ruled states. Nevertheless, the Congress Party and the Muslim League, a community-based political party of Muslims, opposed the bill in the legislature. It was also well known that the prominent leaders of Congress from Malabar were favorably disposed toward the bill. To the great surprise of many, the Nair Service Society chose to welcome the bill.

The Church went all out to oppose the bill at every stage. Volunteers were mobilized to protect the educational institutions. Marches were organized. Prayers and preaching in the Church reached a crescendo.

The revision of school textbooks was also condemned as a ploy to ideologically influence students and spread atheism.[17] Some of the literary works of the most prominent Malayalam writers were also criticized.[18] The agitation waned after a review committee of eminent persons cleared the textbooks with some modifications.[19]

There were misgivings even on the left for the high priority given to passing the Education Bill over implementing land reforms and other welfare measures. The immediate direct beneficiaries of the Education Bill were the seventy-five thousand teachers. Even among them, a section continued to be alienated from the government because of religious concerns.

The Supreme Court annulled certain clauses of the bill, and it was claimed as a great victory. The legislature revised the clauses per judicial ruling and once again passed the bill. The Assembly opposition at this stage was only a shadow of the resistance at the introductory stage. Though the Church was reorganizing its forces to continue the agitation, this looked like a lost cause after the Supreme Court verdict.

The One-Anna Struggle

Of all the antigovernment agitations and incidents during the first two years of the government, perhaps the most damaging to the new ministry was the June 1958 agitation of students for reducing the travel costs of transport boats.

Water transport was the predominant mode of travel in the low-lying lake areas in central Kerala, known as Kuttanadu. The government nationalized water transport. Two annas (one anna is one-sixteenth of a rupee) were fixed as the minimum charge, and students were offered a concession of 50 percent. But students demanded that they be allowed unlimited travel at one anna, as before nationalization. The fact was that unlimited travel at one anna was prevalent in only two of the boats, and only for students traveling to a school that the boat owners wanted to promote. But the agitation was launched and soon gained momentum.

Not only boats but also road buses were picketed. Attempts of

Communist cadres in Alappuzha to confront the students only inflamed the agitation. Public offices were picketed, and destruction of public property became common. The initial demand for a travel concession receded into the background and the students' strike became a general agitation against the government.[20]

The agitation continued with no end in sight. The political parties actively supported the student agitation, which spread all over southern Kerala. A militant, antigovernment student organization, the Kerala Students Union, was born. Finally, the government sought the help of veteran nationalist leader K. Kelappan and reached a compromise. Until a study was completed, the old water transport fee structure would continue to prevail in Kuttanadu. For the first time, the government had been forced to back down. The Communist influence among the students diminished. The number of college unions controlled by the Communist Party–related All India Student Federation declined from thirty to ten.

The Police Excesses

Police atrocities, at times against Communist unions, were a serious embarrassment for the government and a source of high-decibel propaganda for anticommunists. Despite the government's insistence that police stay away from labor disputes, police seemed to be only too eager to wade into them, with the excuse of maintaining law and order.

In the cashew factory at Kilikolloor in Quilon, senior leaders of the Communist trade union were beaten by the police while picketing the factory. An even worse incident was to come on July 25, 1958, at Chandanathoppu in Quilon. Here, a trade union related to the RSP physically prevented the removal of processed cashews by the factory owners. Two workers died in the police firing.

In 1958 Communist trade unions went on strike at the Munnar highlands plantations, demanding bonuses. Their attempt to picket the scabs led to a police officer firing and the death of two workers. Similarly, strikes at the Sitaram Spinning Mill in Thrissur and the Rubber Works in Trivandrum deteriorated into serious confrontations.

The CPI, which prided itself as the party of workers, while upset over these frequent incidents was nevertheless forced to justify police actions. Judicial inquiries gave a clean verdict. Some Communist leaders have since admitted on record how embarrassed they were at facing the workers and trying to explain the Party stand.[21]

The Stunning By-Election Victory at Devikulam

On May 19, 1958, when the EMS ministry had been in power for thirteen months, results were announced for a by-election in Devikulam. This region lies within a highland area where tea plantations employ thousands of workers, most from the neighboring state of Tamil Nadu. Contrary to the expectations of many, the Communist candidate Rosamma Punnose had won by a convincing margin: 55,819 votes to the opposition candidate's 48,730 votes. The polling participation rate had increased from 61.3 percent in 1957 to 84 percent in the 1958 by-election.[22]

The Church and the opposition had thrown themselves into the campaign and worked overtime. Rumors were spread that Tamilian workers would be evicted by the government if the Communists won. The Education Bill was the main theme of the campaign among Christian settlers, and fifteen thousand Christophers from the Kottayam district were deployed to the constituency. Normally, the Christophers were paid daily ₹3 if working within the district, and ₹6 if they had to go outside the district. Though the constituency was inside Kottayam district, everyone was paid daily ₹5 for the election work. There was no dearth of men or material for the opposition. The plantation owners, threatened by higher taxes and possible future land reforms, threw their weight behind the opposition.

The Communists threw their best cadres into the battle under the leadership of V. S. Achuthanandan, who would later become one of the Communist chief ministers in Kerala. The Communist campaign centered around the achievements of government, labor, and welfare measures for the plantation workers. Maternity benefits were extended to plantation workers, and minimum wages were revised upward. For the first time, the Labor Department had taken action against the plantation owners. It was an impressive record for a period of hardly a year and a half.

The resounding Communist victory laid to rest all doubts regarding popular support for the government. Election results were noticed by both the CIA, in its *Current Intelligence Weekly Summary*, and briefly in a *New York Times* article of May 22, 1958, by *Times* India correspondent, who noted the weaknesses in the Congress Party.[23]

Leftist congressman and press attaché H. D. Malaviya put it this way:

> In a way it may be said that the Devikulam by-election was a symbolic struggle between the Communists and the democratic elements supporting them on the one side and the capitalists and anti-Communists on the other. The Devikulam electorate, and symbolically the entire Kerala people, gave their unambiguous verdict.[24]

The victory at Devikulam was not isolated, though perhaps it was the most dramatic. Between 1957 and 1959, by-elections (special elections) were held in 175 Panchayat (village council) wards. Communists won fifty-four and Congress thirty-four. Out of forty-seven independents, twenty-two were Communists, who had nearly doubled their number of seats.

In the municipalities, by-elections were held in nineteen wards. Fifteen of them belonged to the opposition. Communists had only four seats in these wards. After the elections, the number of seats the Communists held increased to ten. In the mayoral election in the capital city of Thiruvananthapuram, though the combined opposition held a majority of twenty-seven seats out of forty, the

Communist independent was elected as the mayor.

Reinventing the Anticommunist Front

Fr. Vadakkan, who was still a seminarian, had taken the initiative to form the Anti-Communist Front (ACF) in 1951. The objectives were through intense propaganda, social mobilization, and social service to prevent the spread of communism in Kerala.[25] With the rise of the ACF, the criticism of communism became virulent and large scale. Anticommunist conventions, on the model of Bible conventions, were organized. EMS, in his pamphlet "Anti-Communist Front and Communists," admitted: "In recent times numerous anti-communist conventions have been organized in various parts of Travancore-Cochin. Thousands of men and women have participated in them. They exhibited deep bias and hatred for communism very similar to what we communists have against imperialism, landlordism, and capitalism."[26]

Despite the hectic programs undertaken by Fr. Vadakkan, which caught national attention, the overall political impact of the ACF remained muted. Its pamphlets emphasizing the importance of a united front against communism did not gather much support from outside the Catholic fold during the run-up to the 1954 Travancore-Cochin election.[27] The ACF was a voice in the wilderness, appealing for a united front of political parties against the Communist Party in the 1956 elections.[28]

Why did the efforts of the ACF not succeed? Dr. P. T. Chacko, a scholar from Louvain University in Belgium, wrote a series of articles in the Catholic newspaper *Deepika* in January and February of 1959 humorously titled "The Contradictions of Anti-ism." The Communists derisively called them "Anti-s" (*virudhanmaar*) and the name stuck, particularly, after the production of P. J. Antony's play, *Children of Revolution* (*Inquilabinte Makkal*), where features of a typical "Anti"-were derided, to the great amusement of the audience.[29] Chacko's arguments were that its image was that of a

Church organization that had inadvertently accepted negativity as the basic feature of its opposition to communism.

Chacko's article offers a long litany of activities of "Anti-s" that would include almost every conceivable agitation method: "Collection of weapons, manufacture of bombs, local resistance projects, rallies, marches, publications, speeches, prayer weeks, penance processions, rosary, Blue Army, Christopher Brigade, Marian Legion, Peace Army, cultural programs, throwing stones, slings, short sticks, long sticks, crackers, assault, foul words, murder, and robbery have all been deployed by the 'Anti-s' at one time or other."[30] But they failed to prevent Communism from advancing in the state.

What had gone wrong? The basic reason was the narrow circle in which the Anti-s operated. They reduced the challenge of Communism to a problem of Catholics alone. Dr. Chacko went on to elaborate:

> It is not possible to eradicate communism from Kerala or India by Catholics alone. Our activities so far were such as to create an impression in other communities that elimination of communism is . . . a vested interest of the Christian community. In a country like ours where there are numerous communities a common danger like communism cannot be eliminated by special organizations of any particular community.[31]

Therefore, Dr. Chacko proposed a united front of Christians, Hindus, and Muslims, to be led by political parties: Congress, Muslim League, Praja Socialist Party, Revolutionary Socialist Party, and Kerala Socialist Party, supported by an alliance of different communities. Only then could the Communists be defeated. The fact that the Catholic Church was willing to devote space for such a lengthy series, despite its highly critical assessment of the existing anticommunist movement, reflected the Church's exasperation with repeated failures to make headway in the anticommunist struggle.

Scaling Up the One-Anna Agitation

The paramount importance of developing a broad anticommunist political alliance became more evident after the Devikulam Communist victory. The Communists had come to power because the opposition had not been united in the 1957 election. Dr. Chacko's approach was to build a united movement around a positive alternative agenda for the state. The assumption was that the Communists would continue in power, possibly for another three years, if they enjoyed a majority in the legislature, and there was a real danger that the Communists would outperform the opposition and become entrenched. Therefore, the objective of the broad political alliance was to oust the government at the earliest opportunity. This was the argument espoused by "another" P. T. Chacko, a devoted Catholic and leader of the opposition in the assembly.

Opposition leader Chacko compared the students' One-Anna Agitation with the ongoing agitation against the Education Bill. While the government conceded to the demands of the students, it was going ahead with the process of finalizing the Education Bill. Why the difference? *Deepika*'s answer was this:

> The education agitators do not disrupt the day-to-day functioning of the government. . . . The leaders adhere to all legal and constitutional democratic norms. There is not even a shadow of violence in the agitation. It is a non-violent agitation pure and simple.
>
> In contrast these students had rejected peaceful methods. They challenged the law without fear. They disrupted the boats and other means of transport. They picketed government offices and roads. The government became helpless to arrest and remove the number of picketers who increased day-by-day. The government was forced to set free a good number of picketers after keeping them under illegal custody for some time. Thus, the enforcement officers of the law were forced to publicly break the law. To put it short, a situation was created making it

impossible for the government to function constitutionally. At least in the last phase of struggle the student agitation became a general agitation against the government.

What is the lesson to be learnt from the above experience? The communists are not going to submit to normal agitations. . . . Only if people apply violence so as to stun the government to a stop can they expect any concession from the communists. This government will not understand the language of democracy. They will understand only the language of violence.[32]

Lessons for Kerala of the Anticommunist Coup in Guatemala

Guatemala in 1954 showed how a mass frenzy can be created to oust a Communist government. *Deepika* argued, in a June 1959 article, "Guatemala and Kerala," that Guatemala was the model for Kerala to emulate:

> Unlike in Kerala the communists had come to power in that country without revealing their true colours. But Guatemala recognized the wolves in sheep's clothing. In 1954 the brave Guatemalan people ousted the communists from power. Guatemala is an example and inspiration for the liberation fighters in Kerala.[33]

We summarized in chapter 2 how the noncommunist but progressive government of Guatemala was removed from power at the instigation of the CIA and American corporations, with the help of the Church and armed mercenaries. The *Deepika* article demonized at length not only Jacobo Arbenz but also his mentor, Juan José Arévalo. It praised Carlos Castillo Armas as a liberator. Aravele, who drew up a constitution banning the Communist Party because of its foreign affiliations, was condemned as a communist because he had attempted, like the Communists in Kerala, to control public education and expropriate the land. Simón

Bolivar's Latin American Confederation, which was resurrected by Aravele, was, for *Deepika*, a Central American Cominform.

Under Arbenz, the true Communist colors came into the open. Castillo was a liberator. The success of his small troop was due to activists, who took to the street for "God, Motherland and Freedom." Rumors spread that the Archbishop was going to be arrested. The upsurge—coupled with mass hysteria aided by armed volunteers of Castillo—had brought down the Communist rule.

Deepika continued: "In our struggle this small country should be our guiding light. We will witness a frightened communism beating the retreat."[34]

British Guiana and the Communist Government in Kerala

The Indian constitution gave a state government the right to continue in power, as long as it enjoyed majority support in the legislature. Attempts to bribe the Communist legislators to defect had failed miserably. EMS had publicly alleged that the opposition offered five members of the Legislative Assembly (MLAs) ₹100,000 each for withdrawing support to the government. The conspiracy to bribe a Trivandrum MLA was exposed, to the great embarrassment of the opposition. The Devikulam by-election defeat appeared to dash hopes of defeating the Communists in by-elections. In such circumstances, the only possible solution was to persuade the central government to dismiss the Communist ministry. The constitution provided for such central intervention in the case of a breakdown of law and order and an elected state government proved incapable of fulfilling its constitutional duties.

The objective of any agitation would therefore be to paralyze the state government and create a constitutional crisis. The central government had a lot of leeway in deciding which party enjoyed the majority in the legislature through the discretionary powers of the governor, who was appointed by the central government and the formal constitutional head of the state government. This right to determine which party had the majority had been used in a partisan manner previously, including in the case of Travancore-Cochin in 1953–1954. But there had been no instance of a state government with a majority in the Assembly being dismissed because of an agitation by the opposition. The idea was not altogether out of the blue; it had come up for discussion in Kerala, in connection with the dismissal of Cheddi Jagan's progressive government in British Guiana by the British Crown.

In chapter 2, we briefly discussed the repeated destabilization of the People's Progressive Party government in British Guiana during the 1950s. That example is relevant here. Even before full independence from Britain, a new constitution, with limited autonomy for Guiana, was enacted and, in the April 1953 election, Cheddi Jagan became prime minister. The British prime minister found Guiana's nationalist and progressive policies unacceptable and, after being in power 133 days, Jagan's government was dismissed by the British Crown.

Meanwhile, the politics in newly formed Travancore-Cochin were rapidly turning in favor of a Communist-Socialist alliance. It was in this context that CPI leader C. Unniraja wrote a pamphlet titled "British Guiana and Elections in Travancore-Cochin." It is a remarkable document, outlining the history of coups in Guiana and includes extensive quotes from the speeches of Cheddi Jagan. Unniraja raised the question: If the Communists gained a majority in the Travancore-Cochin Assembly, would Congress permit the formation of a government?

After he was removed from power, Cheddi Jagan visited India, seeking support from Prime Minister Nehru. Industrialist Madhav Prasad Birla wrote in his business weekly *Eastern Economist*: "If someone is protecting the constitution to establish despotic rule, it is correct to temporarily hold the constitution in abeyance for taking counter measures. . . . The question is whether we should permit communists to come to power in any part of the Commonwealth. . . . It is good that Britain and America have reached a common understanding in this case on the need for limiting the opinion of the people."[35]

There were many indications that some of the Congress leaders were sympathetic to such antidemocratic views. Panampally Govinda Menon, a prominent Congress leader in Travancore-Cochin, asked in a public speech in Thiruvananthapuram, "Is our Travancore-Cochin state a play toy to be given into the hands of a communist united front?" He went on to add that a central minister had opined that Communists will not be allowed to govern even if they win the elections to the Assembly in Travancore-Cochin:[36]

> Is this the official position of the Congress party and the official policy of India's government? asked Unniraja. Are you going to adopt the precedent set by British imperialism in Guiana to bypass the legislature and government elected by the people, suspend the constitution, send army and police and establish a dictatorship?[37]

In 1954 such a crisis had been avoided by manipulating the PSP to defect from the united front and form a government with support of the Congress from outside. This government fell because of infighting and without giving a chance to the Communist opposition to seek an alternative government. The Assembly was dissolved, to the consternation of even some members of the Congress.

Now, in 1959, the question was being raised again: If a constitutional breakdown is created, will the state government be dismissed? It was no secret that Nehru, unlike many of his colleagues, including his daughter Indira, who was the president of the Congress, was against any such misadventure. Therefore, the agitation would have to be of such scope that even Nehru would have no choice other than to dismiss the government. The stage was thus set for the violent upheaval known in Kerala as the *Vimochana Samaram* or "Liberation Struggle."

Our discussion of the events during 1957 and 1958 does not give any hint of the storm that would erupt by mid-1959. Each of the agitations had, by and large, petered out. After the Devikulam Communist victory in May 1958, there were some agitations and police excesses. But from July, the state was relatively calm. The forces of reaction had been blunted—but the opposition was about to step up its work to new and far more dangerous levels.

CHAPTER 6

The Fateful Months of June and July 1959: The Anticommunist "Liberation Struggle" and Dismissal of the Government

In the months of June and July 1959, Kerala was thrown into unparalleled turmoil by the ferocity of the anticommunist agitation, which took everyone by surprise. The government found itself helpless to contain the anticommunist hysteria that erupted. The developments leading to the dismissal of the government can be divided into four phases:

(1) The first half of 1959 saw the forging of a broad antigovernment alliance among major communities and, importantly, among political parties. The anticommunist ideological offensive of a section of the state's secular intellectuals was characteristic of this phase.

(2) The agitation started with a *hartal* (closure of all establishments including trade and services), called by political parties, along with, on June 12, picketing against the opening of schools by community leaders. Police actions and shootings fanned protesters' passions into what Nehru, visiting Kerala on June 22 to study the situation, described as a "mass upsurge."

(3) From the last week of June to the third week of July, the mass upsurge became mass hysteria, with thousands of church-going women and children in the forefront of the agitation. The government was forced to restrain the police, giving the agitators a free hand.

(4) The government was rendered helpless, fulfilling the requirement for a breakdown of law and order as a prerequisite for formal dismissal of the ministry by the central government. The manipulations for a formal central dismissal of the state government succeeded on July 31.

The Catholic Church, Key Player

The Catholic Church, the region's major Christian community, had begun to warn against "atheist communism" even before the formation of the CPI in Kerala. The earliest efforts we were able to trace were anticommunist pamphlets on the danger of atheism, found in the Pontifical Seminary at Aluva,[1] books prohibited by the Church,[2] a critique of socialism,[3] and a catechism on communism.[4]

The opposition of the Catholic Church to Communists in Kerala was most clearly defined by the *Decree Against Communism* issued under Pope Pius XII on July 1, 1951, which declared that Catholics who professed to be Communist would be excommunicated from the Christian faith. The Church in Kerala was irked by the fact that many of the senior Communist leaders in southern Kerala were from Christian communities. However, excommunication and ostracization could not prevent the spread of Communism.

Fr. Vadakkan, who was still a seminarian, took the initiative to found the Anti-Communist Christian Front (ACF) in 1951.[5] With the rise of the ACF, the criticism of Communism became virulent, and large-scale anticommunist conventions on the model of Bible conventions were organized.

The scope and sweep of anticommunist literature spawned during the 1950s is amazing. Though anticommunist literature in the 1950s focused on diversified targets, atheism continued to be an important theme.[6] Class struggle and trade unions were also pilloried.[7] The critique of the Communist ideal of the family and its practice in the Soviet Union was another favorite theme for demonizing Communists.[8] Here is a brief sample:

> Lenin's Russia has declared a woman choosing a single husband as treason. The married women and men were separated and sent to distant factories and fields to work. There they must choose and live with a lover. The self-respecting women who refused to stand with the government were arrested and charge sheeted. Nobody knows what happened to them afterwards. Not satisfied, comrades drew up a glass of water strategy. Women are common property. They do not belong to anyone. They are always for everyone. No man can permanently keep a woman.[9]

The terrible conditions in the Soviet Union and the atrocities committed by Stalin were also described in lurid detail.[10] The Soviet invasion of Hungary was condemned. The Hungarian Cardinal Mindszenty was considered a hero. The foreign connections of the CPI were derided.[11] Obviously, during the 1957–1959 period, the Communist government in Kerala and the Education Bill became favorite targets for hysterical attack.[12]

There were also stray, more temperate voices asking people to "hate communism but love communists."[13] This more positive approach to socialism was much stronger among non-Catholic Christian communities. Some of them, led by M. M. Thomas, who was later to become the most important liberation theologist of Kerala, called a conference in August 1957 "to consider the Christian responsibility in relation to the political and economic and social problems of Kerala in the present situation."[14] P. Govinda Pillai, one of the CPI members in the legislature, also participated in the discussions. The conference came out with a discussion document that covered a wide range of topics, such as education and land reform, Communism, parliamentary democracy, and cooperation with

Communism. But these proved to be voices in the wilderness, and they were swept away in the anticommunist tide.

The Communists also attempted to engage with the criticisms of the Church. K. Damodaran, an important Communist ideologue, published a pamphlet in 1953 titled "Jesus Christ in Moscow."[15] The reply from Fr. Vadakkan was pat: "Jesus Christ Really in Moscow?"[16] Damodaran's rejoinder was "Yes, Jesus Christ in Moscow Itself."[17] During the height of the agitation, Damodaran published another pamphlet, "Christian Religion and Communism." But these polemics had little impact on his adversaries, and the gap between them only continued to widen.

Emergence of an Anticommunist Secular Intelligentsia

Numerous Malayali intellectuals were sympathetic to the Communist cause. The first to break out from the Communist hegemony was P. Kesava Dev, a leading novelist and short story writer. He had, from the 1930s, played an important role in propagating socialist ideas and was involved in trade union activities in Alappuzha. With the ascendancy of the Communists, he fell out with the trade union movement and by the time of independence was a strong critic of the Communist Party. Many of his political pamphlets were published by the Congress Party.[18] Aware of the role of theater in propagating Communism, he penned a series of Malayalam plays attacking the Communist Party.[19]

In 1958 nearly eighty Malayalam literary figures signed a statement criticizing the Soviet Union's treatment of the novelist Boris Pasternak. The intellectual leader of this new critique was M. Govindan, a Madras-based thinker, grounded in the radical humanism expounded by M. N. Roy and mentor of many young literary and artistic talents who came to Madras (today's Chennai). The chief organizer of the platform was C. J. Thomas, a pioneer playwright who experimented with modern trends. He was a Christian socialist and author of the essays "Religion and

Communism" and "Socialism." By the end of the 1940s, he had withdrawn from political work, drifted to Madras, was briefly employed by the U.S. Information Services (USIS), then became involved in book publishing. Returning to Kerala, he immersed himself in theater productions, including several avant-garde plays.[20]

The newly founded South Indian Book Trust in Madras also played an important role in the creation of a broad group of intellectuals opposed to Communism. The Book Trust was funded internationally and was suspected to have links with the U.S.I.S. Nehru refused to participate in its inaugural function upon discovering that it was funded by the Ford Foundation.[21]

Along with Govindan and Thomas, other prominent writers, such as M. V. Devan, Sukumar Azhikode, and M. K. Sanu, drifted to anticommunism based on their idea that Communism was antihumanist. "The Role of Writers in a Free Society," a collection of articles presented at a seminar in Cochin (Kochi), could be considered their manifesto. They were linked to a publishing house called Democratic Publications, and brought out a journal called the *Voice of Kerala*. It is now established that M. Govindan's "Congress for Cultural Freedom" in Madras was financially supported by foreign anticommunist cultural organizations.

The emergence of new intelligentsia platforms gave credibility to the anticommunist literature being spawned in Kerala. Many parodies were written of widely popular Communist plays and cultural productions. C. J. Thomas's *Poison Tree* is a parody on the communist play *You Made Me a Communist*. P. Kesava Dev also wrote a parody, *I Will Really Become a Communist*. Many professional theater groups also produced anticommunist plays. Most popular were the new versions of Kadhaprasangam, using this performing art form of Kerala to create a story-telling performance of music and songs ridiculing Communist policies. Traditionally, Kadhaprasangam festivals provided a cultural space for progressive cultural meetings and performances; now they were captured by anticommunist forces.

The Anticommunist Alliance of Major Communities

In March 1959, the Catholic Bishops Conference at Ernakulam passed a resolution openly stating that "in the present situation, in order to change the unacceptable clauses in the Education Bill, we appeal that our community should take joint actions with other communities."[22] Discussions had been going on for some time about the formation of such a united front. It was clear that the long-standing rift between the dominant caste of Nairs and the Christian community had to be mended for mass mobilization against the Communists. This was the theme of deliberations at the All-India Catholic Bishops Conference at Bangalore in December 1958 and of a subsequent meeting of laity, the Catholic Congress, at Kanyakumari.

The Nair community had to be brought into the fold of the anticommunist front. The Church was willing to accept Mannath Padmanabhan (Mannam), the supremo of the Nair Service Society (NSS), as the leader of the agitation. Mannam had a bloated ego, which the Church enhanced by promoting a series of massive receptions for him in every major center of southern Kerala. Mannam's critiques and declarations became more and more strident.

It was decided that a volunteer force would be raised to protect the schools, and the schools would not be reopened after vacation. On April 25 a pastoral letter from the bishops was issued. The Jacobite and Marthoma sections of the Church joined the school closure movement. On May 7 all the bishops in Kerala issued a joint pastoral letter.

The next step was to rope in the Ezhava community, the largest of the Hindu castes. Already, tensions had risen between the government and the Ezhava caste movement, the Sree Narayana Dharma Paripalana Yogam or SNDP, on the issue of caste reservation. The recommendation of the Administrative Reforms Committee to exclude the elites of the backward castes from the reservation policy was openly challenged. But before damage could be done, the CPI declared that there would be no change in the reservation system. Because the NSS was openly against the reservation system, the new anticommunist community alliance was not an attractive option for backward castes. The Communists' influence among them was also strong. Therefore, the SNDP leadership could not adopt an official anticommunist stance. It was left to the conscience of individual members to decide their stand.

In the intraparty division between Congress Socialists and traditionalists within the national movement, the Muslim leaders generally collaborated with the socialists. This tradition of sympathy toward the left, the Muslim League contesting in Muslim-dominated constituencies; the resulting split in anti-left votes contributed to victories of Communist candidates in some constituencies. But the strident anti-atheist propaganda also made an impact among the Islamic believers.[23] The Muslim community had no serious grievance against the Communists. In fact, the Communist government had lifted many of the discriminatory sanctions imposed on Muslims after the rebellion of 1921. Nonetheless, the Muslim League began to drift toward the anticommunist front.

A United Front Among Political Parties

It was evident that the struggle against the Communist ministry would have to be a political process. Congress, the major opposition party, though eager to be back in power, was constrained in launching an all-out struggle to oust a government that enjoyed a majority in the legislative assembly.

Two factors contributed to change the balance of political forces within Congress. The first, after a hard and bitter fight against northern leaders led by the veteran K. A. Damodara Menon, was the election of R. Sankar, an erstwhile SNDP secretary from southern Kerala, as the Kerala Pradesh Congress Committee (KPCC) president. Menon was at loggerheads with the opposition leader P. T. Chacko, who wanted an all-out struggle against the Communists and had mobilized Christian Congress leaders from southern Kerala in support of Sankar. There was also a growing feeling that the Communist influence among backward castes could be undermined only by having an Ezhava leader as the KPCC president. Sankar, unlike most of the Ezhava community leaders, was strongly anticommunist. His ascension put an end to the vacillations of the Kerala Congress leadership in launching a struggle against the government.

The second factor was the unanimous election, in February 1959, of Indira Gandhi, daughter of Nehru, as president of the All India Congress Committee, replacing U. N. Dhebar. The new president, keen to demonstrate her organizational skill, saw an opportunity in Kerala. If she could rescue the Congress in Kerala from the morass and bring it back to power by ousting the Communists, she could assert her own skill and power. Meanwhile R. Sankar, the new KPCC president, made clear the political line of the Congress Party: "Our aim is to strengthen the agitation of democratic parties. There by force of public opinion we want to compel the communist government to resign."[24]

The message was clear. Whatever might have been Nehru's reservations on anticommunist agitation, the new presidents, both at the center and state, had a different perspective. The two major issues raised by the agitation were the Education Bill and the agrarian bill, which had both passed constitutional scrutiny and due process. Further, Nehru was in sympathy with the broad objectives of the bills. His stand seemed to reflect the formulation of EMS: the bills attempted to implement the accepted positions of the Congress Party, which, for various reasons, it was not able to implement in other states.

In the first week of June 1959, when the Nehru family traveled to the hill station of Ooty in the neighboring state of Tamil Nadu for vacation, the representatives of both groups made a beeline to Ooty. It was evident that a storm was brewing in Kerala. Still, Nehru would not support an unconstitutional struggle in alliance with caste and communal forces.

Therefore, the KPCC had to maintain a facade of independent political protest. The Congress, PSP, and the Muslim League had decided in March to organize joint protests against what they described as the "Andhra Rice Trade Scam." Soon the PSP and even the left RSP decided to launch their own agitations. By June, the Muslim League also decided to join.

Normally, schools reopen in Kerala on the first of June. A section of the school managements had decided not to reopen the schools, and picketing was planned against the schools that did reopen. At this point, the government decided to buy time by extending the school reopening to June 12. On June 8, EMS made it clear that the government was willing to negotiate the implementation of certain controversial clauses in the Education Bill. But the agitators were no longer willing to negotiate: the government had to go. The issue now was not the bills but the continuance of the government itself.

The political parties, Congress, PSP, and the Muslim League issued a public appeal to make a success of Liberation Day, slated for June 12. On that day, their units all over the state would, in public meetings, pass resolutions demanding the resignation of the government. The Liberation Samithi (Committee) of Mannam called for picketing of schools and government offices. The Congress was not to join picketing, but individual members could. The difference between the two streams of agitation was thin. Intense preparations were made by both groups for the fateful day of June 12, when the agitation would be formally launched.

The Volunteers to Spearhead the Agitation

The different types of volunteer forces identified in the previous chapter were brought under a common command. According to *Deepika*, the Church organization claimed more than 250,000 Christophers. Government estimates were smaller, still around 100,000. Once the anticommunist agitation was declared, the Church decided that the Christophers would merge with a general volunteer force. The explanation was the following:

> At this start of the agitation against Education Bill it was feared that Christians would be isolated. It was at this juncture that some of the community leaders took initiative to form Christophers. . . . But today anti-communism has become universal. Christians will not be alone in opposing communism. Christophers have been misunderstood and there is also a possibility of it happening in the future. Therefore, Christophers are disbanded, and its members permitted to join the volunteer forces of opposition parties.[25]

A prominent Congress leader, Panampally Govinda Menon, announced a five-lakh (500,000) force "to resist the goondaism of the communist party and its followers in Kerala." Throughout the struggle, Christophers were prominently visible on the picket lines, at demonstrations, and rallies.

The home minister, Krishna Aiyar, openly stated in the Assembly:

> It is not an isolated activity of some innocent and gullible men. I have materials with me to show that in the early days of this ministry's coming into power two or three top Congressmen who have the authority to represent this organization were getting into touch with policemen. What was the purpose? They told the police that when the time was ripe, they would inform them when their assistance was required. . . . There is being planned what may be described in simple terms as an "operation overthrow" against the present ministry.[26]

THE MALAYALAM NEWSPAPERS

The rapid and exciting turn of events during this period resulted in heightened news interest among the people. The number of newspapers increased from nineteen to thirty and their circulation from 0.25 million to 0.6 million. The largest newspapers, *Malayala Manorama* and *Mathrubhumi*, accounted for 32 percent of the total circulation.²⁷ *Manorama* had always been anticommunist, while *Mathrubhumi*, being the organ of the national movement in Malabar, was softer toward the Communists. During 1957 and 1959, they adopted the stance of the Malabar leadership of Congress, who were not overly enthusiastic about anticommunist agitation. However, after Indira Gandhi gave the greenlight, their attitude toward the ministry changed.

Most of the other newspapers belonged to different communities, such as *Deepika*, of the Syrian Christian community. The other major community newspaper was *Kerala Kaumudi* of the Ezhavas. All political parties had their own mouthpieces. By and large, the only pro-government newspapers were the Communist newspapers *Janayugam* and *Deshabhimani*. *Kerala Kaumudi* had adopted an approach of critical support for the EMS ministry. In short, pro-government newspapers accounted for only 10 percent of the entire circulation.²⁸

Even during the time of the 1957 elections, most of the newspapers were against the Communists, and this antagonism increased over time. One event that soured the relationship was the first budget, which was published in *Kaumudi*, the newspaper mouthpiece of the RSP. The budget, confidential data, was leaked by a trade union worker sympathetic to the RSP. A case was registered against him and the paper's editor, and a court found them guilty. Attempts by the government to reduce the tensions with the press failed. At the All-India Newspaper Editors Conference in 1959, EMS stated point-blank:

> One section of the press is not willing to accept the communist government as a reality. I am afraid that there are newspapers here who are appealing for extra-constitutional methods to remove a constitutionally elected government. Let me point to the instance, of a newspaper editorial that charges the government would understand only the language of violence.²⁹

The Home Minister said in the Assembly:

Such a horrible, gutter type of journalism, which it is difficult to imagine. It is a calculated political campaign. A very large number of newspapers have been cornered by the opposition parties. The press is including vulgar language and vituperative epithets.[30]

Generally, the press played a very important role in creating mass anticommunist hysteria. It was as if more than half a million anticommunist pamphlets were distributed to the households in Kerala.

Mobilization of Finance

There was no shortage of money for the agitation, although no overall estimates of the total expenditures involved or how they were raised exist. In chapter 1 we cited American ambassadors Moynihan and Bunker referring to CIA money being channeled to fight Communists in Kerala and West Bengal. But, apart from these remarks, we do not have any details. A contemporary account of the overthrow of Kerala's Communist government includes this statement:

> There is a persistent impression in the mind of the public that American money has come through subterranean sources. Dame Rumour has it that money from the United States has come to Bombay from where it has been distributed through the church in Kerala. Direct channeling into Kerala of dollars has also taken place according to some sources. The food parcels, including butter, oil and milk powder, have come under an innocent garb from the United States to the Kerala churches in enormous quantities. They have been used for political purposes, one may assert almost without doubt. The great interest evinced by the Americans in the Kerala battle is natural and well known. An American embassy official from Karachi is said to have come to Trivandrum during the agitation period without previous notice.[31]

In the run-up to the agitation, formal fund mobilization campaigns were organized. The Kollam bishop set a quota of ₹50 due from every household. On May 5, Mannam issued a call for funds: "We must collect money. Lakhs and lakhs are required . . . we are mobilizing for a war. Our enemies are communists. Therefore, we must be prepared."

The planters and big landlords who were threatened by Communist rule were an important source of funds. Colonel Mackay, then general manager of Kanan Devan plantations in Kerala, which were subsidiaries of the UK-based plantation giant James Finlay, was elated by the agitation, writing in his memoir: "It was here that EMS met his Waterloo!" He recalls that William Roy, visiting agent of James Finlay, had met then prime minister Nehru, along with George Sutter, acting general manager.[32]

Fr. Vadakkan in his memoir recalled:

> I have not even taken a paise from America. The donations from big industrialists were collected to Bishop houses. I know of people who received hundreds of thousands of dollars from America. One priest toured America in my name and collected money. I learned this when I visited America in 1965. There were big opportunities to collect huge sums of money in that period.[33]

Police Firings and the Shift in Popular Mood

The *hartal* (closure of all establishments) on June 12 was total and quiet but for a *lathi* (nightstick) charge at Pala. Huge rallies were held in the capital and in selected towns. Then a charge sheet against the government was released in the capital by the opposition leader. Peaceful picketing turned into a violent confrontation with the police in Angamali, and seven persons were killed by police firing. Police had taken into custody a group of people who had destroyed toddy palms in retaliation for a ruckus at a toddy shop between workers and volunteers. A protest meeting was held in the evening of June 12 and a crowd of two thousand strong marched to the police station to free those arrested. Cornered by a violent mob, the police opened fire, resulting in the deaths of seven people and injuries to more than two dozen.

Circumstances indicate that the violence was provoked and premeditated. Church mouthpiece *Deepika*, on June 2, in an editorial, had hailed the preparedness of volunteers at Angamali:

> Angamali is the place, where on the spur of the call for the formation of a volunteer corps, 5,000 young men instantaneously came forward and lined up. . . . A big crowd armed with spades, knives, pickaxes and other implements surrounded the police station. The arrested persons were produced in court and at once let free on bail. This Angamali incident goes to show that the very presence of a big crowd can arrest police high handedness and injustice even without their resorting to violence.[34]

The *Deepika* editorial ended with a strong warning to the police: "When the lathi-loving police officers start wandering in the streets sick and coughing, understand that people have put an end to their high-handedness."

The tragic events of June 12 were the outcome of the tactics that Church newspapers had lauded a week earlier. This time it was not a spontaneous reaction but a planned march to the police station after a public meeting. A crowd had gathered, summoned by the ringing of the church bells.

Obviously, there were widely different versions of what transpired at Angamali. Fr. Vadakkan, in his autobiography, confessed:

> Let me make a factual statement. Communists were violent in many instances. But the situation of Angamali firing was created by the strikers themselves. Hundreds of people, most of them drunk, pelted stones at the police station; the police were forced to open fire. One of the injured died in Thrissur hospital. Before he closed his eyes he told me with excitement, "Father let me die. But the agitation must succeed."[35]

The deaths of the seven protesters was a shocker. Their burial service was led by the bishops. Their graves were visited by leaders and followers. On June 15, two more incidents of firings at two sites of school picketing resulted in the deaths of five more persons. The firings transformed the volunteer picketing into mass picketing, which became more and more provocative:

> The Trivandrum district collectorate was almost in a state of siege for about an hour and a half this morning when antigovernment demonstrators entered the premises in batches and shouted slogans. . . . Demonstrators went upstairs to the first floor of the building and hoisted three party flags as the police, armed with lathis and rifles, looked on. The doors of the office rooms in the collectorate remained closed and the demonstrators began shouting that the collectorate had surrendered.[36]

THE ROLE OF STUDENTS

The role of students in the anticommunist agitation in Kerala would be second only to the Indonesian experience. A strategic vision of agitation was scaling up the one-anna transport struggle organized by students in 1957. The same joint council of students gave a call on June 3,1959, appealing to students for direct action. The appeal referred to the boat transport struggle, and organizers seemed confident that, if the same unity and enthusiasm could be carried forward, the government would fall. For the present, the pro-communist Student Federation (SF) remained isolated.

Meanwhile, a dramatic change was taking place in the political orientation of the student community. The pro-communist SF, the PSP's Independent Student Organization, and the RSP's Progressive Student Organization constituted the major student organizations, while the Student Congress was the formal student wing of the Congress Party. The 1958 boat transport struggle had given birth to the Kerala Students Union (KSU), which had a new generation of student leaders, drawn mostly from the leadership of the Malayala Manorama-sponsored children's organization, the Bala Jana Sakhyam (Alliance of Children). Most of these student leaders later became key political leaders of the Congress Party, including chief ministers and central ministers. The support given by Manorama newspapers was an important reason for their rise to prominence. The anticommunist KSU replaced the Students Congress and grew into the most important student organization, outpacing even the SF, so that the number of college unions controlled by the SF declined from thirty in 1957 to eight in 1960.

The students' socioeconomic background was a major influence in the rise of the KSU, as well as the decline of radicalism among students. The share of Student Congress and backward students among those who appeared for the School Leaving Certificate exam was less than 10 percent. In the colleges, their proportion was only around 2 to 3 percent. The emergence of the KSU and an anticommunist intelligentsia gave voice to a silent conservative majority among the students.[37] These students were in the forefront of picketing the schools. The students joined in large numbers in picketing offices and buses, often escalating to violence. All the colleges were closed.

Women and Mass Hysteria

As the situation in Kerala deteriorated, Nehru decided to make a visit to the state to make a personal assessment. He arrived on July 22 in a special air force plane and was welcomed by protesters who stood silently holding English placards demanding central intervention on both sides of the road, from the airport to Raj Bhavan (Government House). This was an important psychological move that seems to have made a deep impression on Nehru. He still did not hide his reservations about an unconstitutional dismissal of an elected ministry, but he admitted that there was a "mass upsurge" in the state. The CPI retorted that Kerala was witnessing a case of "mass hysteria."

The question is: how did such a mass hysteria come to engulf the state in such a short period? The answer lies in the intense propaganda, particularly focusing on women. Annie Joseph, one of the most articulate pamphleteers of the agitation, addressed women: "Christ specially loved women. Therefore, we have a special responsibility to take up the protection of the church. . . . Need not fear anybody. Must come forward in masses to break the law. Let the jails be filled by patriotic women."[38]

Women participated in large numbers in torch processions from the tombs of those killed by police fire, who were labeled the "Trivandrum Martyrs Column." The wives of the martyrs lit the torches. Big receptions were also organized at various centers for the torch jathas, and they contributed to rousing the passions of the crowds. Women holding brooms to sweep out Communists were organized. A special committee was formed for the women's wing of the agitation with (Nair leader) Mannam's daughter as president.

The predominance of Christian women in protest actions after the police shootings is clear in the photographic album of the agitation published by *Deepika*.[39] Aroused by incessant sermons, tens of thousands of women walked with rosaries to the pickets, ready to suffer martyrdom for the Church. Fr. Vadakkan offers the following description of women picketing the Thrissur collectorate (office):

> Nearly 5,000 women and men came to picket. There were armed police lined up in front of the gate. Women rushed the gate and caught police by their belts and pushed them back. I had to firmly intervene and quieten them. Simple women who know nothing about politics! After some time, police officers declared that they were all under arrest. Armed police surrounded them. Women thought that they were going to be quartered in the public place itself. A granny came up and her concern was whether I would offer mass in the morning tomorrow![40]

The police were at a loss how to deal with this mass of women, old and young. There was no way to arrest and jail them all. *Deepika* album photos also reveal women charging into tense sites, patiently suffering water jets and booing the police when the water was exhausted.[41]

The hysteria peaked after Flory, a pregnant fisherwoman standing in front of her hut in a coastal village, was killed by a stray bullet in Thiruvananthapuram on July 3, which happened to be Women's Day, as designated by the Vimochana Samithi (Liberation Committee). Two other persons also died in the firing. Flory became the symbol of women's sacrifice and an icon, representing how Communist police murdered innocent women throughout Kerala. Hundreds of thousands of posters showing a photograph of Flory's husband and family weeping around her dead body were printed and distributed. The photo, showing the wailing husband, his mother consoling him in front of Flory's dead body, surrounded by her children, left a lasting impression in the minds of viewers. It was a masterpiece of propaganda.

Nearly five decades later, the police head constable who had pulled the trigger to shoot Flory came out with a narrative of the event, which was published in *Malayala Manorama*.[42] The police team on patrol, the constable said, had stopped by the church because the police inspector, who had come from a neighboring station, was a friend of the parish priest and wanted to visit him. As he walked toward the church he was attacked—totally unprovoked—by a band of people, who stoned the police vehicle. The church bell rang, and the crowd began to swell. There was no other way to disburse the crowd than to open fire. The constable also doubted if Flory had been standing in front of her hut. Since he had fired into the air and directly into the crowd, Flory must have joined the crowd. The fisherfolk were under the conviction that police attacks against the Church and Church institutions could happen any time, and they were there to rally to protect their church.

The Final Assault

Nehru, who spent four days in Kerala, held parleys with all interest groups. He put forward three proposals before the state ministry:

(1) Postpone the implementation of the Education Bill until a compromise could be reached; (2) Hold an inquiry against police firings; (3) Hold an inquiry regarding the thirty-two allegations raised by Ashok Mehta in the national parliament. EMS accepted all the proposals. But Congress and the Vimochana Samithi were unwilling to consider any compromise.

Malayala Manorama had published an English editorial while Nehru was in Kerala, explaining why the state government should be dismissed. They argued that there would be six adverse consequences if the government were allowed to complete its term: (1) The unrest would increase; (2) The Communists would capture important posts in the government machinery; (3) People would be forced to accept Communism against their better judgment; (4) The Communists would manipulate voter lists and render the next election a farce; (5) Kerala would become a source of finance for Communist propaganda in the rest of the country; and (6) If moral and spiritual values were undermined, it would be very difficult to recover them.

On July 1, EMS invited the Education Council for a discussion, which was rejected by the council outright. Instead, a suggestion was made by the central government that the ministry resign on its own. This undemocratic proposal was outright rejected by the CPI. Thus, the stalemate continued, as did the widespread violence against government property and against Communists. A record of the six weeks of agitation led to the following summary:

> 245 transport buses were damaged. 15 schools burnt. 42 toddy liquor shops run by workers co-operatives were attacked. 20 boats were damaged. There were 31 attacks against teachers and students. 5 bridges subverted to block traffic. 93 houses of communist activists and sympathizers attacked. 112 police were hurt in the agitation.[43]

The Vimochana Samithi declared a march to the government secretariat. The Samithi decided to start a "Save India Struggle" for the banishment of Communism from Kerala and India on August 9, the memorable day when Gandhi had launched his Quit India Movement. Over one lakh (100,000) volunteers from different parts of the state were to march into the capital and completely paralyze all activities at all levels of government, achieving liberation by August 15—national Independence Day.[44]

The same declaration was repeated by KPCC president R. Sankar, addressing a public meeting in Bombay. According to the Press Trust of India (PTI), Sankar said that "the people of Kerala would observe a Save India Day on August 9 when every man in the state would march on to the secretariat in Trivandrum and will not return to their homes till the communist government is thrown out."[45]

It was a declaration of an open coup d'état. No government could bow to such a challenge. There would be a bloodbath and anarchy. The agitation had foreclosed all options other than a direct central intervention. Available evidence points to the role of India's Central Intelligence Bureau (CIB) in bringing matters to such a denouement.

Central Intelligence Behind the Scenes

According to some observers, the CIB "had a very good organization in Kerala under M. Gopalakrishna Menon and came to know actions of the party and government as soon as they were planned." The CIB worked hand-in-glove with the CIA, a relationship that was admitted by U.S. ambassador Ellsworth Bunker: "Our intelligence people, CIA, worked very closely with the Indian intelligence people."[46]

B. N. Mullik, director of the CIB, was deeply prejudiced against communism and was highly critical of the policies of the new Communist government.[47] The CIB kept close watch over Kerala developments. On July 5, Mullik was asked by Home Minister Govind Ballabh Pant for an assessment of the Kerala situation, and whether the central government should take any action.

Mullik was of the opinion that "the time had not yet arrived for the government of India to take action, which would take place in due course, and that it would be better to let the Kerala ministry collapse by force of events than by any action of the central government."[48] Every day, there would be an evening meeting with the Home Minister.

By July 18, the CIB's assessment changed to a need for central action, as Mullik feared, "there would be widespread bloodshed and civil war in Kerala."[49] At the same time, there was strong opposition from Home Secretary Aditya Nath Jha against dismissing a government that enjoyed a majority in the legislature. But the situation changed again after the Vimochana Samithi declared the August 9 march to Trivandrum—a bloodbath in Kerala could be avoided only through central intervention.

According to Mullik, on July 23, a charge sheet was prepared against the Kerala government by a team involving him, the Home Minister, and the Law Minister, and then flown to the Kerala governor. The governor had only to rubber-stamp it. Three days later, Mullik, on the instructions of the Home Minister, phoned the governor regarding his response. The Home Secretary still maintained his reservations.

It was at this juncture that the CIB produced its ace card. "Namboothiripad himself was keen that the central government should step in and terminate the suspense that was hanging over Kerala."[50] Mullik's claim was that he had discussed the situation with leading Communists. This information seems to have been fabricated, as no Communist leader has ever, so far, admitted to any such discussions in subsequent decades, and Nehru's reference to it was hotly contested by the Communist members.

Thereafter, events moved fast. A report from the governor was requested The report was opened in Madras, while in transit, and its contents communicated over the phone to the CIB, enabling the Home Minister to receive the report on the night of July 29. The report formally arrived on July 30, and the next day orders were issued by the president dismissing the Kerala government.

Dismissal and After

Many expected the Communists to react violently to the ministry's dismissal. But, after receiving the formal communiqué, Chief Minister EMS and other ministers in the capital merely led a peaceful demonstration in the city and a protest meeting. Similar demonstrations took place in major centers and, in subsequent weeks, receptions were organized for the erstwhile ministers. It was the victorious rightists who continued to be on the rampage, mocking the left workers and attacking their houses and offices. The post-dismissal violence continued for months.

The CPI state committee that met in September 1959 protested the widespread organized violence in the state. An important feature of the violence was the targeting of agricultural workers, scheduled castes, and the Ezhava community. The dismissal resolution mentioned specific areas in the state where such attacks were intense. Kelappan, a freedom fighter and Congress member who toured the troubled areas, testified to the generalized attack against agricultural workers. K. R. Narayanan, who was a Congress man, SNDP leader, and a participant in the anticommunist agitation, came out in public against revenge attacks on Ezhava families, narrating many tragic incidents. Not only did this low-caste, poor group side with the Communists, but they had also become more assertive regarding local powers under the Communist government. Now they were being brought back into submission. *Kerala Kaumudi*, the mouthpiece of the Ezhava caste, editorialized against the violence selectively targeted against backward-caste people and the inaction of the government to stop it.[51]

A group of journalists led by the editor of *Deepam* and, incidentally, the secretary of the Editor's Guild, toured troubled areas in the Ernakulam and Thrissur districts. *Deepam* published a detailed report on the repression in the now infamous Angamali region.[52] The pro-communist writer Pavanan described the treatment meted out to the journalists participating in the inquiry:

"Blocking the journalists from holding their enquiry, threaten and attack them and finally, tear up the reports. . . . These are being done by rowdy elements who are aware that their actions are too vile to be reported. But their respectable leaders do not utter a word against them."[53]

Initially, the general belief was that it was only natural that the victors would attempt to overpower the vanquished, and that the violence would subside. But the statement of K. R. Narayanan publicly countered that the violence was only becoming more aggravated over time. The reason for this was summarized by the Election Review Report of the CPI in 1960: "During the last three years their strategy was to inflame the anti-communist hatred among the people. The object was to divide the people into two camps of communists and anti-communists. For this purpose, violence and government machinery was used." The post-dismissal violence was part of a conscious strategy to keep up the anticommunist tempo of antigovernment agitation in the run-up to the 1960 election.

The organizers of the anticommunist agitation in Kerala had visions of extending it to Communists in other states. After all, the name of the direct action on August 9 was "Save India Day." Mannam declared that having completed the job in Kerala he would now lead the anticommunist campaign in the rest of India. But such wild imaginings were put to rest by Nehru, who expressed to KPCC president R. Sankar displeasure and stern disapproval of any such plan.

A curious incident took place after the dismissal of the Communist government. R. Sankar held a press conference, where he thanked the participants and supporters of the anticommunist agitation. At the end, he reportedly thanked the United States of America for the support extended. But immediately after the press conference, the USIS released a denial, and no press carried the remarks the next day. Robin Jeffrey is on record that *The Hindu* reporter, who was present at the conference, testified to the accuracy of the report.[54] What was the role of the CIA in Kerala, which it was so keen to deny? We shall attempt to answer this question in subsequent chapters.

CHAPTER 7

Creating Anticommunist Hysteria: The Christian Anti-Communism Crusade and Moral Re-Armament

Some components of the typical template for describing CIA interventions and toppling of administrations (presented in chapter 2) could have taken place with the CIA in the background. That is, the classical "covert" actions, such as paying bribes, would not have been visible to the public. Further, military operations might not even be necessary or feasible in certain cases.

In general, although the hand of the CIA might not always be apparent, plenty of public CIA action takes place. The CIA's first step is to target public opinion. This can include infiltration or control of the local press and media. In the Kerala case, much of this activity was generated by the Catholic Church. However, in addition to the conservative, anticommunist Church, two unanticipated CIA allies emerged to play roles in the campaign against the EMS ministry. These are the Christian Anti-Communism Crusade (CACC) and the Moral Re-Armament movement (MRA).

Fred Schwarz and the Christian Anti-Communism Crusade

In 1953 an obscure Australian M.D. founded the Christian Anti-Communism Crusade. Never actually ordained in any Christian denomination and self-taught as to the theory and practice of Communism, Fred Schwarz had emerged on speaking tours in the United States in 1950 and 1952 as a dynamic and persuasive lay lecturer. To his followers, he instilled enthusiasm and excitement about what he saw as the worldwide dangers of the Communist movement. He gained acceptance as a rising star in U.S. evangelical circles and had soon set up headquarters in Southern California, one of the country's right-wing strongholds at the time.

Billy Graham was then at the height of his popularity. He advised Schwarz to form a ministry of his own, welding anticommunism and evangelism. In Graham's early years, anticommunism was also a feature of his evangelism, but he gradually moved into more liberal postures, leaving the extreme anticommunism platform to preachers like Schwarz. Journalist and media critic Ben Bagdikian, in his study, *The Media Monopoly*,[1] gave Billy Graham as an example of how the media could transform a low-profile Baptist minister into an evangelical superhero. Schwarz[2] held Billy Graham to be "the prince of Christian evangelists" and, in his 56-page booklet "Communism: Diagnosis and Treatment,"[3] includes a picture of Graham preaching to Red Volunteers in India. We do not know exactly where in India Graham's sermon took place, but it was somewhere in Travancore or some other South Indian state. Billy Graham and Fred Schwarz both benefited from the "media monopoly."

HUAC Testimony and the Rise to Stardom

On May 27, 1957, Fred Schwarz was called to testify before the House Unamerican Activities Committee (HUAC), the notorious body that had ruined the lives and careers of numerous Americans in its ruthless search to root out Communist Party members and sympathizers. Schwarz, however, was called not as a target for blacklisting but as an expert witness on the theory and practice of communism.[4] He spoke on the record with HUAC chair Richard Ahrens for two and a half hours.[5]

Schwarz's smooth and direct performance bowled over the already sympathetic Ahrens. In explaining the appeal of Communism in India, Schwarz asserted that Christians in India who voted for the Communists did so because "Red propaganda operated by targeting very specific subgroups and exploiting narrow issues to their advantage." The "Reds," Schwarz stated, also knew how to present a friendly image. People in India voted Communist "because the Communists sent a very fine young student to their village with glorious magazines showing them how much their life will be improved under Communism."[6]

Two spectacular points helped propel Schwarz's HUAC testimony into right-wing stardom. First, Schwarz claimed that Stalin and Mao had set 1973 either as the year when Communist countries would overtake the West, or when the entire world would succumb to Communism.[7] In the wake of the projected Communist takeover, for which he had no evidence,[8] Schwarz also predicted that the Communist worldwide victory would lead to the massacre of hundreds of millions of people, as entire classes of humanity would have to be destroyed to make way for Communist-introduced atheism. Schwarz remarked: "Inherent within the theory of Communism is the greatest program of murder, slaughter, and insanity conceivable."[9]

By 1957 HUAC's political impact was on the wane. Nonetheless, the committee printed Schwarz's testimony as a booklet and sent it out to their mailing list. Within months, thousands of right-wing business leaders and politicians were paying to distribute copies, buying expensive full-text, full-page newspaper ads, and recommending the booklet to their mostly right-wing friends and readers.[10] So viral did the tract go that Schwarz began calling it "Operation Testimony" in the CACC newsletter. As knowledge of the booklet spread in right-wing circles, Schwarz documented requests for copies or reprintings by American Legion posts, small-town newspapers across the country, and local Christian ministers in otherwise obscure publications and places such as *The Christian Beacon* and the Bible Presbyterian Church of Collingswood, New Jersey. One request asked for enough copies "to place one in the hands of every student at the [Bozeman] Montana State College here, some 3,000," then went on to report, "The Texas Power and Light Company reprinted 7,000 copies to send to all their employees . . . [and] the Southwestern Savings and Loan Association of Houston, Texas, has requested 10,000 copies to be mailed to all their accounts."[11]

How many ordinary Americans became convinced that doomsday for capitalism would occur by 1973 may never be known, but, in terms of toppling the EMS ministry, one very important follower emerged: Harry Bradley of the Allen-Bradley Company of Milwaukee, Wisconsin. Impressed by Schwarz's ability with words, Bradley began an investment splurge in Schwarz and his Christian Anti-Communism Crusade that ended in donations over several years totaling "in the neighborhood of $150,000"—nearly $1.5 million in today's money.[12]

In June 1958, Bradley, with several company executives and board members, hosted Schwarz for lunch and a talk. As Schwarz tells it:

> There was a wonderful sequel to the meeting. Shortly afterwards there came through the mail a check for the Crusade for $10,000 from the Lynde-Bradley Foundation.[13]

This check made it possible for Schwarz and his colleague George Thomas back in Kerala to make a down payment on an additional printing press to expand their anticommunist literature production. Schwarz:

> We immediately called George Thomas to secure the printing

establishment. It is now working for Christ and freedom. I cannot find words adequate to thank Mr. Bradley and his associates. I sincerely thank God for them and their generous devotion to freedom.[14]

George Thomas and the "Light of the World"

In what appears to be a coincidence, a Malayali named George Thomas who, in 1957, was studying at the University of Washington, attended one of Schwarz's lectures in Seattle and decided to speak with Schwarz after the presentation.[15] George's father was a missionary working in Kerala with the so-called Plymouth Brethren, also known as the Kerala Brethren. He was also associated with a small evangelical missionary group, the Indian Gospel Mission (IGM), that ran an orphanage in nearby Andhra Pradesh and had a few small congregations in Kottayam, Kerala.[16] Schwarz and George Thomas decided to work together.

On his return to Kerala in 1957, George Thomas shifted the evangelical newsletter *Vishwa Deepam* (The Light of the World), which was published by his father in a nearby small town, to Kottayam and converted it into an anticommunist magazine, whose circulation grew to more than 10,000. He built a new headquarters for the magazine and also purchased a printing press.

In 1955 Schwarz started publishing a newsletter. In its October 1957 issue, just a few months after the CPI election victory and the installation of the EMS ministry, Schwarz recounted what came to be one of his typical scare-stories about the CPI ministry. Taking his information from "a report from the United Planters Association of Southern India," he accused the ministry of having introduced "an Education Bill that has stirred up wide opposition throughout India. It aims at giving the Communist government a monopoly of the educational process." Schwarz further claimed that "they have reduced the police force and have given the go-ahead sign to organizing gangs to force the workers into Communist controlled unions."[17] More specifically, we have received a report from the Manager of Hereford Estate, Thenmally, Kerala, about the forcible conversion of workers, made by gangs of outsiders, to join the local Communist union, which was organized only two months ago. It is reported that the workers have been given to understand that the Communist organizers of the union could do anything and the police would not interfere. Those who waver were helped along by the free supply of liquor distilled in the jungles.... In some cases those who refuse to join the union are brought before "tribunals" appointed by the gang and fined or warned. Workers are harassed and some molestations have taken place.... It is also reported that one of the leaders who happens to be one who had served a term of imprisonment at Punalur is the most active in the gang.... Since the formation of the new union, the workers have been freely collecting the crops of the estate, and staff who have been threatened are gradually leaving the estate. The manager concludes in his report that the workers are in full possession of the property.

On the following page, Schwarz made his first mention of the need for a bigger printing capability for the "Indian Christian Crusade . . . [which is] carrying on its work of proclaiming the story of Christ and exposing the godless emaciations [sic] of the Communists."[18]

Back in Kerala, the $10,000 check was supplemented by other donations from the United States, based on sales from Schwarz's HUAC testimony booklet. This led to the prospect of purchasing a building in Kottayam, where a new daily paper and its printing press could be centralized. Although an appeal to the Ford Foundation appears to have failed,[19] the discovery of an old but workable English press brought great excitement. Even so, the project stalled until further funding could be arranged.

In January 1959, a member of the CACC named Charles Sarvis visited Kerala. Among his observations on the road to Kottayam:

> I saw there many bookstands and their red flags with hammer

and sickle flying. I heard them shout their menacing slogans as they gathered for a parade. . . . Near the end our taxi driver honked the horn to pull by them and the crowd parted as we started to leave, but before we knew it our car was surrounded by them and angry faces were peering in the windows. Both George [Thomas] and I bowed in prayer for our safety as they knew who George was and I was an unwelcome American. We were both breathing easier as the crowd parted when some police (Communist also) arrived and we were given room to leave the area and go home. The Communist menace looms larger and closer every day . . . I firmly believe the answer lies in supplying George Thomas with the equipment necessary to publish a daily newspaper. This paper will print the truth to the people in Kerala of the Communist menace.[20]

A Newspaper, "The Voice of Kerala"

On August 20, 1959, *Keraladhwani*, "The Voice of Kerala," published its first issue. Daily circulation was estimated at 20,000 copies and was costing its supporters $5,000 to $8,000 per month in labor.[21] Altogether, the paper hired up to ten journalists and "a gallant crew of over 120 employees working inside the plant," supplemented by over five hundred agents and distribution workers. Shortly after the paper's launch, CACC director Fred Schwarz estimated its circulation as 27,000, making it Kerala's fourth-largest newspaper.[22] Dr. George Thomas also received a monthly allowance, which was increased from $250 to $400 per month in 1958. Overall, the "truth" newspaper ended up costing CACC around $270,000. How the difference was made up from the original Allen-Bradley check for $10,000 was not fully explained in the CACC *Newsletter*.[23]

At the newspaper's opening, Schwarz proclaimed:

> God provided the capital through His humble servant, Dr. Fred Schwarz, and Dr. George Thomas became the Editor-in-Chief.

> The daily output of the "Voice of Kerala" grew from 10,000 in August '59 to 28,000 copies at the present time [March 1960] with a reading coverage of ten times that number. Statistics indicate that at least 10 persons read each copy of the "Voice of Kerala." Every day of the week the "Voice of Kerala" penetrates into the homes of Hindus, Roman Catholics, Moslems and Protestants alike with its three-fold objective: Education, Dedication and Evangelization for Christian freedom and democracy. . . . The motto of "The Voice of Kerala" is "Truth Be Victorious," and Communist literature and propaganda is replaced by its readable and lucid articles. The "Voice of Kerala" excels all papers in Kerala state in both content and quality and has a profound influence upon the lives and thinking of 280,000 people now.[24]

The statistical basis or any other criteria for these success claims was not divulged. Schwarz did, however, claim that, along with anticommunism, the spread of Christianity was also being facilitated by the Crusade's publications:

> Over 700 letters of inquiry were received at The Voice of Kerala headquarters in a 7-month period of time. A full time Evangelist is employed to correspond with those who desire to know Him. Follow-up work is handled methodically and every 6 months a new church body is born for the Kingdom of God. Is this not marvelous and rewarding for our sacrifice?

And in a moment of heady self-reflection:

> With all humility, I boldly say that this work in South India is the greatest Evangelistic endeavor of the 20th century to be shouldered by an organization like the Christian Anti-Communism Crusade. Eternity alone will reveal the extent of their endeavors.[25]

Around 1965, the CACC seems to have stopped its subsidies, and the paper's subsequent demise was apparently not chronicled.[26]

But in March 1960 the CACC *Newsletter* could still look back at the paper's functioning from August 1959 through the February 1960 election to proclaim, "From Tragedy to Triumph—Kerala, India," and further:

> Since victories in the battle against Communism have been so few, the defeat of the Communist Government in Kerala, India, is certainly an occasion for rejoicing. A review of the Communist rule of Kerala and the methods by which they were expelled without major violence should be helpful for those eager to repeat this achievement in other areas.[27]

As to the role of the CACC and its monthly and daily publications, Schwarz quoted from a letter he received from George Thomas, originally sent to Bill Stube, a CACC leader:

> I have the satisfaction that we have played our reasonable share in the victory of the democratic parties. During the election campaigns we gave full coverage for statements and speeches of the leaders of the democratic parties. We wrote editorial after editorial bringing before the people the dangers of Communism. . . . I consider the prayers of the children of God around the world as the main fact which brought the Communists down. I should be thankful to all of you who have upheld us in prayer through the past critical months.[28]

This was followed with an appeal for several thousand dollars in donations to help cover the various costs of operating the newspaper.

From Taste of Victory in Kerala to Guiana

In the November 1963 issue of the CACC *Newsletter*, Schwarz notified readers of the availability of a film titled *A Taste of Victory*. He described the film as showing the part played by the Christian Anti-Communism Crusade in the support of the Indian Christian leader and publisher, George Thomas, Ph. D. and the means by which the Communist Government of Kerala was overthrown. The film is in color, splendidly produced and is narrated by our Director of Missions, James Colbert. The methods used to combat Communism in Kerala are described in this film, and these can be used successfully to meet the Communist threat all over the world.[29]

Schwarz, deeply perturbed by the reelection of Cheddi Jagan as prime minister of British Guiana in 1957, invoked the domino theory, arguing that the capture of Guiana would open Brazil and Venezuela to Communism. Given its strategic location, Guiana became the most important arena of CACC's campaign, and the country was flooded with pamphlets. Preachers from the United States continuously visited the country and, in 1962, Schwarz himself visited Guiana. His right-hand man, Dr. Joost Sluis, was in charge of the operations and visited Guiana six times in 1961 and 1962. It was on one of these visits that three anticommunist veterans from Kerala accompanied him, with the film *A Taste of Victory*.

The Guianese government raised objection to the CACC's activities at the UN Special Committee on Decolonization. They also expelled Sluis from Guiana. But reports in CACC newsletters reveal that the anticommunist activities continued. It was also claimed by critics that these propaganda activities were in collaboration with the U.S. government and enjoyed the support of the U.S. ambassador.

CACC's July 1964 newsletter noted three major victories for their anticommunist crusade so far: "When we review the world today there are three centers where we can claim victory over communism. They are Brazil, British Guiana, and Kerala in India. We proudly claim that CACC was deeply involved in all three victories."

Regarding Brazil, the following was the assessment:

The developments in Brazil are highly optimistic.... All the free world can be exalted with what happened in Brazil. In particular, you, of the Christian Anti-Communism Crusade can rejoice because for ten months you have supported putting in the hands of the university students 12,000 copies of the book "You Can Trust the Communists (to Be) Communists."... With sorrow in my heart I see people trying to spoil victory in Brazil by saying that the revolution was done by the army to install a dictatorship there. This is not true. The revolution in Brazil was started by 100,000 religious women. They went into the streets praying and singing religious songs. I remember one day Goulart's brother-in-law Brizola had scheduled a rally in Belo Horizonte. The meeting should have started at 8:00 p.m., but when Brizola got there with his people in the public auditorium, they had no place to sit. One hour before the meeting started, those religious women had taken all the seats, and in a loud voice singing and praying their rosary they refused to leave the place. The moments just like that made Goulart realize that he did not have the people's support to make a social revolution in Brazil. Then he had to leave the country and the shedding of blood was not necessary.[30]

George Thomas, A Postscript

Despite Schwarz's accolades for George Thomas, a careful viewing of the film, and consideration of the many claims made in the newsletter as well as in other Crusade publications,[31] the actual impact and the "lessons learned" in the Crusade are questionable. The Crusade's main accomplishment appears to have been the publication of the monthly bulletin *Vishwa Deepam*, from at least 1957, and the daily newspaper *Keraladhwani*, from August 1959 to sometime shortly after the 1967 elections, which were won overwhelmingly by the Left Democratic Front, which was composed mainly of Communist supporters.

Tax documents obtained by researcher Hubert Villeneuve indicate that, after reaching a high point financially in 1961, *Ker-*

aladhwani became an increasing drain on the overall Crusade finances, never achieving self-sufficiency. In one final blast of fundraising in 1964, Schwarz organized an "Urgent Projects Banquet" at the Hollywood Palladium in the United States, attended by such high-visibility personalities as Ronald Reagan and Herbert Philbrick, a famous FBI infiltrator of U.S. Communist Party organizations, attending.[32] But after 1965, the Crusade stopped subsidizing its Kottayam publishing project.

A closer look at Crusade finances in India raised questions about George Thomas's management of some funds he was receiving from the United States to support the publications. In 1966 he was arrested and briefly detained "for fraud after a series of complaints on the part of *Keraladhwani* employees to the effect that they had not been regularly paid for long periods of time."[33] A Kottayam journalist reported rumors that George Thomas had spent many of the funds on "personal use," which may have included purchase of plantation land and loans to family members. He also lost a tax fraud case in court and was made to pay an unknown penalty.[34] None of these controversial matters appear to have been recounted in the CACC newsletter.

The anticommunist fronts supported by people like George Thomas broke up in 1963, and the Congress Party itself split. Thomas became an office-bearer of the breakaway group, Kerala Congress. After failing to be elected in the 1965 assembly by-elections, he shifted to the main Congress Party faction and was elected to the Kerala Legislative Assembly. We carefully perused all the speeches and interventions made by George Thomas in the Assembly, to see if he referred to his role in the anticommunist agitation. There was none that we could discover. Toppling the Communist government had already become an episode that nobody wanted to remember and take pride in.

Whither the CACC?

Back in the United States, the CACC reached its own apogee in

1962, when its activities were significant enough to merit twenty-eight citations in the *New York Times*. These included coverage of debates and rallies on the West Coast,[35] rallies and anticommunism "schools" in New York City,[36] and a Madison Square Garden high point event attracting an audience of eight thousand.[37]

After its 1962 peak, the CACC gradually lost appeal, replaced, perhaps in part by the Goldwater 1963 and 1964 presidential campaign, and changes in how people viewed Communism and anticommunism, and by competition from other evangelical groups. By 1964 the CACC had disappeared from the *Times*. Fred Schwarz retired as executive director in 1998. He passed away in 2009. In his honor, the newsletter was renamed *The Schwarz Report*. It remains in publication.

The Moral Re-Armament Movement

In May of 1957, Fred Schwarz and the Christian Anti-Communism Crusade got their shot at fame and influence through a meeting with the chair of the House Un-American Activities Committee. Similarly, on March 31, 1960, the Moral Re-Armament movement, headed by Frank Buchman, reached its own apogee of fame and influence when U.S. Congress member Leonard G. Wolf of Iowa read into the *Congressional Record* what might be considered the ultimate Cold War anticommunist screed. We quote from committee proceedings:

> THE SPEAKER . . . "The Gentleman from Iowa [Mr. WOLF] is recognized for 1 hour and 20 minutes."[38]
>
> [Mr. WOLF]: "Mr. Speaker—'A nation without an ideology is self-satisfied and dead . . .' So stated Konrad Adenauer in his statement released in the *New York Journal American,* Sunday, January 31, 1960.
>
> "There followed quotes from the Prime Minister of Japan, a U.S. former Ambassador to Moscow, the Executive Director of the National Academy of Sciences plus a small list of newspapers

from around the U.S. Today as I speak, 75 million copies of a booklet entitled '*Ideology and Co-Existence*' have been distributed in 24 languages in many areas of the world . . . (from the *Suburban* Record of 24 March, 1960). Every home in the Washington area will receive a handbook next week which is clarifying for hundreds of millions of people across the world the issues created by the cold war . . . prepared by Moral Re-Armament. [It is] a 31-page handbook which describes the Communist plan for world takeover and explains how democracy can become an effective force to answer it. It has been published as a weapon to put America and the free world on the offensive in the ideological struggle . . . [several more accolades and overviews of the booklet], then on the following page (7091) of the House Record, Cong. Wolf . . . Mr. Speaker, at this point I include the entire booklet in the Record."[39]

The 31-page booklet, "Ideology and Co-Existence," was soon to be deposited in the homes of tens of millions in North America, Europe, and several other locations, in one of the most widespread mass mailings in history. And yet, like the CACC, within a couple of years of its peak, MRA began a steep decline and today plays a minor role in world history.

The booklet was one among thousands of informational pieces distributed by the Moral Re-Armament movement, across six decades, from 1938, when it took the name Moral Re-Armament, to 2001, when it was renamed Initiatives of Change. Before 1938 it had been known mostly as the Oxford Group, and before that, in the 1920s and earlier, it often went by the name First Century Christian Fellowship.

Besides its trajectory of sudden impact—a high point around 1960 to 1962—and rapid decline, MRA shared other features with the CACC. Both depended heavily on the charisma of a dynamic leader. Both seemed to emerge almost from nowhere and capture the imagination and enthusiasm of large numbers of people. Both depended on right-wing money, and espoused an apocalyptic and hysterical hatred of communism. And both were intimately involved in toppling the elected EMS ministry in Kerala, or at least in the celebrations after the toppling.

But there were also important differences. The CACC never came close in worldwide influence, compared to MRA. While the CACC depended heavily on a somewhat limited base of Southern California rightists, MRA, at one time or another, had offices and conference centers on four continents; Caux, Switzerland; Mackinac Island, Michigan; Armagh, Australia; and Panchgani, India.[40] The CACC was mostly a large-rallies movement, while MRA developed theater groups that could supplement the rallies and spread its message to a wider range of audiences. Furthermore, MRA offered its followers a vision of self-improvement that went somewhat beyond the simplistic anticommunism that both groups fostered.

From the Keswick Epiphany to the Oxford Group

Like Fred Schwarz, founder and head of the CACC, Frank Buchman emerged from obscurity. A not very successful Lutheran minister from a small town in the state of Pennsylvania, Buchman, while working at a hospice for poor boys in Philadelphia, had argued with his board of directors and stormed out of the meeting, and the organization.

Vacationing in Europe on doctor's orders, on a long walk one afternoon in Keswick, England, he happened upon a small church, where an impassioned sermon was being delivered to a small audience by Jessie Penn-Lewis, one of many evangelists who practiced in the English countryside in that time. For reasons never well explained, Buchman suddenly realized, as he absorbed her words, that the anger and depression from his Philadelphia experience were based at least partially on his own arrogance and self-centeredness. He immediately returned to his lodging and wrote letters of apology to the former board members.

Suddenly, he was a different man:

The Keswick experience had a permanent effect on Buchman's whole outlook on life. One could almost say that it was like St. Paul's Damascus Road experience. He saw the cost of his own pride, i.e. the human factor. He faced the consequences by taking remedial action.[41]

The post-epiphany Frank Buchman seems to have become highly charismatic and, by the 1920s, was drawing dozens, sometimes hundreds, to a Christian discussion group he founded at Oxford. A focus developed on implementing a set of Christian-based ideals: absolute honesty, absolute purity, absolute unselfishness, and absolute love (said to derive from Jesus' Sermon on the Mount and some other verses).[42] This focus was, in turn, supposed to lead to a happier and more satisfying life. Two U.S. members of the local Oxford Group, Bill Wilson and Bob Smith, went back to the United States and founded Alcoholics Anonymous, influenced in part by their experience in the Oxford Group discussions.

From the 1920s to the Cold War

For four decades, Frank Buchman wandered the globe, visiting numerous countries and spreading his message of self-improvement spirituality to thousands. In 1938, on the eve of the Second World War, he announced a change in the Oxford Group's name to "Moral Re-Armament." An essential feature of his teaching was the idea of finding a quiet time each day to listen for instructions from God, to help solve whatever problems the person was experiencing. The emerging philosophy suggested activism of some kind in the material world, as opposed to "armchair Christianity." Perhaps because of a certain vagueness, Buchman's ideas spread rapidly, and he became, according to a follower, "a focus of hope for millions and was exerting influence on governments in many countries."[43] However, Buchman's influence was often limited: he was not able to get a meeting with Adolf Hitler despite several attempts, and he obviously failed to prevent the Second World War. In the aftermath of the war, Buchman led Moral Re-Armament, and he played a role in getting leaders and politicians of formerly warring states, particularly France and Germany, to seek reconciliation.[44]

A feature that set MRA apart from many movements—certainly including the CACC—was its use of staged dramas as a means of communicating its messages. Between 1940 and 1964, at least thirty-six such plays were performed, some of them hundreds of times, in locations around the world.[45] From 1946 to 1997, MRA actually owned the Westminster Theatre in London.

On August 27, 1939, MRA leader Frank Buchman delivered a radio address from Boston titled *The Forgotten Factor*.[46] By 1940 one of MRA's top playwrights, Alan Thornhill, had turned the concept of the forgotten factor into MRA's most successful and probably its most influential drama. *The Forgotten Factor* is the play that most exemplifies the MRA theatrical tradition of propaganda-plus-morality-play. The plot concerns two families, one of a corporate CEO; the other of a shop floor worker, who learn to acknowledge their own individual responsibilities for the tensions created around a labor strike situation. Somehow, they come to realize that guidance from God—the forgotten factor—is needed to make things work right. Once this realization takes hold, all problems between management and labor dissolve. As MRA supporter and analyst Philip Boobbyer notes, *The Forgotten Factor* links up "industrial strife with conflict in family life . . . [and] failings of character."[47] The drama was shown to thousands of workers, many bussed in from surrounding areas of London with free tickets.[48] From its opening in 1940, *The Forgotten Factor* is said to have been seen by over 850,000 people in its first ten years.[49]

Ideology and Coexistence: The Anticommunist Essence

By the time of its apogee in the late 1950s to early 1960s, MRA was, at its base, an overwhelmingly anticommunist political movement fed by an apocalyptic near-hysteria about Communism's likely world takeover. Equally important, MRA posited that the "West" was succumbing to Communism virtually without a fight, wallowing instead in mindless, self-satisfied materialism, and desperately in need of an ideology that—not surprisingly—could only be provided by MRA.

In the summer of 1959, on the eve of Indian prime minister Nehru's decision to dismiss the EMS ministry in faraway Kerala, the MRA conference center on Mackinac Island, near the northernmost point of Michigan in the Midwest, became the site of one of MRA's most successful summer conferences. About one thousand guests from forty-eight nations gathered at the Grand Hotel and nearby buildings to attend meetings, seminars, and drama performances built around MRA's forgotten-factor message.[50]

This 1959 summer conference provided the impetus for much of the content of the aforementioned booklet, *Ideology and Co-Existence*. Unlike MRA's usual public face of calmness, tolerance, and self-improvement, *Ideology and Co-Existence* is harsh and confrontational. Much of the text consists of proclamations that MRA is the only force capable of bringing about a better world. But to accomplish this betterment, the booklet condemns Communism in words both truculent and fearsome. The opening lines read: "We are at war. World War III has begun. Even while we were celebrating the end of the war of arms in 1918, the Soviet Union was planning to defeat and enslave the free world through the war of ideas."[51]

The booklet continues with a description of what Moral Re-Armament itself is for: "Moral Re-Armament . . . believes that God's Mind should control the world through human nature that has been changed." By contrast, "Communism . . . believes that man's mind should control the world through human nature that has been exploited." The booklet goes on to state: "One or the other must win."

BUCHMAN, INDIA, AND THE MRA MOVEMENT

Frank Buchman and MRA had a long-term presence in India. Over several decades, Buchman made nine visits. At least twice, he met with Mahatma Gandhi, and at least once with Jawaharlal Nehru. He stayed for six months on one visit, traveling across much of the country and converting some officials to the MRA perspective.[52] Several national Indian newspapers printed special supplements about MRA. *The Hindu* put out a special ten-page supplement that included interviews with four former Communist trade union activists, telling how MRA had changed their lives and pulled them away from Communist teachings.[53]

In 1953 a large delegation of Indians attended the MRA World Assembly in Caux, Switzerland, which led to an invitation to Buchman and colleagues to come again to India. This time, Buchman brought four MRA dramas, including *The Forgotten Factor*, and two hundred representatives from thirty-five nations.[54] They toured the country, giving performances to thousands of people.

MRA and the EMS Ministry

It is unclear whether Mannath Padmanabhan was directly involved in connecting MRA with anticommunist agitation and the toppling of the EMS ministry. However, the Nair leader was apparently present for the post-EMS toppling celebrations. After the dismissal of the Communist ministry, there was a beeline of visitors from Kerala visiting Caux as part of different delegations. Most important among them was a five-member team headed by Mannath Padmanabhan, whose one-month tour of Europe was reported daily by the Malayalam press. A member of another group, led by C. H. Muhammed Koya, speaker of the Kerala Assembly, recorded his impressions in a travelogue titled "Caux—London—Cairo." During Mannam's visit, the home minister P. T. Chacko was also present in Caux. Fr. Vadakkan also visited Caux during his European tour. Reports of these visits in the Malayalam press made MRA a familiar name in Kerala.

Caux was a center of intensive psychological pressure exerted through music, drama, official dinners, and personal interactions. Though everything seemed informal, there was an army of well-trained personnel who knew how to influence and win people. Mannam's visit to Caux deeply influenced him, and he spoke in laudatory terms of Buchman and MRA during his European tour and after returning home. C. H. Muhammad Koya, the Musim League leader and Assembly Speaker after the 1961 election and also later one of the chief ministers in Kerala for a brief period, recalls an audience's standing ovation when he was introduced as a Muslim leader who selflessly sacrificed for the victory over Communism.[55]

The Kerala newspaper *Malayala Manorama* was the biggest source of media support for MRA in Kerala. After the anticommunist agitation's success, K. M. Cherian, the editor, visited the MRA center at Mackinac Island and, from there, traveled to Brazil to participate in the MRA World Conference, where delegates from thirty-five countries were present. Cherian suggested that Kerala should be used as the Asian base for MRA: "It was because of misrule that Communists were thrown out. Communists have trained their agents to go to the rest of India and South Asia. With the help of MRA we have to launch a counterattack from Kerala and Japan. This two-pronged attack will save Asia."[56]

The *Malayalarajyam* newspaper published a curious story of how the opposition leader P. T. Chacko was so deeply touched by the MRA drama *Pickle Hill* that he approached another Congress leader, who was also at Caux and with whom he was not on best terms, with apologies for being unfriendly.[57] But back home, Chacko never said anything about his conversion and confession at Caux. Even *Deepika* gave only a short report. The Catholic Church always suspected that MRA was a Protestant project and rejected its theology. Its lukewarm approach was an important reason why MRA did not develop a mass influence in Kerala.

All these vignettes constitute evidence of a close connection between top anticommunist leaders in Kerala and MRA. The closest connection of all seems to have been with Padmanabhan. In the supplementary documents to *Remaking the World*, a 1961 edition of Frank Buchman's speeches, Padmanabhan, Nair community leader and elder statesman, recounted his role in the February 1960 election that sealed the end of the EMS ministry:

> Eight days before the poll I introduced the MRA manifesto *Ideology and Co-Existence* to the people of Kerala in their own mother-tongue. It was distributed on a state-wide basis and had an additional coverage of three million through the medium of the press. Most of the Malayalam daily papers—there are thirty of them—brought it out in bold headlines. The *Malayala Manorama,* Kerala's largest daily, wrote an editorial entitled "True Patriotism" based on Dr. Buchman's definition, "A true patriot gives his life to bring his country under God's control."[58]

Here, then, is a major leader in Kerala helping make available to the people, just before a crucial election, MRA's most truculent statement on the topic of the election. Thirty-eight days later, this manifesto would be entered into the *Congressional Record* of the United States House of Representatives.[59]

At this same time, Padmanabhan and colleagues "decided to cable [West German] Chancellor Adenauer requesting that the Ruhr miners with the MRA ideological drama *Hoffnung* come to Kerala." At the reception given by the governor of the state, two hundred members of the Kerala elite were present, hearing the governor declare: "All our problems, economic, political, social and individual must be solved in the spirit of MRA."[60]

Over the course of a few days, fifteen thousand persons are said to have attended showings of the play. Padmanabhan concluded his report by stating: "MRA has taken root in Kerala and we have decided to invite a permanent international force to help carry forward this battle."[61]

U.S. congressmember Wolf presented a lengthy addendum to the MRA anticommunist booklet he was reading into the *Congressional Record*. Included were several observations and reports from various sources. One states:

There is no doubt that the handbook had a real influence in the defeat of the Communists in the recent [1960] Kerala elections. . . . Fifteen thousand copies reached the key men of the city of Trivandrum and throughout the state. . . .. A man helping with the distribution reported that in his village it changed the outlook of a number of men who had previously supported the Communists. He himself spent two evenings reading the book to a night class of 180 people. A thousand local councils received copies as did 2,500 libraries and towns throughout the state.

A foreword to this Malayalam edition was written by Mannath Padmanabhan, a leader of the liberation movement, who used his organization to secure maximum distribution. A further edition of 100,000 is now being printed.[62]

One big-name endorser, Rajmohan Gandhi, grandson of Mahatma Gandhi, was quoted as stating: "The real choice before the world is Moral Re-Armament or communism. The free nations of Asia look today to Moral Re-Armament as the one hope."[63]

Longtime MRA activist David Young claims:

The Malayalam edition of the booklet was sent to the entire leadership of the state including members of the legislative assembly, government officials, all members of over a thousand village councils, the lecturers and principals of 73 university colleges, [and] 1,000 high schools. [64]

Self-Congratulation or Genuine Impact?

A certain amount of hyperbole seems to typify MRA documents. In 1964 British journalist and Labour Party MP Tom Driberg came out with a book that gave a detailed critique of MRA, infused with labels such as "greatly exaggerated" (86), "shrill" (151), "bombastic" (157), "megalomaniacal" (192), and "exuberant overconfidence" (227).[65] He specifically cast doubts on MRA's claims to have influenced the 1960 special election in Kerala (158), but his

CREATING ANTICOMMUNIST HYSTERIA 169

only evidence on that score is the stated opinion of U.S. ambassador John Kenneth Galbraith (1961–1963). The intensity of the MRA self-celebration makes one wonder how much MRA spokespersons actually understood about what the 1960 special election in Kerala was about. But there can be little doubt that MRA had put on a mobilization that dwarfed Fred Schwarz and the CACC. It also failed to prevent the EMS ministry from garnering a million new votes. Celebrating the unity of the various factions within the anticommunist coalition and attributing that unity to MRA turned out to be premature.

Rejoicing Over a Win

We have noted the vindictive terror unleashed against supporters of the EMS ministry, once that ministry had been toppled. At the same time, vast displays of anticommunist fervor took place. The dismissal of the ministry on July 31, 1959, followed by the anti-EMS special election victory in February 1960, led to a round of anticommunist demonstrations involving large sections of the public. One of them was a production of the MRA propaganda play *Hoffnung*, accompanied by West German miners invited to Kerala to act in the play. For opening night a big event was organized.

On February 29, 1960, just seven days after the formation of the new anti-EMS government, four special planes carrying the cast and equipment, and an eighty-strong MRA force from fourteen nations landed in Trivandrum, led by Rajmohan Gandhi and a group of Indians committed to making MRA their nation's policy. Mannath Padmanabhan, at a dinner in honor of the visitors, also attended by cabinet ministers of the newly elected government, declared:

> Kerala and MRA are going to stand together and fight for the betterment of the world. We will pattern for East and West a unity that bridges all differences of race, class and nationality.

Not to be outdone in the MRA style, Archbishop Mar Gregorious of Trivandrum, who had also played a major role in leading the opposition to the EMS ministry, said:

> History will record our permanent gratitude to Mannath Padmanabhan not only for having ousted the Communists from Kerala but for creating unity in all the communities following his return from Caux.[66]

For the next six days, thousands—eventually totaling as many as fifteen thousand—packed Trivandrum's University Convocation Hall to view *Hoffnung*. Use of the performance hall was given free of charge on order of the governor and members of Parliament flew in from New Delhi to see the play. Newspapers daily carried stories about the production, and about MRA as an alternative to Communism. The theater troupe, traveling to Kottayam, a Christian center and a major center of opposition to the EMS ministry, received enthusiastic accolades. Performances were also given in the nearby South Indian city of Madras. In New Delhi, Rajmohan Gandhi and Peter Howard, an MRA playwright, were received for an audience with India's national president, Dr. Rajendra Prasad.[67]

The 1962 MRA World Assembly in Kerala

From its very beginning, the post-EMS, Congress-led ministry dissolved into bickering and infighting. But MRA continued to focus its anticommunist energy on the state. In January 1962, MRA held a World Assembly in Thiruvananthapuram (previously known in English as Trivandrum). From MRA activist David Young's account, it appears to have been a spectacular event, running for five days, with representatives from thirty-seven nations, including sports and political figures and trade union leaders. The World Assembly ended in a massive public procession led by five caparisoned elephants, a Kerala five-piece orchestra, and a hundred girls marching with lighted lamps in the front

CREATING ANTICOMMUNIST HYSTERIA 171

to an open-air stadium where a crowd of over 90,000 stood for two hours and heard international speakers and the evidence of the worldwide advance of MRA. They saw the premiere of *The Final Revolution*, a play in Malayalam written and enacted by students showing how communists and non-communists are captured by a superior ideology.

Mannath Padmanabhan, who had led the procession on foot, addressing the ocean of humanity, said, "Today I have seen what I wished to see in my own dear Kerala before I died. We are grateful for the strength, unity and clarity which has come as a result of the work of MRA. I want to see what happened here repeated in every part of India."[68]

After the Assembly concluded, an "MRA force crisscrossed" the state, said to have addressed over a quarter of a million people.

WHITHER MRA?

David Young's glowing account of the January 1962 MRA World Assembly in Kerala might lead one to think that the MRA was still expanding its influence and ready to do battle with Communists everywhere. To an extent, that is the case. On December 10, 1961, the *Los Angeles Times* reported on an MRA conference that took place in Petropolis, Brazil. K. M. Cherian of the *Malayala Manorama* spoke about the need for a "superior ideology" to combat Communism in Kerala and around the world and delegates from thirty-five countries heard him identify the MRA as that ideology. Furthermore, "If Kerala is lost to communism, India is lost and if India is lost, China and Russia will overrun the world." Cherian went on to state: "I am putting my newspaper and all its resources at the disposal of the great Moral Re-Armament force."[69]

In 1963, Rajmohan Gandhi and several Kerala leaders organized a "March-on-Wheels" to draw greater public attention to the MRA message. They began on October 2, from Kanyakumari at India's southern tip, traveling in buses and stopping at various towns and villages, finally, on November 24, reaching New Delhi, where they held one of their trademark events, an "Assembly of Nations."[70] In 1965 MRA began purchase of land for an international "Asia Plateau" training and conference center in Panchgani (Maharashtra State), to parallel those in Caux, Switzerland, and Mackinac Island, Michigan. The center opened in 1972 but has mainly been involved since with contracted interpersonal skills training on commissions for businesses[71] and for government officials.[72]

Declining Revenues, Declining Impact

The glory days of MRA's worldwide influence and its vast anticommunist endeavors did not last. Beginning around 1966, it began experiencing a decline in donations. Operating revenues declined: $3.5 million in 1967; $2.7 million in 1968; less than $2 million in 1969. An attempt in 1966 to convert the Mackinac Island conference center into a college failed, and in 1970, the facilities were sold. Other properties, including an estate in Mount Kisco, New York, were also sold and various MRA publications were discontinued. The *MRA Information Service Bulletin* stopped publishing in 1964 and the production of new films was halted about the same time.[73] An MRA spinoff—Up with People—continued to draw in young singers but got a bumpy reception at Harvard University in 1967. The clean-cut 1950s' look of optimistic American patriotism was about to give way to the counterculture.[74] MRA withdrew to England, where it has maintained a low profile,[75] although it currently also maintains an address in the state of Virginia. In 2001 MRA was renamed "Initiatives of Change." Its website proclaims the four MRA "absolutes" in more modern phrasings—for example, unselfishness over greed—and claims to promote inclusiveness as well as "relationships and resources as a resounding form of equity justice. We take risks, own our failures, and engender new learnings through deep listening and purposeful actions." This results in "transforming communities from the ground up."

The CACC and MRA both played roles in toppling the EMS ministry. Both used the individual charisma of their leaders and some organizing activities to perpetuate and intensify the anticommunism that swept over parts of Kerala in the form of anticommunist hysteria. But neither movement had the organized strength of a formal, paid bureaucracy that could watch over events as the EMS ministry launched its various reforms and weathered—or failed to weather—its challenges. For that, institutions such as the Indian Intelligence Bureau or the CIA would be necessary. In the next chapter we sample much of that intelligence work and examine how the CIA kept a watchful eye on the unfolding drama of the EMS ministry and its opponents.

CHAPTER 8

Through CIA Eyes: Information and Instructions for Toppling the Ministry

Even before the formation of the state of Kerala, the CIA had started to eye with suspicion the spread of Communist influence in the region. The 1954 elections for the Travancore-Cochin Assembly produced a socialist-Communist majority. On March 9 and 10, 1954,[1] the CIA alerted the U.S. National Security Council (NSC) to hold meetings to discuss this state of affairs.

These two alerts were the first of ten during the time period covered by the sixty-three CIA reports we located via the Freedom of Information Act (FOIA) collection and the CIA electronic reading room. The NSC is the body set up to manage and control the actions of the CIA, and would be the body to authorize a covert action. In the intelligence world, alerting the NSC to meet is probably the highest level of action other than a CIA covert operation itself, which would presumably require NSC authorization, along with that of the president. President Eisenhower established during his administration (1953–1961) an "Operations Control Board" that was to formally manage and control the CIA, but it did not function effectively and was disbanded by President Kennedy in 1961.

The two CIA-NSC documents give a general overview of India's 1954 election and its outcome: Communists and their allies won sixty of 118 assembly seats. The discussion briefly notes that the Central Indian government could "invoke President's Rule" to bypass the formation of a ministry, as had been done in Andhra Pradesh State. A period of instability was predicted, amid concerns about popular disillusionment with the Congress Party at the local level. It is noted in the report that this 1954 situation may have been the first time that the Communists participated in forming a state government in India. But the danger was averted by the Congress Party extending support for a socialist ministry from outside. The Communists were excluded from power. On February 19, 1955, however, the socialist ministry fell and President's Rule was imposed on the state of Travancore-Cochin, owing to weakness in the Congress Party, which, according to the CIA report, could engineer the Communists' fall but not supply a meaningful alternative. The report expresses some concern that the Communists will now appear as the best alternative in the upcoming elections.[2]

Threats to the Empire? Ongoing Concerns

The CIA's next note of concern was disseminated (internally) by the CIA on August 2, 1951 (SN 04) and released to the U.S. public on August 2, 1982. This 7-page report came from the office of National Intelligence Estimates and is titled "India's Position in the East-West Conflict." Much of the document is a complaint against what the authors see as Indian appeasement of the Communist bloc and displaying of "the utmost contempt for those Asian regimes which accept Western leadership." The document—originally classified as SECRET—also considers that "A right-wing government . . . would be more intent on obtaining U.S. economic assistance."[3] Furthermore, despite setbacks, the Communists would benefit from "a powerful appeal to the intellectuals who mould politically effective opinion." Concern was also expressed that "Communist control of India would deny the

West a major source of manganese, mica, shellac, kyanite, and jute products. The loss of these supplies would in the short run confront the US with serious problems of procurement." Much of the rest of the document bemoans India's economic weakness and the need for major injections of economic aid.

More on The Threat of Communist Control

Just a year later, on 5 September 1952, the CIA released to its internal list a secret report on the "Consequences of Communist Control Over South Asia." This 8-page document repeats some of the projections of the previous report but adds a more detailed and an even gloomier prognosis of cascading Western resource losses, adding rubber and monazite (used in nuclear technology) to the list of strategic commodities lost. The document invokes the now well-worn domino theory: "Communist control over South Asia would be speedily followed by the loss of much of Southeast Asia." According to this intelligence estimate, Communist forces would gain control over "strategically located air and submarine bases and would gain control of the military potential of South Asia." This includes "a large number of excellent airfields and air base sites. . . . Major ports, air bases and other facilities." Further, "The British would lose their substantial investments in India," and significant trading losses would accrue to Australia, New Zealand, and Japan. The document notes that "India and Ceylon together produce close to 85 percent of the tea entering international trade and about two-thirds of the black pepper."[4]

Kerala As Part of the Struggle for Domination in South Asia

On January 1, 1953, the State Department's Office of Intelligence Research came out with a major intelligence report on *Communism in the Free World*. This 569-page document includes 31 pages evaluating the capabilities of the Indian Communist Party. The report starts with a summary of the CPI's own overview, based on an article by its general secretary, A. K. Ghosh, in the December 1952 issue of *For a Lasting Peace, For a People's Democracy*. CPI leader Ghosh is quoted as writing that the goals of the Party's program are "the liquidation of all vestiges of British rule, defense of the National independence and sovereignty threatened by the American aggressors, the preservation of Peace, and the promotion of a life of happiness for the people." According to the report, the CPI connects these ideals to its opposition to U.S. financial and technical aid and to U.S.-sponsored community development projects. The Party proposes to realize its goals through various means including alliances with other left-wing groups and work among peasants, workers (trade unions), students and intellectuals, utilizing constitutional procedures. An additional component is work via members of state legislative assemblies.

The report goes on to give details of CPI strength and weaknesses in membership numbers, education and leadership skills of its officers, electoral strength, military strength, influence in government and labor unions, cultural and professional organizations, public opinion formation (publications), radio broadcasts from Soviet bloc sites, and finances. It was within these expressions of concern for the empire that Kerala State came into being. For the CIA it was a cause of instant worry.[5]

Despite the CIA's warnings, the people of Kerala seem to have had a mind of their own.

CIA Prediction of the 1957 Communist Victory and Initial Assessments

On November 1, 1956, the new state of Kerala was branded by the CIA as "the most likely of all Indian states to escape from Congress control as a result of the [upcoming in February 1957] elections. . . . Dissatisfaction within the party's own organization may become a serious weakness."[6] On January 24, 1957,[7] the Agency's *Current Intelligence Weekly Summary* (CIWS) predicted that "Prime

Minister Nehru's Congress Party will retain control of the national Parliament and of the governments of all states, except possibly Kerala." On January 26, 1957,[8] the CIA pronounced the "Indian Congress Party in Election Difficulties," and identified West Bengal, Orissa, and Kerala as problem areas, further noting that in these areas, Congress Party "district organizations were still not in close contact with the people...."

In a memorandum from the U.S. Office of National Estimates, Staff Memorandum No. 20-57, dated April 2,1957,[9] the Agency opined:

> The elections reemphasized the point that the Congress Party is an old and often listless organization which leans heavily on Nehru and the comparative weakness of its opponents to win elections... its most important defeat was in Kerala [where]... the Communists won 60 seats, and with allied independents, are expected to form the state government.[10]

The report goes on to state:

> EMS Namboodiripad, who has been given the Communist mandate to form a ministry, is among the most competent of the Communist leaders and has a good chance of bettering the record of the previous ineffectual Congress government of the state.[11]

On April 5, 1957, EMS took the oath of office as the first Chief Minister of Kerala.

The CIA clearly saw the EMS ministry as a threat to U.S. interests in India. This came about because the Agency viewed the CPI—especially in Kerala—as a possibly more competent and certainly more organized and disciplined organization, in contrast with the Congress Party. The CIA identified "the economic difficulties in which the [national Indian] Government finds itself" as the most threatening aspect of the situation at the time: a fall of foreign exchange holdings, despite IMF loans and a lack of foreign aid funds in amounts necessary to make possible the carrying out of the second five-year plan. On top of this, Kerala's Communists had made an apparently successful overture to industrialist G. D. Birla to start a pulp and rayon factory in the state. The Agency predicted:

> Any Communist success in improving conditions in Kerala would reflect adversely on the Congress Party's past record.... Congress leaders hope the Communists will fail but cannot take an overt stand against their efforts to improve the economy.[12]

The CIA was keenly watching the onset of the EMS ministry. On April 11, 1957,[13] in a lengthy report on the prospects of the new ministry, the Agency wrote of the ministry:

> Its freedom of action is limited by the powers of the federal government, and failure by the local authorities to improve conditions might lead to a reimposition of President's Rule—direct administration from New Delhi.[14]

The idea of a New Delhi takeover appears throughout CIA reporting, from the onset of the EMS ministry to the actual takeover on July 31, 1959.

The April 11 *Current Intelligence Weekly Summary* (CIWS) goes on to note that the EMS cabinet

> includes representatives of trade unions, peasants, lawyers, educators, writers, and women's groups but is not highly experienced in administrative matters.[15]

It is likely to undertake

> nationalization of foreign-owned tea and rubber plantations in Kerala, commutation of death sentences and release of political prisoners.

but

> Neither land reform nor emigration is likely to ease materially the population pressure on the land. . . . By achieving some superficial success in eliminating corruption, improving administration, and attacking minor problems, however, the Communist regime may be able to retain power for some time if it does not come into outright conflict with the national government in New Delhi.[16]

In its April 25, 1957,[17] CIWS, the Agency took up the possibility of widening Communist influence in India, noting that the Party had doubled its popular national vote in recent elections. The weekly summary report concluded:

> The government of India is aware of the problem it faces in Kerala, and will probably take discreet but firm steps to discredit the Communists and return the Congress Party to a dominant position. Madhavan Nair, one of the three Congress general secretaries, is going to resign his party position in order to devote full time to the job of revitalizing the state party machine.[18]

On May 8 and 9, 1957, the Eisenhower administration held two briefings of the National Security Council, with Kerala on the agenda. The briefings mostly went over the material from April 11 and 25, but included some additional points of suspicion and concern in the CIA's view of the EMS ministry:

> "Moderation" is announced Commie watch-word, and operation within limits of Indian constitution their declared intent. In bids for popular favor, Commies have cut ministerial wages, stayed eviction proceedings for peasants, declared war on corruption, solicited investment [of] private capital in state industrial development . . . some attempt at land reform is obvious long-range Commie aim . . . any local economic gains will have nation-wide

appeal.... Meanwhile Congress-dominated Central Government can be expected to fight hard against Commies, although avoiding open harassment . . . cannot force Commies out of office unless breakdown of "law and order" occurs.[19]

We note again the reference to a law-and-order breakdown as a means to topple the ministry, which the CIA acknowledges has taken some popular and effective steps.

In that regard, here is the report's final discussion point:

In interim, U.S. faces embarrassing problem regarding ICA [International Cooperation Administration, now USAID], USIA and similar U.S.-sponsored activities in State, since normal pattern involves active cooperation with State (now Commie) officialdom.[20]

A Key Document Declassified in 2013: Document 171

On July 3, 1957, the "Operations Coordinating Board" issued a report titled "Operations Plan for India and Nepal,"[21] which updated the National Security Council Report of January 10, 1957.[22] That document made no mention of Kerala by name and limited its Cold War anticommunism to noting the competition between India and Communist China in inspiring alternative paths to economic development.

The document of July 3, however, devoted three full paragraphs to the CPI victory, including the observation:

This victory of the Communists within a democratic, constitutional framework gives them an important foothold from which to expand in India, and enhances their respectability and prestige as a successful, parliamentary party which may have a far-reaching effect on their future capabilities. Their victory also introduces a new element in the psychological battle for Asia which is clearly advantageous to international Communism.[23]

There follows an excision in the public record of unknown length, and then a note on the modest U.S. operations in Kerala. a USIS Library at Trivandrum and two ICA employees engaged in agricultural education and research work. The concern was that the Kerala Communists would demand the United States end its operations in their state. But it was the next telegram, on August 1, 1957, that set in motion the forces that would play a major role in toppling the EMS ministry.

The Operations Coordinating Board Report and the earlier National Security Council's "Statement of Policy on U.S. Policy Toward South Asia" seemed to point toward a vigorous U.S. response to the CPI election victory in Kerala. But the NSC statement was issued before the elections and, as noted above, did not include reference to Kerala. But the Operations Coordinating Board (OCB) report made available in the online electronic CIA Reading Room had a serious weakness: between paragraphs two and three, four dots were inserted, indicating that something was left out.

The only materials left out in the July 3 telegram were those within the section on Kerala. Presumably, this excision was done when the document was originally classified, as most sensitive materials were routinely classified prior to the Freedom of Information Act, and many were kept secret after the FOIA was implemented. How much was excised we do not know. It could be a single line of text, such as a person's name, or several paragraphs. In some of the CIA documents consulted for this project, up to fifteen pages have been removed.

There is, however, a procedure for requesting, via the U.S. National Archives National Declassification Center, that some to all of the text withheld in a document be reclassified at a lower security level, and thus be made available to the public. A problem with this procedure is that it may take a long time for a decision to be rendered and communicated.[24]

But the wait may be worth it. In the case of a telegram sent from Washington to New Delhi on August 1, 1957,[25] we filed for a declassification in 2007, and received word of its acceptance in 2013. This document indicates the U.S. government's willingness—now on the record—to apply covert action against the EMS ministry. The next several paragraphs summarize Document 171 with the newly declassified materials included and in some cases highlighted.[26]

This telegram is titled "Instruction from the Department of State to the Diplomatic Missions in India," and its subject line reads "United States Policy with Regard to Kerala. SECRET." The document is approximately five pages long, of which about two full pages constitute declassified material. The one original page and a copy of the letter from the National Declassification Center, confirming acceptance of our request, follows. As far as we can tell, this entire document has been declassified, as there are no marks indicating remaining excisions.

Document 171 Declassified: CIA Outlines Strategy for Subversion in Kerala

The first approximately one-half page of the document had been labeled SECRET and not available for viewing until 2013. It begins:

> It is in the U.S. national interest that a moderate, non-Communist government, basically oriented toward the Free World, succeed in consolidating the allegiance of the Indian people. . . . It is, therefore, in the interests of U.S. policy objectives in India, as well as South Asia, *that the present Communist Government in Kerala fail to achieve any further successes which might enhance its prestige, and that it be removed from power with the least possible delay.* To this end, any attempts by the Congress Party or the Government of India to undermine and bring about the fall of the Kerala Communists should receive encouragement and to the extent practicable, assistance from the United States. [Emphasis added.][27]

The document continues:

> Should the Government of India or the Congress Party fail to move effectively against the Kerala Communists within a reasonable period, perhaps due to their unawareness of the full implications of this Communist victory, it is in the U.S. interest to attempt, with caution and tact, to convince Indian leaders of the dangers to India of a Communist Government in Kerala.

This is followed by a paragraph on ICA and USIS operations in Kerala:

> Although the Communist authorities in Kerala are, for tactical reasons, currently pursuing a moderate policy towards American activities in the State, there is no reason to believe that this policy will not change when the Communists determine it politically advantageous to do so. They may eventually demand the removal from their State of ICA advisors and USIS personnel, as well as to insist that all U.S. activities in these fields cease. Unless the Government of India is willing to oppose such moves by the Communists, the United States should be prepared to withdraw ICA and USIS operations from Kerala. For the present, however, no change should be made by the United States in the level of ICA activities in that State, thus avoiding any situation which would benefit the Communists, by giving them the opportunity either to allege American discrimination or to claim that they succeeded in obtaining more technical assistance than did previous State administrations. By the same token, USIS operations should be maintained at the current level to avoid either a U.S. retreat in the face of Communist opposition or charges in Kerala and elsewhere that U.S. anti-Communist propaganda has been increased to a marked degree.

There follows a section of about two pages on information-gathering by the U.S. Embassy:

> Obtain as complete information as possible on, and ensure

continuing coverage of, events in Kerala, with particular reference to economic, political and administrative programs and tactics of the Communist Government, an assessment of opposition parties and their future capabilities, especially the Congress Party, and detailed information on key political figures in the State.

A. General: While maintaining the present level of staffs in India, all offices should make special efforts to implement the above course of action. The Embassy at New Delhi shall have primary responsibility for reporting on the attitude of Central Government and of Congress Party headquarters towards Kerala; the Consulate General at Madras shall have primary responsibility for reporting on developments within Kerala.

B. Politico-economic reporting by Madras Consulate General:
1. Selective dispatch or telegraphic reporting only on most significant developments;
2. Preparation of a weekly (or bi-weekly at the Consulate General's discretion) classified round-up dispatch, including analytical comment where appropriate, on Kerala Government and State developments (this might later be submitted on a less frequent basis if the situation should warrant such a change);
3. Continuing contribution to the Embassy for inclusion in the wake of any important developments, which should also be covered in greater detail under 2, above; and
4. Submission of a bi-weekly, unclassified despatch reporting appropriate coverage of the press with respect to Kerala. (*Note:* Submission of similar information from other posts in India, when appropriate.)

This is followed by a discussion of protocols for U.S. officials visiting Kerala. The basic principle was: "The United States must avoid taking any action which (1) contributes to the Communist effort to gain respectability, or (2) might render the U.S. vulnerable to future Communist maneuvers against U.S. personnel in the area." Travel to Kerala was to be kept at minimum, and visits to the chief minister and other ministers on call of business should be limited to government officials of civil service status.

Next comes approximately one page of declassified material on the need to

> convince Indian leaders of the dangers to India as a democratic nation which a Communist Government in Kerala presents, and, through such attempts to encourage Indian political and governmental leaders to counter this threat as soon as possible.
>
> It is recognized that the removal of the Communists from power in Kerala is primarily dependent upon the attitude of the Government of India and the Congress Party leadership, and, in the final analysis, upon the attitude of Prime Minister Nehru himself. Any action by the United States to encourage Indian leaders to counter the Communist threat in Kerala is, therefore, a matter which requires the most careful handling. If Mr. Nehru or various other Indian public leaders were to become aware of any such attempts on our part, they could charge us with unwarranted intervention in Indian internal affairs, and the entire effort would be counterproductive. Any steps in this direction should, therefore, be taken only at the Ambassador's discretion, and in such manner, and to such extent, as he may consider appropriate . . .

Drawing up a program of action, the document offers the following suggestions for the ambassador's consideration:

> A. Discreet approaches by such U.S. officers as may be specifically designated by the Ambassador to these officials in the Government of India in a position to influence their superiors at the ministerial level, taking advantage of the general anti-Communist stand of ICS career public servants and officers of the Indian Armed Services.
>
> B. Such informal approaches as the Ambassador may deem

appropriate by U.S. officers at the highest level to those anti-Communist, Indian government and political leaders who are in a position to bring influence directly to bear on Mr. Nehru. Among Indian leaders who might be considered in this connection are Vice President Radhakrishnan, Education Minister Maulana Azad, Home Minister G. B. Pant, Commerce and Industry Minister Morarji Desai, Finance Minister T. T. Krishnamachari, Irrigation and Power Minister S. K. Patil, West Bengal Chief Minister B. C. Roy, General K. S. Thimayya, Rear Admiral Katari, and Congress Party President U. N. Dhebar.

C. Discreet and continuing attempts as directed by the Ambassador to influence such non-official, leading Indian figures as authors, economists, educators and professional men.

D. As appropriate and with utmost discretion, but without expanding USIS activities, attempt to influence sympathetic elements of the press to take a stronger editorial stand on: (1) the real danger to India of the Communist regime in Kerala, and (2) the weaknesses of the "wait-and-see" policy of the GOI [Government of India] and the Congress Party regarding the future of Kerala.

E. At the highest level, inform appropriate Indian leaders of the sympathetic interest of the U.S. and its people in any attempts by the Congress Party or the Government of India to bring about the fall of the Kerala Communists.

F. Recommend to the Department, as appropriate, steps that might be taken to render *discreet assistance, including that of a covert nature*, which might lead to the overthrow of the Communists in Kerala. (Emphasis added.)

It is significant that, in Section II, Part F, reference is made to "discreet assistance, including that of a covert nature," which might lead to the overthrow of the Communists in Kerala.

There follows a newly declassified section on "withholding, reducing or terminating, for plausible reasons those [U.S.-financed] projects for which the Communist government could take credit."

It is further suggested that any projects in neighboring states should emphasize their capacity to function "to the disadvantage of the Kerala Government."

Finally, a newly declassified section requests that "every effort should be made to accede to requests for USIS assistance, *overt or covert* by the Government of India." (Emphasis added.)

As can be seen, this puts the United States clearly on record as supporting the use of covert action against the EMS ministry. Indeed, the overall tenor of the document suggests that the United States actively *encouraged* the use of covert action by the Indian government to "overthrow" the Kerala ministry. It was promoting covert action as long as it could remain discreet.

The CIA also had a clear assessment of the key weakness of the government that underlay their toppling strategy:

First: "This regime, in contrast to communist governments in other parts of the world, functions without the backing of the state police here."

Second: "The Indian Constitution and the strong central government impose serious restrictions on party's activities in Kerala and on its ability to adopt dramatic postures."

Third: "The endemic economic problems of Kerala cannot be solved quickly, and the communist ministry has not been able to make a striking improvement in the living conditions in the state."

Fourth: "The party realizes that it depends on a narrow two-vote majority in the legislature . . . and the maintenance of discipline within the party and continued support of five independents are thus of utmost importance."

Fifth: "The Kerala government prospects could be affected by left-right controversy within CPI."

After Document 171: Monitoring Kerala

Document 171 laid out the basic policy framework that the CIA was to follow in dealing with the Kerala situation. Kerala was monitored at the highest levels. President Eisenhower commented, in his own handwriting, on an April 9, 1958, discussion held at the White House: "The most important part of this informal report is that dealing with Kerala. It could be sent to [CIA Director] Allen Dulles."[28]

Warnings, Feelings, and Actions

On August 25, 1957,[29] the CIA's Current Intelligence Bulletin (CIB) reported that Indian prime minister Nehru had issued a warning to various leaders about the motives of Kerala's Communists. The CIA observer claimed that Nehru had not warned about this enough, implying that he tended to leave the impression that he was not sufficiently critical of the CPI. Then in the *Current Intelligence Weekly Summary* of August 29,[30] the author reported on one of the first public protests against the EMS ministry, ostensibly against the new Education Bill and the hands-off policy toward the police in labor disputes.

The *Summary*, regarding the Education Bill, includes the following: "The bill is bitterly opposed by the powerful Catholic elements in Kerala, which own approximately two thirds of the state's unusually well-developed educational facilities."[31] Regarding the police and labor disputes, the source states that there have been "widespread reports of 'terroristic' activities by Communist-dominated labor groups, particularly directed toward foreign managers of the state's many large plantations." These two factors led to a "much-publicized protest march on the state capital staged by Congress Party and Catholic leaders on 26 August." There follow several lines whited out from the otherwise declassified document. Also noted: "The size and strength of this popular opposition in Kerala has not been reliably reported."[32]

A month later, the CIA reported: "The national president of India's Congress party, U. N. Dhebar, told an American consular officer at Madras that both he and Prime Minister Nehru regarded the outlook for the country's ruling party with considerable pessimism."[33] Also noted:

> The Congress leader expressed his belief that the Communist government in Kerala State will last "at least two to three years." He ruled out any immediate attempt to overthrow the Communists, saying the Congress party is "not yet ready to face the Kerala electorate."[34]

A week after that,[35] the National Intelligence Estimate came out with a special report, "Consequences of Economic Crisis in India." This 9-page document contained a gloomy analysis of the economic situation. Duly noted was the Kerala election, viewed here as partly a "protest vote" against rising prices and poor living conditions. Also presented was a brief overview of rising leftist protests, including work stoppages.

By February 12, 1958,[36] the CIA was reporting, with slight skepticism, CPI claims that membership had doubled and that the Party was loosening the prerequisites for joining. On May 6,[37] the CIA reported that the Congress Party top leadership was despondent: "Nehru has not been able to halt the party's decline. . . . it has lost six out of eight by-elections since March 1957." Meanwhile, the EMS ministry was on the verge of receiving aid from Hungary to start an aluminum plant and assist a porcelain factory.[38] (The report on this was combined with other countries, the document was marked SECRET, and fifteen pages were marked "Exempt.")

On June 27, 1958, the U.S Embassy in New Delhi sent a dispatch to the State Department. This was a response and an update to the telegram State had sent to the Embassy on August 1, 1957, outlining strong U.S. actions, including covert actions, to overthrow the EMS ministry. The 3-page dispatch proposed adding a staff person with a secretary to the consulate in Madras. They would travel around Kerala, gathering information, solidifying relations with local anticommunist activists, and bring Congress Party officials from around India to observe U.S. elections. According to the dispatch's analysis:

> It has become clear over the last year that the removal of the communists from power in Kerala is related to the problem of combatting communism in India as a whole.... The key factors in the struggle are the Government of India and the Congress Party.

The dispatch praises four cabinet officers: Pandit Pant (Home Ministry), Morarji Desai (former Commerce, now Finance Ministry), A. K. Sen (Law Minister), and S. K. Patil (Transport and Communications Ministry) for discrediting the Communists. Conversely, harsh words were in order for Shrimali (Education) and Dey (Community Development), who "most recently continue to make public statements praising the record of the Government of Kerala." More generally, the dispatch criticizes the upper levels of the Congress Party "and its executive arm [which appears] to be lacking in the necessary organizational talent"—not including the Party president, U. N. Dhebar, and Prime Minister Nehru. Finally, the dispatch pledges to "discourage economic expansion [less than 2 lines of text not declassified] that is likely to produce benefits to Kerala while the communists are in power."

STRENGTHENING THE USIS OFFICE AT MADRAS

We have noted the August 1, 1957, Instruction from the U.S. Department of State on Kerala and the role assigned to the USIS in influencing the press. In June 1958, the U.S. Embassy took up the recommendation for strengthening the USIS:

> The Embassy believes that under prevailing circumstances it is desirable for the United States to have more direct access to and contact with developments in Kerala. To do this, consideration has been given to the possibility of establishing a

consulate-cum-reading room at Cochin. While our analysis indicates that there appears to be sufficient economic and commercial activity in which U.S. interests are involved to give us legitimate grounds for requesting the Government of India's permission to establish a consulate, we are inclined to believe that, for the immediate future at any rate, our interests can best be served by augmenting the staff of the Madras consulate by one officer with political and economic reporting experience (plus secretary) and by providing him with sufficient travel funds to enable him to spend a portion of every month in the various parts of Kerala. This should be accompanied by stepped-up USIS activity from Madras. The total cost should be less than that of establishing a consulate.

It was argued that the establishment of a new consulate would be time consuming, could arouse suspicions, would be superfluous after the Kerala regime is overthrown, might contribute to increasing the respectability of the government, become a target of attack as an espionage center, and result in establishment of similar institutions by Communist countries. "Thus, the augmentation of the Madras staff would give us the maximum flexibility of action while enabling us to increase our coverage while we are making up our minds on the question of the consulate."

Strengthening the U.S. consulate at Madras was to play an important role in anticommunist propaganda in Kerala. The South Indian Book Trust, established in Madras, became the pole that attracted anticommunist writers and intellectuals in Kerala. K. M. George, an erudite scholar and literary critic with astute organizational capabilities, was the Book Trust's director. The intervention of the Madras consulate played an important role in the emergence of a secular anticommunist intelligentsia.

We do not know of the other internal rearrangements at the embassy level, except for a reference in *A Spy for All Seasons: My Life in the CIA*, an autobiography by CIA operative Duane R. Clarridge. Clarridge began his career in South Asia, later helped to fund the CIA's Counterterrorism Mission Center, and was notorious for his alleged role in helping develop local terrorist groups in Nicaragua:

> Our CIA objectives in New Delhi were several. The overarching one was to keep India out of the Soviets' imperial clutches whether the Indians liked it or not. . . . It required the penetration of institutions with clandestine agents.[39]

The "Nehru-Awakening" Document

In the midst of the mid-1958 Congress Party gloom and some gains by the EMS ministry, a CIA operative in India posted a 15-page commentary, reproducing and extensively annotating an essay by P. Nehru, which had been published at the request of friends in the Congress Party in the official Party organ on August 15, 1958. The CIA version in the *A.I.C.C. Economic Review*, extensively edited and annotated, was released to the public several decades later on July 31, 1998.

"At last he [Nehru] sees Communism as it really is . . . he publicly condemns Communism for the first time," read excerpts from the second paragraph. There follows a discussion of Soviet suppression in Hungary and Nehru's then unwillingness to criticize the Soviet Union leadership for it. The CIA commentator accuses Nehru of having "partiality towards the Soviet bloc" and of frequently using the terms "colonialism" and "imperialism," despite the fact that those very "colonialist" and "imperialist" countries "granted" (author's term) independence to India and other nations. Nehru is criticized for holding contradictory views toward Communism by admiring its theory but criticizing the CPI's practice. Nehru is quoted as saying that international Communism's ideas "are in many ways out of date," that "Communism has definitely allied itself to the approach of violence." Further, Nehru had written, Communism's

> contempt for what might be called the moral and spiritual side

of life not only ignores something that is basic in man, but also deprives human behavior of standards and values. Its unfortunate association with violence encourages a certain evil tendency in human beings.[40]

The CIA analyst then takes up the question of why Nehru made this supposed complete turnabout in his views on Communism:

> The most logical answer seems to lie in the political situation in the south Indian state of Kerala, where the Communists have been in power for the past 20 months.... The terrorism, subversion and other illegal activities carried out by the CPI he could and did excuse as the misapplication of Communist principles by a small unimportant party overly eager to gain power.... The actions of the present regime in Kerala, however, have been such that Nehru can no longer deceive himself.[41]

There follows an overview of Kerala geography, history, and politics leading up to the election victory of 1957 and the rise of the EMS ministry. Once that ministry achieved power, the CIA claims, it began a reign of terror and malfeasance that forced Nehru to his current understanding. The CIA states that the EMS ministry's proposal to nationalize foreign plantations was all a ruse, since the CPI leaders well knew that compensation would be required and they did not have any funds for it. The CPI's charges that Kerala was being unfairly treated in the distribution of food is tossed off as a lie. The anti-eviction law, which could be seen as a means to protect the poor and vulnerable, is presented as a means to undermine law and order, something further supported by the policy of police neutrality in labor disputes. Again and again, the EMS ministry is attacked for "lawlessness"—reinforced by the local village committees, which could otherwise be seen as steps to decentralize power. Quoting from Congress or other opposition party spokespersons, the CIA commentary lists additional charges. Then comes an attack on the Education Bill, perhaps the lightning rod for the opposition, as "designed to give the state complete control over the private school receiving state funds—which includes virtually every private school in the state." The CIA commentary's concluding paragraph begins:

> It is probable that the situation in Kerala is going to get worse before it improves.... Nehru, despite his reluctance to interfere with any state's sovereign rights, may feel compelled to suspend the state's constitution and *impose President's Rule*, which the Union constitution permits in emergency situations.... His new realization of the true nature of Communism and its inherent evils gives grounds for hope. [Emphasis added.][42]

How accurate the CIA report was may be open to debate. Two things can be safely said, however. It gave rather a small amount of space to Nehru, despite the title of the work and, as later events would demonstrate this essay might have worked well to rile up anticommunist forces and to help create an atmosphere of hysteria about the EMS ministry. As we saw in previous chapters 5, 6, and 7, such hysteria, coming from a variety of sources, did indeed play a role in toppling the ministry.

Aid to India and the Indian Economy vs. "A Deteriorating Political Situation Within India"

On August 26, 1958, the U.S. Embassy sent a telegram to the State Department. While not containing an official subject line, it referenced various matters "designed to achieve U.S. objectives in India." As usual, at the top of the list was the "need for India to have a stable, non-communist government, economically sound and favoring the free world, which will give hope for building an Asian bulwark against challenges of international communism, especially Communist Chinese strength and ideology." U.S. Ambassador Ellsworth Bunker, author of the telegram, took an upbeat stance: "I am convinced India can make truly effective use of U.S. aid." Most of the following three pages of text are various pleas for more aid, in view of India's worsening economic situation. Along with expansion of PL-480 food aid, Ambassador Bunker noted the cooperation of the Ford and Rockefeller Foundations. On the other hand:

> Opportunities for Communist use of trade for specific purposes have been found in Kerala. In event further drop in Indian exports, India may be forced increases its volume of trade with Communist countries.[43]

And

> Through our program execution and consultation with the GOI, we must also stimulate more development in south India to mitigate India's "north vs south" conflicts and to lay ground for demonstration superior Congress Party economic capabilities as compared Kerala Communists.[44]

Ambassador Bunker worried about the lack of United States steel technology trainees from India, fearing "a dangerous flood of Communist-trained technicians." And finally, he expressed concern about "Communist Chinese trade penetration of Southeast Asia."[45]

The United States was already concerned about EMS ministry political successes that had led to a spectacular by-election victory by the CPI in May 1958 in Devikulam constituency. The CIA explained the Congress Party loss as a result of putting their best officers into administration so that "a gap gradually developed between the government and the people, which hard work by Congress Party national leaders since early 1956 has failed to fill."[46]

On September 2, 1958,[47] a National Intelligence Estimate appeared under the title "To Estimate Probable Economic and Political Consequences of India's Financial Problems." This 6-page-plus account of India's "increasingly serious economic difficulties" noted India's continuing dependence on foreign assistance. If the second five-year plan failed to achieve at least a few high-profile goals—large increases in steel production, for example—"political stability would probably deteriorate fairly rapidly." The report describes Kerala as the "showpiece Communist-governed State," and predicts that its impact on other parts of India would probably be reduced "if it were to lose control . . . after failing to provide good government and economic improvement."[48]

On November 3, 1958,[49] the CIA held a "deputies meeting" that included Director Allen Dulles. Much of the record is whited out, but it does include reference to a remark by Dulles about "aid for Indians killed by the Communists at Kerala and commented this might be an appropriate item to be followed up." No further information was provided.

The Communist Showpiece

The next declassified item is the India Central Intelligence Bureau (CIB) report of February 21, 1959. According to this report, Soviet Bloc leaders are concerned that the "Kerala Government had a good record during its first year in office, but has lost prestige since last summer due to its attempts to repress opposition elements and its inability to reduce the state's high level of unemployment." A team of Polish experts was to visit the state to survey business possibilities. Several lines are whited out.[50]

On March 3, 1959,[51] the Agency issued Intelligence Report No. 5650.75: "International Communism: Annual Review–1958–The Nonorbit Communist Parties." This 155-page report contains eight pages specifically about India and the Indian Communist Party, of which three pages are devoted specifically to Kerala, labeled as "The Communists' Showpiece." According to the report, in Kerala the CPI is pursuing a

> 5-pronged attack designed to (1) infiltrate and tighten control over the governmental services, including the police; (2)

consolidate the party's position among teachers and mold the school curriculum toward the Communists' way of thinking; (3) strengthen 'people's committees' as a potential parallel government apparatus controlled by the Communists at the local level; (4) enhance the party's prestige by publicizing Kerala's accomplishments within the state and throughout India; and (5) strengthen the Kerala branch of the CPI organizationally and financially through its present hold on the government structure.[52]

The report describes the Devikulam by-election victory won by the CPI, and claims that the Indian national government "has apparently become aware of the danger which Kerala poses for the future stability of India."[53] The report goes on to mention disputes between students and the CPI ministry that led to open hostilities around ferry rates and among striking tea plantation workers. It recalls that "firing on workers was a major reason for the downfall of a Praja socialist government in Kerala in 1955." Nehru himself had noted the "sense of insecurity" that exists in Kerala. Even so, the report concludes that "the opposition parties in the state are not sufficiently strong to defeat and replace the present ministry."[54] Also suggested is that the CPI is the only effective national opposition party in India.

On March 17, 1959,[55] a CIB report noted that the EMS ministry had survived a confidence vote of 64 to 58, indicating that the Party's independent supporters were not wavering. But "developments during recent months stimulated active collaboration between influential Hindu and Christian leaders and Congress Party politicians."

> This attempt to bring down the ministry by parliamentary means was apparently organized by "the Christian business community . . . powerful elements of the Nair community . . . and reliably reported to have been supported 'unofficially' by the Indian Central Intelligence Bureau. Indian Home Minister Pant is said

personally to have told a Kerala police official on 14 March to go ahead with the plan, which would receive his full support. The Communist government may have learned of the opposition plot and forced a confidence vote before the antigovernment leaders were able to omplete their arrangements."[56]

Three to four lines of whited-out text follow. On April 16, 1959, the Central Intelligence Weekly Summary (CIWS) included an assessment of the first two years of the EMS ministry. The report covered pluses and minuses and ran to 22 paragraphs along with a photo of EMS. Mentioned among several achievements of the ministry are raising the minimum wage; gaining some support among the police; organizing local committees in the villages; passage of an agrarian reform act; better organization and dedication when contrasted with the Congress Party. On the negative side, three pages of details about striking tea plantation workers and other rehashes of negative points about the ministry are followed by at least two full pages of "Page Denied" white-outs. As overall summary, the, report states:

> Most of the Kerala electorate appeared satisfied with the ministry's performance during its first year in office. The Communist Party may even have increased its popular support.[57]

On the other hand, owing to heavy-handed tactics in some confrontations, "opposition sentiment in the state rose sharply and national attention was focused on the problem of Kerala." The report criticizes the CPI for failing to bring about significant economic growth while it criticizes the opposition for failure to unite the various factions into a force that would be able to throw the CPI out.[58]

On May 19, 1959,[59] the NSC held a briefing on Soviet activities in India. The meeting focused in part on the extensive Soviet publishing activities, in several Indian languages, on radio broadcasts and their technical assistance in steel production, fertilizer, and heavy machinery building. Two sentences are whited out.

Anti-EMS Forces Unite

On May 28, 1959, the U.S. Embassy in New Delhi sent a telegram to Washington, updating the situation in Kerala. Of greatest consequence is the observation: "Both Congress High Command and KPCC [Kerala Pradesh Congress] seem to have now adopted greater realism and agree that CPI is dangerous to India and should be ousted from power in Kerala. . . . AICC [All India Congress Committee] met in Delhi with Kerala Congress Party May 10–13 . . . green light from AICC to proceed with 'charge-sheet' agitation." The text goes on to describe differences between older leaders and impatient Congress Party Young Turks open to any means to remove the Kerala ministry from power.[60]

> Impending agitations may easily lead violence that GOK [Government of Kerala] unable control and leave way open GOI [Government of India], if it desires, *impose President's Rule*. . . . greater determination and confidence derived from tacit High Command support. . . . These leaders fully aware that ultimately GOI assistance needed if CPI is to be successfully ousted summer 1959. [Emphasis added.][61]

The text then refers back to Document 171, containing the instruction sent out on August 1, 1957, which should be re-examined

> to consider possible U.S. assistance to non-Communist GOK re supply food grains via PL 480, increased trade in such products as corn, cashew, pepper in order strengthen indigenous industries, increased participation U.S. private investment medium-size industries. . . . U.S. financial assistance for "impact projects" in area . . . if opportunity presents itself we shall explore discreetly, with selected GOI and diplomatic personnel especially from NATO countries, possibilities of effective and immediate cooperation with new non-Communist GOK.[62]

THE BATTLE BEGINS

Then, on June 9, 1959[63] in the CIB, a heavily whited-out page includes the following:

> The Congress Party branch in Kerala State plans, in cooperation with other groups opposing the Communist government there, to launch a major campaign on 12 June aimed at eventually forcing the Communists out of office. This drive is expected to tie in with separate agitation planned by the Hindu Nair and Catholic communities to begin on 15 June to protest the Communists' unpopular education policies. . . . A showdown in Kerala seems likely in the near future. Continued demonstrations by various groups may lead to violence, particularly if extremist agitators provoke Communist police units into using force. Serious disturbances as could lead New Delhi to suspend parliamentary government in Kerala and *invoke President's Rule*. [Emphasis added.][64]

Further, on June 15, 1959,[65] in the CIB, an overview of the first three days of the agitation was given, noting:

> Further violence is likely when the intensive agitation planned by the Catholic and Hindu Nair communities against Communist education policies begins on 15 June. These groups have long planned an all-out effort to challenge the Communist government and apparently have been amassing weapons in anticipation of clashes with Communist security forces.

Six-plus lines are whited out here. Then, it is noted that Chief Minister EMS had offered some compromises on the education act, but

> Anti-Communist leaders in Kerala are unlikely to accept the compromise offer, since they hope that a serious breakdown of

law and order will either force the Communists to resign or cause New Delhi to suspend parliamentary government in the state and *institute direct rule*. If the Communist position deteriorates drastically, party leaders may also conclude that direct President's Rule—with the onus for intervention on New Delhi—is the best way out of an unfavorable situation. [Emphasis added.]⁶⁶

On June 15, 1959, a meeting was held in Washington with Ambassador Ellsworth Bunker and several directors and other high officials of the ICA (International Cooperation Administration, now USAID) to discuss the situation in Kerala. Ambassador Bunker felt the agitation had been premature and might not succeed. There was also further discussion of Soviet aid to India and of U.S. aid slowly increasing, to be more competitive with them.⁶⁷

Identifying the Opposition

This was followed on June 17, 1959, by another NSC briefing, which identified the main actors in the anticommunist agitation as Catholics and upper-caste Hindus, and included a charge sheet submitted by the Congress Party, with thirty-seven charges published against the EMS ministry. "Local police fired on several crowds; to date 12 killed, many injured, and hundreds arrested. . . . National and state Communist party bosses agreed at meeting on 7 June to avoid police firing until clearly needed to prevent severe disorder. . . . Anti-Communists now likely to exploit casualties to incite further 'direct action' against government." This was followed, once again, by reference to the possibility of a "breakdown in law and order [that] will cause New Delhi to suspend parliamentary government and impose direct rule."⁶⁸

On June 19, 1959, a conversation took place between Ambassador Bunker and the under secretary of state for political affairs, Robert D. Murphy, regarding U.S. relations with India. After discussing India's concerns about the quantity and quality of U.S. military aid to Pakistan, the talk turned to Kerala, where Bunker gave an update on recent events. The ambassador noted that he "felt that Mrs. Indira Gandhi was a considerable improvement as President of the Congress Party over her predecessor, U. N. Dhebar. Bunker also reiterated his view that the agitation in Kerala might be premature, as the Congress Party is not likely to be able to form an effective ministry if the Communists are thrown out."[69]

On June 23, 1959,[70] the Central Intelligence Bureau submitted a full-page report, "The Situation in Kerala." This was mostly a rehash of the recent events in previous documents with the additional information that up to three thousand persons had been arrested, and that the younger activists in the Congress Party were disappointed at Nehru's tepid remarks about the problems in Kerala. Nehru had arrived for a three-day visit and "publicized plans to talk to members of the Communist administration." Rumors had it that Nehru was proposing a roundtable of discussions, rather than outright support of the agitation. Of note, a comment in the text reads: "If further violence does not occur, and if the anti-Communist campaign loses additional momentum, Nehru would find it difficult to institute President's Rule—direct rule from New Delhi—in Kerala on grounds of a breakdown of law and order." There follow more than six lines, whited out.[71]

The following day, June 24, an additional National Security Council briefing took place in Washington. Among the items presented: agitations to bring down the EMS ministry had been going on for two weeks; five thousand persons arrested, fourteen killed; students, labor unions, small socialist splinter parties, and Moslem League have joined the agitation; indecisiveness in Nehru's top circles might weaken the campaign; Nehru perturbed by British press comment about the wisdom of trying to force the Kerala government to resign by mass action; latest reports suggest Nehru looking for a compromise; however, local anticommunist leaders in Kerala to press their campaign. Therefore, there is still a chance that New Delhi may feel forced to step in and take over direct administration of the state.[72]

On June 25, CIA Director Allen Dulles briefed the 411th

meeting of the NSC on developments in Kerala: Agitations quite strong; EMS ministry made a number of grave mistakes—6,300 people in prison; guess is that Nehru will do nothing; Congress Party is split on "whether to throw out the Kerala Communists or not."[73]

On June 25, at the 411th meeting of the National Security Council, Allen Dulles

> discussed developments in Kerala. . . . We do not know precisely what Nehru will do but our guess is that he will do nothing. If this guess is correct, it is very unlikely that local agitation alone will prove sufficient to oust the Communist government. Meanwhile, these developments have posed a very grave issue for the entire Congress Party in India. The Party is split right down the middle as to whether to throw out the Kerala Communists or not.[74]

Agitations Reach High Mark

SN 42, published June 30, 1959, included the claim that the Kerala Communists will not resign and there is no need for further elections: "Kerala State Congress leaders are determined to carry on their agitation in an effort to bring about the fall of the Communist government—apparently even to the point of disregarding the advice of the national leadership—and are continuing their opposition activities."

A report published July 3, 1959, states that

> Nehru apparently anticipates that the continuing demonstrations will force the central government to *impose President's Rule* in Communist-governed Kerala State about mid-August. Lengthy discussions of the Kerala situation by the Congress Party high command on 29 June, during which Nehru expressed this view, resulted in a directive to Kerala Congress leaders to intensify their agitation against the Communist government, but without

violence. An immediate election is now the anti-Communist coalition's major demand. Clashes between demonstrators and police continue.[75]

SN 44, the CIA document published July 4, 1959, as "TOP SECRET," reported that the agitation had been stepped up. Congress Party high command "overrode Defense Minister Krishna Menon's objections and advised the state branch to proceed with efforts to work out an electoral alliance.... Communist leaders rejected the Congress executive's call for elections in Kerala, condemning the party resolution issued on 29 June as 'dishonest' and a 'complete endorsement' of the agitators 'undemocratic demand.' The Communist government maintains there is no proof that it does not represent majority sentiment in the state and insists it will not resign under pressure."[76]

> Clashes between demonstrators and Communist-directed police continue. Some 25,000 have been arrested thus far in the three-week-old campaign, and about 6,000 are still in jail. The hardening attitudes of both sides in the conflict increases the likelihood of further serious violence. Extremists may try to touch off widespread disturbances to provide New Delhi with sufficient grounds for intervention, which could cause the national government to act prior to mid-August.[77]

On July 8, 1959,[78] an NSC briefing included the observations that Congress high command was supporting intensification of the campaign, and that Nehru now felt he will have to "impose President's Rule" sometime in August.[79]

On July 14, 1959,[80] a further NSC meeting noted that no decision might be made until late July. "Moscow directive ... promised to support Indian Communists in undertaking widespread agitation—presumably non-violent." Meanwhile, Congress leaders were preparing the legal basis for President's Rule. The CIA document reports:

Most Congress and Communist party leaders now expect New Delhi to impose President's Rule in Kerala State within a month. Formal government decision not likely until late July; Congress leaders meanwhile are trying to prepare strong legal case for intervention and gear up party for Kerala elections which would follow imposition of President's Rule. Communists planning retaliatory agitation in other key states, including West Bengal, Bombay, Punjab, but in line with 3 July "advice" from Moscow apparently will avoid "drastic program." Moscow directive, [several words blacked out] promised to support Indian Communists in undertaking widespread agitation—presumably non-violent.[81]

On July 20, 1959,[82] a CIA officer proposed a general background study on Kerala, while on July 28, 1959,[83] in a CIB memo, it was reported that demonstrations in Kerala and other key states were taking on a more violent tone, with two lines of text blacked out. On July 31, 1959,[84] the CIB reported that "Prime Minister Nehru on 30 July advised President Prasad, on the recommendation of the Indian cabinet, to take over direct administration of Communist-governed Kerala State under his emergency powers. Prasad is expected to issue a formal proclamation imposing President's Rule shortly."

New Delhi's intervention will climax a bitter struggle begun by combined anti-Communist groups on 12 June to unseat the Communist government. Suspension of parliamentary government in Kerala—probably accompanied by the dismissal of the Communist ministry—on grounds that it was unable to function constitutionally and maintain internal stability will be a serious setback to Communist prestige throughout India. The party may succeed in saving some face, however, by claiming it was victimized by the central government acting in collusion with the anti-Communist opposition leaders in Kerala. The Communists also plan to launch large-scale retaliatory agitation against Congress Party governments in such key states as West Bengal, Andhra Pradesh, and Bombay. Party leaders reportedly have decided, however, to limit their campaign to nonviolent action in order to avoid any further loss of popular support.[85]

There follows a paragraph of speculation about the image of the CPI, followed by three-plus lines of whited-out text. Then, "The Communists retain considerable strength in the state, and the present close cooperation among anti-Communist groups may deteriorate once the Communist government is ousted."

Then, on August 6, 1959,[86] the CIWS reported:

> New Delhi's take-over of the administration of Kerala State on 31 July brought to a successful conclusion the six-week struggle by combined anti-Communist groups to oust the Communist government. President Prasad's dismissal of the Communists and the scheduling of new elections under President's Rule have been a serious setback to Communist prestige throughout India. In turn, Prime Minister Nehru's Congress Party now faces a critical test of its ability to win the elections and provide a more effective and stable government. . . .

The report goes on to describe the logic of the dismissal, followed by statements of concern within the Congress Party, which had a weak base in Kerala. Also speculated: the CPI may be split into moderate and hardline supporters, with the moderates ascendant at this time. One line of text is whited out.[87]

The Deed Is Done

Two days later, on August 8, 1959,[88] the CIB reported that Soviet leaders again cautioned Indian Communists to avoid violence. Several lines are blacked out in this one-page report. The author also notes that Soviet accounts of the dismissal are muted, whereas Chinese sources gave "detailed, slanted reports on Kerala." This is followed by a seven-page report from the Office of Research and reports on the results[89] of a background information research proposal about Kerala,[90] covering geographical, demographic, economic (production and employment), historic, caste, religious, and other information. An unusual inclusion was some brief information about landholdings and the EMS ministry's land reform bill. Also of note:

> Kerala produces about 90 percent of the rubber of India, 92 percent of the pepper, 70 percent of the cashew nuts, 69 percent of the ginger, and 60 percent of the cardamom; it also includes 95 percent of India's tapioca acreage.[91]

A major portion of the report was devoted to political activities, including recent voting patterns in the state. Three and a half pages at the end are blank and marked "Exempt." They have not been declassified.

On August 27, 1959, a set of notes advise a CIA author about the text of a speech he was to give in Wisconsin.[92] The speaker was advised to avoid using the term "Commies" and replace it with "Communists." Two or more lines on this page are also blacked out.

On September 9, 1959,[93] a CIB memo was devoted to comments on the various responses that CPI officers in Moscow received, versus comments received by officers in Peiping (now Beijing), about the dismissal of the EMS ministry. While Moscow continued to urge caution and nonviolence, the Chinese and their supporters in the CPI were critical of Soviet aid to India, which they viewed as supporting Nehru—whom they blamed for carrying out the takeover. About five lines of text are blacked out at the end of this report.

Mutual Security Appropriations finance hearings in the U.S. Congress were noted in the report of September 12, 1959,[94] in which a U.S. congressmember is quoted as stating:

> We have read reports of riots instigated against the Nehru

government by the Communist Party in Calcutta. These riots are probably meant as retaliation for the dissolution, under constitutional procedures, of the Communist regime in the State of Kerala.[95]

The congressmember appears to support higher levels of aid to India, to be used against the Communists.

On November 5, 1959,[96] the CIWS included an update on China-India border disputes, but also a separate update on the problems faced by the CPI, partly as a result of the border issues:

> Chinese Communist action along the Tibetan frontier has highlighted divisions in the Indian party along "nationalist" and "internationalist" lines, while the failure of the "Kerala experiment" emphasized the conflict between proponents of a "peaceful, parliamentary" approach to power and those advocating more aggressive tactics. Party Secretary Ajoy Ghosh, caught in the middle, leads a faction favoring a policy which in effect compromises differences between the extreme positions on both internal and external questions.[97]

The update goes on to describe the "increasing isolation of the Communist Party in India" and the problems created for Moscow and for Nehru by Chinese actions.

On December 7, 1959,[98] the CIA's *Biweekly Propaganda Guidance* devoted most of a page (one-third of the page is whited out) to reporting on the defection of a certain Dhani Ram, "one of the 8 Communist members of the 80-man New Delhi Municipal Assembly. The defector, who had been a leader of lowest caste former untouchable Indians, declared his allegiance to the Congress Party. It appears his actions were at least partly connected with the failure of the CPI to take a strong stance against the Chinese border incursions that were in the news a lot at the time." The CIA document notes:

> There are about 50,000 Harijans in Outer Delhi, as well as large

numbers almost everywhere in India. Those in Delhi, like almost all Harijans, live in hovels which have sprung up in the old city, in the shadow of the residences of caste Hindus, carrying out for a few pennies a day the most menial tasks.[99]

Looking for a Win

According to "the CIB" report of December 28, 1959,[100] conditions for the elections in Kerala to be held under President's Rule favor the anticommunist forces. Anticommunist parties were attempting to create coalitions and Congress Party activists are "organizing down to the precinct level. The Hindu and Christian communal organizations that spearheaded the agitations in June and July of 1959 will continue to work towards an election victory. They will be joined by Muslim League and Praja Socialist Party workers. They may also be aided by the India-China border disputes that have led many Indians to consider the national CPI leadership to have made an 'unpatriotic' response to Chinese border incursions in the mountain areas around Tibet." The CPI remained, however, "the best organized and best financed group in Kerala . . . and already have an impressive campaign apparatus in the field."

The December 30, 1959,[101] Central Intelligence Weekly Summary predicted an election loss for EMS followers in the February 1 special elections to choose who would form the next Kerala ministry. A key factor:

> National leaders, including Prime Minister Nehru, *now are providing the state party with the material support* and direction which was previously lacking. [Even so]. . . Congress planners apparently still have some doubt that the funds and equipment supplied by their national headquarters will be adequate. [Emphasis added.][102]

The label "United Democratic Front" of Kerala (UDF) gave the forces joined together an identity, along with "widespread disillusionment with the Communist Party in Kerala," fueled by continuing economic problems and the India-China border dispute. Even so, the CPI and its allies were ahead of the UDF in organizing for the special elections. And sufficient unity among the anticommunist forces may yet prove hard to achieve. One and a half lines are blacked out.[103]

On January 1, 1960, the CIA produced a 29-page "SECRET" report titled "Establishment or Strengthening of Illegal Apparats by Free World Communist Parties." Pages 16 to 18 deal with the situation in India—with a caveat that the information emanates "from a source of questionable reliability." A visit to Moscow and return via Peiping by Party leader Ajoy Ghosh is cited as evidence of consultation on this issue. The "Kerala crisis" is cited as further reason to think that the CPI was planning to establish such a unit.

An NSC briefing was called on February 3, 1960,[104] to report that a "Coalition of anti-Communist parties in Kerala State scored decisive victories over Communists in elections on 1 February." Records of the briefing note that the CPI maintained significant "potential" in Kerala, and that the new ministry will have many weaknesses and a difficult economic situation to address. At a luncheon meeting on the same day, the Operations Coordinating Board held a "discussion of how the OCB could best exploit propaganda targets-of-opportunity, with specific reference to the results of the Kerala elections." No particular conclusions were reached, so the meeting passed off the issue to the "Working Group on South Asia" to see what could be done to further U.S. interests and those of the free world in general. A CIB for the same date reported much of the same information.

On the next day, February 4, 1960,[105] CIB summarized the election outcome as about three-fourths of the seats going to the coalition, and about thirty seats of the 127 total still held by the Communists and their allies. The report reiterated the weaknesses in the winning coalition: bitter rivalry between Praja Socialists and Indian National Congress; and wondered if they could work together to produce any meaningful improvements in the lives of

Kerala's people. The CIB also proclaimed that "the extent of the majority won by the anti-Communist coalition is a serious setback to the Communist party. Despite their loss of many seats, however, the Communists retained a sizable share of the popular vote, indicating they still have a firm hold on the lower classes and can effectively exploit any shortcomings of the new government." Two lines are blacked out.

On February 22, 1960, a ministry was formed in Kerala, made up of the Congress Party, the Praja Socialists, and the Muslim League, under Chief Minister Pillai of the Praja Socialist Party.

Lessons from the Documents: One Mystery Solved?

What can we learn from this survey of CIA and State Department materials? First, we see that the United States has enormous resources to devote to watching any opposition movement almost anywhere around the world. If they could maintain eyes on the Communist movement in one state of India, they could do it anywhere.

Second, we see that the CIA's watch on Kerala was almost completely focused on preventing the CPI from expanding its base. Watching events in Kerala was devoted to that. Across approximately ten years of excerpted documents—from 1950 to 1960—almost all the reports were devoted in some way to estimating the capabilities and weaknesses of the Communists and the EMS ministry, in particular.

Third, our survey of these documents has identified more details about the role of U.S. intelligence agencies in toppling the EMS ministry. Daniel Patrick Moynihan's 1975 revelation, and Ellsworth Bunker's further acknowledgment in 1979, provided proof that covert action had been at work in toppling the EMS ministry. However, no details emerged, and there are inconsistencies in what the two U.S. ambassadors at the time said they remembered. Testimony by David Burgess (recounted in chapter 1, along with that of the ambassadors), gives us a bit more knowledge. But in Document 171, the "instruction" sent from the

State Department to the U.S. Embassy in New Delhi adds a rich dimension that clearly greenlights covert action to bring down the ministry. In fact, the instruction seems even to propose that, as long as the main perpetrators were from the Indian side.

While reviewing the CIA Reading Room documents, we were struck by the entry on December 30, 1959,[106] in connection with the upcoming special election on February 1, that "National leaders, including Prime Minister Nehru, now are providing the state [Congress] party with the material support and direction which was previously lacking." Evidence points to a CIA contribution to the much better "material support in the runup to the election." That election could well have been the February 1, 1960, election, for which preparations were taking place near the end of 1959. But there is one more piece of evidence to present.

The Empty Box at Abilene

The Dwight D. Eisenhower Presidential Library in Abilene, Kansas, has walls of boxes and standalone shelves filled with materials from the president's life and his 1953–1961 tenure of office. Dozens of the boxes contain materials concerning U.S. relations with India, which was a major foreign relations partner—and not always on the same political page, as the United States might have desired. Indian prime minister Nehru visited the United States in December 1956, and "Ike" returned the favor in December 1959. Both visits generated enormous publicity and the creation of documents and news releases.

Among boxes stuffed with reports, letters, telegrams, and press releases are materials on an "Administration" series, a Cabinet series, a Speech series, and thirty-seven categories under the names of various Eisenhower administration officers. Most—perhaps all—of these series and categories have at least one document filed under "India,"—so many that "India" has its own research topic guide.

At least thirty-three boxes appear to contain materials from the National Security Council or the Operations Coordinating Board (discussed in chapter 2, as well as earlier in this chapter). Eight boxes have materials from the "Dulles-Herter Series," with materials on the activities of Eisenhower's secretary of state John Foster Dulles, and under secretary of state Christian Herter, while several boxes contain materials under the heading "Ann Whitman Diary Series," referring to the President's private secretary.

One box, however, is notable for what it does NOT contain. This is the "Withdrawal Sheet (Presidential Libraries)." The text,

FORM OF DOCUMENT	CORRESPONDENTS OR TITLE	DATE	RESTRICTION
1. Docs	NSC Case #L02-34 Documents #133-136 Exempted 5/17/2011 Exempted 5/16/14 JVL Exemption appeal 7/6/15 JVL	unknown	A

FILE LOCATION
U.S. National Security Council Presidential Records, Intelligence Files: 1953-1961; Box 2
Folder: Country Files/INT Subject Files (15) [Kerala]

RESTRICTION CODES
(A) Closed by applicable Executive order governing access to national security information.
(B) Closed by statute or by the agency which originated the document.
(C) Closed in accordance with restrictions contained in the donor's deed of gift.

NATIONAL ARCHIVES AND RECORDS ADMINISTRATION NA 14029 (1-98)

in capital letters, reads: "ALL DOCUMENTS WITHIN THIS FOLDER ARE **EXEMPTED IN FULL** FROM DECLASSIFICATION AND RELEASE BY THE NSC STAFF," and continues, "UNDER Sec.3.3 (b) of E. O. 12958." This is the Executive Order that permits withholding of Freedom of Information Act documents for national security purposes. Also marked is the "CASE# 10200034" and the "DOCUMENT #s 133–136." On the left-hand page is the "NSC case #102–34" and the documents numbers 133–136 on the

NSC Files, Continuity files maintained by the Intelligence Director of the National Security Council, Box 1001, Kerala Jul 1959 - 19 Aug 1959

ALL DOCUMENTS WITHIN THIS

FOLDER ARE **EXEMPTED IN FULL**

FROM DECLASSIFICATION AND

RELEASE BY THE NSC STAFF

UNDER Sec. 3.3(b) 1 of E.O.12958

DATE REVIEWED/REVIEWER:

CASE#: 10200034
DOCUMENT #s: 133-136

right-hand side. The exemption date is given as "5/4/2011" or "04 May, 2011." Note, then, that there are two more exemptions. These are apparently references to requests for declassification and a further denial of an appeal to that previous request. Notice, too, the materials at the left-hand bottom for Box number 2 and the designation that these are National Security files.

Now look at the upper-right part of the folder, which identifies the contents in more detail: "NSC Files, Continuity files maintained by the Intelligence Director of the National Security Council, Box 1001. Kerala Jul 1959–19 Aug 1959."

These dates correspond closely to the dates of the so-called Vimochana Samaram, or "Liberation Struggle," the period during which anticommunist forces rejected all compromises and led a series of violent actions to create a law-and-order crisis—a key element in the typical CIA playbook described by Vijay Prashad. These documents may well relate to that movement; their carefully maintained absence suggests that the National Security Council has something to hide.

A Plausible Scenario

This folder, with this particular information, makes it possible to suggest a historical connection among three documents, and three sets of plausible information:

1. In Document 171, issued by the State Department on August 1, 1957, barely six months into its tenure, we see the insistence that "the EMS ministry must be removed from power with the least possible delay." That same State Department "Instruction" greenlights covert actions in two separate places—and the removal of the word "covert" in the public presentation of the document that lasted several decades, until we were able to get it declassified on request in 2013.
2. We also see in the CIA CIB of December 30, 1959, released to the public in 2005, that the Congress Party leaders "are providing

the [Kerala] state party with the material support and direction which was previously lacking." This fits with the observations made, off and on, throughout the CIA reports concerning the weaknesses in the Congress Party and the importance of those weaknesses in making the EMS ministry possible in the first place. Could that "material support" have been the cash that David Burgess refused to spread around to labor leaders in the run-up to the February 1, 1960, special election?
3. And the documents describing connections among the factors leading to the toppling of the EMS ministry—are those perhaps the files or documents 133 to 136 that contain details and additional information about how "Washington bullets"—to cite Vijay Prashad—brought down Kerala's first state government?

We don't know where these three key documents are housed. The folder in Box 2 in Abilene only tells us that they exist and that at least two requests for even partial declassification have been denied. If Box 2 is someday declassified, we should have a fuller picture of the role played by U.S. agencies and actors in toppling the EMS ministry.

Kerala in Long-Term Perspective

The consequences of the toppling of the EMS ministry and the subsequent anticommunist election victory in 1960 were many. In the next chapter we suggest how the continuing struggle for social justice in Kerala has fared across the decades, with a somewhat surprising outcome.

CHAPTER 9

The Aftermath of the Dismissal of the EMS Ministry

Every one of the left-oriented democratic governments that came to power after the Second World War was overthrown by the CIA, with terrible and tragic consequences. In most cases, the democratic electoral process through which these governments came to power were the first casualty, giving way to decades-long military regimes, such as those in Indonesia, Guatemala, Congo, and the royal dynasty in Iran; or to rigged elections, such as in British Guiana. There is not a single example of a CIA coup leading to a democratic outcome.

The brutal savagery of these regimes is reflected in their death tolls. In Indonesia, as many as one million Communists were butchered. In Guatemala, 150,000 to 250,000 citizens were killed by CIA-trained paramilitaries and armies over four decades before relative peace returned. The Catholic Church, which had played a pivotal role in the coup against Jacobo Arbenz, later implemented the "Recovery of Historical Memory" project, in which survivors testified to atrocities before the UN-sponsored Truth Commission. In East Timor, the death toll from famine and death squads was estimated at 200,000 to 300,000. Elected leaders such as Patrice Lumumba, prime minister of the Republic of the Congo, were murdered, while Iran's Prime Minster Mohammad Mosaddegh was deposed and kept under surveillance until his death. Foreign corporations such as the United Fruit Company in Guatemala and the Anglo-Iranian Oil Company continued the plunder of natural resources. Decades of undemocratic governance and violence distorted social and economic development.

Journalist Vincent Bevins concluded that "in the years 1945–1990 a loose network of US-backed anti-communist extermination programs emerged around the world, and they carried out mass murder in at least twenty-two countries."[1] The main vehicle for this mass murder was the CIA's National Clandestine Service, which often used the information collected by the intelligence wing of that organization to identify and target victims. Finally, after forty-eight years, in 2023 a commercially available publisher brought out the Church Committee findings, which documented various abuses committed by U.S. intelligence agencies and the Internal Revenue Service.[2]

Kerala was fortunate to escape the gruesome fate of so many nations because of India's democratic federal constitution, although it was through the misuse of its constitutional provisions in 1959 that the Kerala government was dismissed. Nehru nipped in the bud plans to escalate the Kerala agitation to the national scale "Save India" campaign. Nevertheless, the abrupt end of the Communist government and disruption of key reforms left a strong imprint on the evolution of Kerala's economy and polity.

In an analysis of the results of the 1960 special state Assembly election, the Communists were trounced, and their number of seats in the Assembly was reduced from sixty-five to twenty-nine. The Communists, though crestfallen by the defeat, pointed to their increase in votes from 34.98 percent to 39.04 percent. Regarding the reduction of CPI seats, there is no dispute, but the increase in the vote share needed to be recalculated because the CPI did not contest (sought to win elections) in all the constituencies in 1957.

What were the regional, community, and class voting patterns? How did the anticommunist agitation and defeat in 1960 impact CPI advance in the state?

Despite the clear majority of the anticommunist front's ministry, governing proved to be troublesome because of interparty rivalries in the front. The new ministry modified or scuttled the key reforms of the Communist ministry in agriculture, education, and decentralization. What was the impact of the disruption of these policies on the long-term development of the state? We will use this discussion as an opportunity to draw attention to the democratic achievements of Kerala in subsequent decades.

The 1960 Assembly Election

The February 1960 Assembly election aroused so much passion on both sides that voter participation increased from 7.51 million in 1957 to 8.04 million in 1960—more than half a million votes. The votes polled increased from 66.52 percent to 84.84 percent of voters.[3] The CPI's share in the votes polled improved, but not to the extent claimed by its supporters.

In 1960 the CPI and its independents had contested in all the seats, while it had not contested for seven seats in 1957. Therefore, simple comparison of voting percentages will not give an accurate picture. We recalculated the figures by assuming that the CPI received in the uncontested constituencies the same number of votes as it received in the constituency with lowest votes in the district. In the case of twelve dual member constituencies, we have considered the average number of votes for candidates of the same party.

The anticommunist front (Congress, Muslim League, and Praja Socialist Party) received 53.1 percent of the votes in 1957 and 53.79 percent in 1960, nearly the same. The share of votes for the CPI and independents supporting it grew from 42.21 percent to 43.82 percent, an increase of 1.61 percent. It is obvious that, in 1957, the CPI won the majority of seats in the Assembly because of a split in the opposition votes. But it is surprising that the improvement of the CPI's vote share was only marginal, despite its pro-people radical policies. The anticommunist agitation, with its associated propaganda, is the key factor responsible for the muted improvement in popular support.

The agitation put a break on the upswing of the Communist support base in Kerala. If we take the CPI votes in the 1952 election to the Madras Provincial Assembly in Malabar and add to it the votes received by the CPI in the 1954 Assembly election in Travancore-Cochin (after deleting the votes received in the Tamil constituencies, which were merged with Tamil Nadu in 1956), we get a broad picture of the balance of political forces in the Kerala region during the 1952–1954 period. The share of votes for Congress was 42.3 percent, that of PSP 20.3 percent, and the CPI 17.5 percent. The others, including independents, got 19.9 percent. By 1957 the CPI vote share had increased to 42.21 percent. In short, the 1950s witnessed a rather meteoric rise in the support base of the CPI in Kerala. This trend was broken by the anticommunist agitation of 1959.[4] Another surprising incident may be referred to in this context: Rosamma Ponnuse, who had won the Devikulam constituency in 1958. with more than seven thousand votes, was defeated by a relatively unknown Congress candidate.

In which regions did the CPI suffer setbacks? A detailed analysis of district votes shows that the CPI vote share in Travancore declined from 44.52 percent to 43.84, and Cochin from 45.73 to 44.09 percent. In contrast, in the Malabar region the CPI vote sharply increased from 37.07 percent to 43.64 percent. The anticommunist agitation was relatively weaker in Malabar.[5]

How did the vote shares break down, relative to the class character of constituencies? On the basis of agricultural workers to farmers, the constituencies were categorized into four types, in descending order of proportion of agricultural workers in the population. The sharpest increase in CPI support was in constituencies dominated by agricultural workers.[6] CPI influence was relatively higher in rural areas and smaller towns. This pattern continued into 1960, but the improvement in the vote shares was higher in the urban centers, pointing to increased influence among urban workers.[7]

We do not have data based on caste voting patterns. There is a near consensus that CPI influence among the upper castes declined, but it was more than made good by the improvement in the support of Dalits and lower castes. We have already noted the unsuccessful effort to rope in the Sree Narayana Dharma Paripalana Yogam to the anticommunist alliance. Pamphlets were published pointing to the high-caste background of EMS, his role in Namboodiri caste organizations, and alleged disrespect to Ezhava-caste literary figures.[8] It is pertinent to quote from the preface of A. P. Udayabhanu, a freedom fighter, journalist, and Congress leader in a pamphlet addressing Dalits:

> Let us start with the address of communists, "comrade." It rouses self-respect and points to the ideal of equality and prepares Dalits and backward castes for self-sacrifice. They may starve but they would yet give a share of their wages earned working from morning to night without any hesitation for the party. They are willing to kill and get killed. We who understand the real character of the communists realize the call of "comrade" and the passion for equality it rouses is a myth. But they fall to illusion and become the puppets—head loaders—sacrificial offerings of the communists. This book is an attempt to tell the truth.[9]

But obviously, their efforts failed.

Setback Among the Christian Minority

A major reason for the contrasting performance of the CPI in Travancore-Cochin, compared to Malabar, was the sharp decline in vote shares in twenty-three Christian-dominated constituencies in Travancore and Cochin. The CPI vote share in these constituencies declined from 43.31 percent to 38.63 percent. In Malabar, there were no Christian-dominated constituencies. The anticommunist propaganda spread by the Church was effective in blocking the inroads of the CPI into the Christian community. Despite opposition from the Church, there was a long line of Communist leaders, such as K. V. Pathrose (first secretary of the CPI Travancore Committee), K. C. George (secretary who succeeded Pathrose), T. V. Thomas (industries minister), P. T. Punnoose (one of the best CPI orators), Simon Asan, and P. S. Solomon (both later members of Parliament), O. J. Joseph, and George Chadayanmuri. But after 1959, recruitment from the Christian community sharply waned until the advance of the Communist student wing in the latter half of the 1970s. The Communist influence in the Christian constituencies has continued to be much lower in recent decades.

The role of agitation in whipping up anticommunist religious hysteria led to ostracizing Communists from the community. It even affected the thinking of religious leaders who had dared to take radical positions in 1957. In chapter 6, we referred to the Marxist Christian dialogue held at Aluva in 1957; a similar conference was organized in 1959. The documents of the 1959 conference published under the title "Church, Society and Government in Kerala—A Christian Assessment" was critical of the Communist ministry.[10]

The Muslim Minority Community

Surprisingly, it would appear that the anticommunist agitation did not have an immediate impact on Kerala's Muslim minority. We examined the voting pattern in ten Muslim-dominated constituencies in Malabar. The vote share of the CPI increased from 21.01 percent in 1957 to 33.32 percent in 1960.[11] All these constituencies but three were won by the Muslim League. In 1957, in all these constituencies, the Muslim League and Congress opposed each other. Both polled nearly the same number of votes, 0.15 million. The PSP polled 0.07 million votes. The three parties together polled 75.8 percent of the votes. These Muslim-dominated constituencies were among the weakest pockets of Communist influence.

In 1960 the Congress contested in the three constituencies it had won in 1957, and in the rest of the constituencies, the Muslim League contested. The CPI lost all ten seats, but their votes increased from 84,007 to 189,243. Their vote share went from 21.01 percent to 33.32 percent. The CPI's vote share in other constituencies of Malabar increased from 44.5 to 46.13 percent. Though the vote share of the CPI in Muslim-dominated areas was relatively lower than in other Malabar constituencies, there was a startling improvement of vote share in Muslim-dominated constituencies.[12]

The CPI campaign in the Muslim community was simple and straightforward: "Which side should the Muslim community take? With the government that has addressed long-run grievances of the community or on the side of those who want to subvert the government?"[13] The long list included separate 10 percent reservation (affirmative action or allotment) for Muslims, 50 percent education fee concession, full-time Arabic teachers, removal of restrictions on construction of mosques in Malabar, and so on. Muslim tenants had also been set to be major beneficiaries of the land reforms. None of these proposals were contributed by the Muslim League; they came from the Communists, but the arguments struck a sympathetic chord in the Muslim community.

However, the formation of the new ministry in 1960 gave an official stamp to the Muslim League sharing power. The tactics adopted by the CPI, of aligning with the Muslim League in elections, strengthened CPI's legitimacy with both the left and right alliances, and paved the way for its influence to spread from areas of marginal Muslim concentration to communities in other parts of Kerala.

The Central Intelligence Bureau's Role in the Formation of the 1960 Ministry

The troubles began immediately after the February 1960 victory of the anticommunist front. The Congress Party, with its independents, had an absolute majority in the Assembly, but it developed cold feet about a coalition government. The national level Central Intelligence Bureau was upset over this development. In the words of its chief, B. N. Mullik, "We felt that all that had been achieved during the struggle as well as the election fight was going to be thrown away and there was no doubt in our minds that within a few months of the formation of the ministry by the Congress, it would break up and there would be another President's Rule in Kerala."[14]

The history of the Congress in Kerala was notorious for creating unstable governments. From 1949, when the interim government of Travancore-Cochin state was formed until Kerala's emergence in 1956, five ministries were turned over, even though Congress held a majority in the Assembly. Mullik personally had a meeting with the national Congress leadership and the Home Minister and vigorously argued for an alliance government, even if the post of Chief Minister had to be given to an alliance partner to keep the CPI at bay. He won the case. But Nehru was opposed to sharing power with the Muslim League and therefore a compromise had to be made. The PSP leader, Pattom Thanu Pillai, would become the Chief Minister, sharing power with the Congress. The Muslim League would not be included in the ministry, but its leader, C. H. Muhammed Koya, would be the speaker of the legislative assembly.

The words of Mullik betray the extent of involvement of the Central Intelligence Bureau in toppling the Communist ministry and installing an alternative government. "In the IB we were happy, because our struggle last[ed] nearly three years, during the first twenty-eight months of which we had often been threatened with expulsion from Kerala by the Communist Government, but had ultimately succeeded."[15]

Kerala Politics in Subsequent Decades

It did not take long for the differences among the ruling partners to come out into the open. The Muslim League was ousted from the alliance in 1961. The next year Pattom Thanu Pillai, the Chief Minister belonging to the Socialist Party, was given the post of governor of Punjab and a new Congress government with R. Sankar assuming power as Chief Minister. Then began a factional fight within the Congress between R. Sankar and P. T. Chacko, which ultimately led to the fall of the Congress government. President's Rule was reimposed in 1964.

The Congress Party split, giving rise to a breakaway group called the Kerala Congress. The CPI also split at the national level, leading to the formation of the Communist Party of India (Marxist) (CPI(M)). The basic difference between the CPI and the new CPI(M) was with respect to the relationship with Congress. The CPI wanted an alliance with Congress, which, they argued, was pursuing many progressive policies. The CPI(M) wanted to confront Congress, which they considered to be a reactionary ruling party. The by-elections for the Assembly in 1965 were conducted without any alliances, and the CPI(M) emerged as the single largest party. But the governor decided not to offer a chance to the leader of the CPI(M) to form the government, but instead dissolved the Assembly.

In the 1967 election, the CPI(M) took the initiative for a grand alliance against Congress, including the Muslim League, and won a thumping victory. Ten years after 1957, EMS was once again Chief Minister of Kerala. But his government fell after two years because of strains between the CPI and the CPI(M). The CPI then formed a government with the support of Congress.

This new coalition, which included Congress, the CPI, and some other minor parties, was continuously in power until 1980. It broke up under the weight of national level realignment after the fiasco of the national emergency (1975–1977), and the subsequent dictatorial rule imposed by Congress during that period. This realignment also took place in Kerala, with both the Communist parties coming together, in a Left Democratic Front (LDF) versus Congress, leading a United Democratic Front (UDF) against the Communists. Since then, the coalitions of LDF and UDF, with each front alternating in power in every consecutive election to the Assembly, has characterized Kerala.

The LDF governments have been in power from 1987 to 1991; 1996 to 2001; 2006 to 2011; and 2016 to 2021, alternating with UDF governments in the intervening periods. In 2021 the LDF broke the jinx when it returned to power for a second consecutive term. Each of the LDF ministries proved to be nodal points in Kerala's development, implementing such major progressive programs as the Total Literacy Program,[16] the People's Plan Campaign, and Kudumbashree Women Neighborhood Group network, established by the Kudumbashree anti-poverty program.[17] The most recent in this series has been an innovative financial institution, the Kerala Infrastructure Investment Fund Board (KIIFB), that raises funds from the market and undertakes large-scale infrastructure construction based on guaranteed annuity payment from the government. A mission has also been launched for transforming Kerala into a knowledge economy by encouraging investment in knowledge-intensive sectors, upskilling the workforce, and overhauling higher education.[18]

The tendency of the two fronts to alternate in power reflects the fact that popular support for the two has been relatively stable and narrow. Therefore, the normal anti-incumbency that would exist in any government in a highly demanding political environment would be sufficient for a change. The left has found itself trapped in a 40 percent popular support base, something they had achieved at the end of the EMS government in 1959. The left's failure to become a political formation with a firm absolute majority has been considerably discussed.

The failure by the left to increase influence among the minority communities that constitute nearly half the population in the state is a major impediment to gaining majority support. In the Christian community, this lack of progress was a clear outcome of the anticommunist agitation of 1959. The average share of votes that the two fronts received from Christian and Muslim communities in elections between 2004 and 2019 is a revealing contrast. The vote share of the left in the Christian community is less than 30 percent, while it is nearly 65 percent for the UDF. The vote share of the LDF in the Muslim community is 31 percent, while that of the Congress-led UDF is 63.38 percent.[19] Of course, there are other factors, such as Kerala's peculiar agrarian structure and the rapid growth of a middle class, discussed below.

Delayed Land Reform and Its Implications

Though the agrarian bill was legislated by the first Communist ministry, by the time it got the sanction of the president the state government had been dismissed. It took more than a decade, until 1971, before the process would be completed: 1.4 million tenants became the owners of their leased land,[20] and 400,000 landless households received around ten cents (about one-tenth of an acre) of land for their hutment.[21]

The land reforms have had a profound impact, not only on land ownership but also on social structure. The landlords almost entirely belonged to the upper castes, and the tenants were mostly from lower castes and non-Hindu communities. As a result, the land reforms significantly undermined the economic base of upper-caste domination and strengthened upward social mobility. The provision of hutment land removed the insecurity of eviction of the landless from their abodes and improved their wage bargaining power.

The major drawback of the reforms was that cultivable lands could not be provided to landless agricultural workers, most of whom were from the Dalit and backward (lower-caste) communities. In the original scheme of the 1957 agrarian bill, these communities were to be provided with cultivable land from the surplus land owned above a family ceiling of fifteen acres. The estimate was that at least five lakh (500,000) acres of surplus land would be available for distribution.

Between 1959 and 1971, a major portion of this surplus land was transferred either through sale or gifts. The surplus land clauses in the 1971 act were further watered down by Congress governments.[22] Until now, less than forty thousand acres of land have been taken over by the government and distributed. As a result, the agricultural workers received only ten cents for the hutment land on which they lived. Generally, the Kerala land reforms failed to resolve the question of landless agricultural workers. Providing cultivable land to all of them today is no longer practical, except for tribal workers in the hill tracts, where wastelands of plantations and forest can be distributed.

Currently the landowners in the midlands and coastal areas are mostly smallholders who employ wage workers to cultivate the land, while they themselves engage in non-agricultural salary-wage employment or self-employment. Because the major source of income of these landowners is non-agricultural, landowners are not under compulsion to maximize the income from their small parcels of land. Unlike typical self-employed small agricultural holders in agrarian economies, these smallholders would employ wage laborers only to the extent that the wage paid is higher than the incremental income generated by the additional employment.

If the increase in productivity does not keep pace with the increase in wages, the situation would discourage investment and expansion of production. Strong agricultural workers' unions and the increase in wages from migration have impacted labor sectors and have been responsible for the rapid rise in agricultural wages. Productivity did not keep up with the increase in wages. The result has been a decline in cultivation intensity, withdrawal from labor-intensive crops, and expansion of fallow land. Land is held in possession more with an eye to capital gains, given the rapid rise in land prices in Kerala. As a result, the agrarian question has become complicated and extremely difficult to solve. Problems have been aggravated by the fall in prices of commercial crops, which constitute more than 75 percent of cropped area after the neoliberal reforms in the 1990s.

This situation makes it very difficult for the united mobilization of farmers and agricultural workers. Demand for higher wages can alienate the farmers, and restraining wage demands can alienate the agricultural workers. The high level of underemployment and multiple jobs that rural laborers are forced to take also make their unionization difficult.

Institutions of Collective Bargaining and Labor Welfare

In chapter 4, we discussed measures adopted by the 1957–1959 government, such as the policy of noninterference by police in trade union disputes, strengthening of the labor department, promotion of workers' cooperatives, formation of tripartite committees, and appointment of minimum wage committees, boosted unionization and the collective bargaining power of the workers. The dismissal of the ministry was a setback to this process. Employers and landlords sought to put down the workers and lower castes by force, but these actions were only temporary. The trade union movement reasserted itself. With land reforms, the hutment dwellers' movement to capture their ten-cent land plots spread through Kerala like wildfire. The 1960s and 1970s also witnessed rapid unionization of agricultural workers and workers employed in small-scale informal sectors.

An important outcome was a rapid rise in wages. Besides the pressure from the sweep of the trade union movement, two factors helped facilitate a continuous rise in wages. One was the expansion of the coverage of minimum wage legislation to more sectors, so that today there are more than eighty domains of employment, both in agriculture and non-farm sectors, which together account for almost the entire workforce of the state.[23] These legally enforceable minimum wages became rallying points for the mobilization of workers in unorganized sectors. The other factor was massive migration to the Gulf countries, where construction workers—initially scarce—were able to achieve improvements in their wages. Because of the interlinked nature of labor markets in Kerala, spillover improvements also took place in other employment sectors.[24]

Today, average wages in Kerala are the highest in the country.

The daily wages of construction workers in Kerala are ₹838—more than double the national average of ₹373. For agricultural workers, the rates are ₹727 and ₹323, respectively. Similarly, the wages of non-agricultural workers in Kerala are ₹682, while the national average is ₹327.[25]

Another important innovation in labor welfare was the establishment of an Agricultural Labor Welfare Fund by the 1980 left government. Over ensuing decades, new welfare funds were also set up in other unorganized sectors, so that a large proportion of workers in the unorganized sectors are covered by social security programs. The rates and benefits may vary, but generally the funds are created by contributions from employees and employers, with matching contributions from the government providing benefits such as a monthly pension on retirement, medical and education support, maternity benefits, and marriage allowance. For some of the welfare funds, such as the Agricultural Labour Welfare Fund, the entire thrift contribution of workers is returned to them on retirement.[26] There is also direct pension coverage for people outside the welfare funds. The beneficiaries of the pension schemes today benefit more than five million aged, differently abled, and widows in the state. This is the largest social security system operational in India.

Education in Knots, Yet Highest Quality in the Country

The redistribution of assets through the land reforms and the redistribution of income through collective bargaining were the two major elements of the redistribution strategy of development of the 1957–1959 government. A third redistribution factor was the public provisioning of universal health care and schooling, which, along with the reservation (affirmative action) tremendously increased access to upward social mobility. The Education Bill of 1957 was a radical step in this direction. The government was carrying forward the tradition of the relatively high priority that was accorded to these sectors by the princely states of Travancore and Cochin, even before independence.

The Education Bill of 1957, passed by the Assembly and approved by judicial scrutiny, was scrapped by the 1960 government. The private school managers had their way in disputing the extent of social control over public education. This dispute continues even today, without resolution. With recent neoliberal reforms, the general trend is for greater autonomy and powers for management.

A decade later, Congress Party leaders were forced to take to the streets against private management. This time, the controversy was regarding the management of colleges. Here was a situation where both Congress and the left were mobilized against private education management. In fact, the same student leaders who had led the agitation against education reforms during the EMS ministry were now in the role of protesters. Youth Congress leaders violently confronted private managements in the education sector in the early 1970s. Finally, Prime Minister Indira Gandhi was forced to visit Kerala, hold discussions with the private managements, and broker an agreement.[27] There could not have been a better deal for managements: the teachers would be directly paid by the government. The fees collected by the managements would be remitted to the Treasury and the managements would have control of teacher appointments, with, as a fig leaf, the presence of a representative of the university on the selection board.

The anticommunist agitation of 1959 had pushed Kerala education into intractable knots. Nevertheless, the public education system has expanded in coverage and quality. In the School Education Quality Index (SEQI) of Niti Aayog in 2021, Kerala, with a score of 77.64, was ranked number one in India.[28]

Similarly, Kerala ranks number one among the states on the Health Index (HI) of Niti Aayog in 2015–2016, with the score of 74.65. The main contribution to this outcome has been from the public health system, the most comprehensive in the country.[29] The health and education achievements of the state have also given

Kerala top ranking on the Child Development Index (CDI) with a score of 0.76.[30]

Paradox of Low Economic Development and High Social Attainment

At the time it was formed in 1956, Kerala was one of the poorer states in India with a per capita income of ₹259—lower than the national average of ₹306. It was characterized by low productivity, small-scale production, and services that accounted for 44 percent of the workforce.[31] The GDP growth of the state was also low, averaging, between 1961 and 1987, only 2.93 percent per annum.

Though economically backward, Kerala was ahead of other states in social sector development. The prime mover was the spread of education, although that is often attributed to the nineteenth-century policies of royal families and missionaries. The major actors were the powerful socioreligious reform movements that, beginning in the late nineteenth century, swept Kerala and generated powerful demand from below for education, health care, and significantly influenced public policy. The political process in the post-independence period strengthened this tradition.

As a result, today Kerala has the highest rank among the states on the Human Development Index (HDI). In 2018, according to the UNDP, Kerala's score on the HDI was the highest, at 0.79, while the national average score was 0.65. Similarly, on the Sustainable Development Goals Index (SDGI), in 2020 Kerala ranked first, with an average score of 75 as against a national average score of 66.

The contrast becomes even sharper when comparing the level of multidimensional poverty between the states. In 2015 and 2016, whereas 25 percent of Indians were poor, Kerala's poverty rate was only 0.71 percent.[32]

There have been debates about whether there is a tradeoff between equity and growth. Kerala's slow pace of GDP growth was nearly negative during the 1970s. Was this an outcome of overzealous efforts for welfare and equity? Scholars have explored the "Limits to the Kerala Model of Development,"[33] but Kerala's investment in human resources ultimately paid off by enabling the skilled workers of Kerala to take the lead in the Gulf migration boom beginning in the mid-1970s. As a result, the inflow of remittances ballooned to 25 to 30 percent of the state's GDP. As a result, Kerala became a top-ranking state in per capita consumption, savings, rapid expansion of finance, and consumption-led services. As a result, the state's GDP growth rate increased from 2.93 percent per annum between 1961 and 1987, to 6.71 percent between 1988 and 2018. The rate of growth in per capita income was even more remarkable, rising from 0.99 percent to 6 percent per annum, so that Kerala's per capita income today is 40 percent above the national average.

However, the surge in economic development also raised new challenges. One important set of problems is related to what have come to be known as "second-generation problems." The public sector was not able to meet the demand for higher-quality education and health care and, as a result, an elite private sector began to thrive, undermining the public sector. Furthermore, the agricultural sector continued to stagnate despite land reforms, because of neoliberal reforms and the importation of products that compete with Kerala's commercial crops. What was the solution? The answer was found in a radical decentralization program to empower local governments to take leadership in local-level participatory planning in addressing the above challenges. The solution to the crisis in service delivery was not privatization but popular participation. Decentralization had been an important agenda item of the 1957–1959 government. Kerala began rediscovering it in the 1990s.

The local government bills introduced in the Assembly under the EMS ministry were the most comprehensive and radical among the decentralization laws enacted in India. They put forward the concept of the elected district government being in charge of the district administration and responsible for coordinating lower levels of local government. This vision can no longer be realized because the Seventy-Third and Seventy-fourth Constitutional

Amendments, enacted in 1994, gave constitutional status to the third (most local) tier of government. These reforms, though radical in many respects, segregated the rural local bodies and urban local bodies into two separate compartments. As a result, the district administration has remained independent of local governments, as an appendage of state government. Further, the functions allotted to local governments are mostly developmental, with few regulatory powers.

Instead of a comprehensive overhaul of local bodies and their powers, only modifications and integration of the existing laws were made by successive governments. The exception was the District Administration Bill that was passed in 1974 but remained unimplemented until 1999. The expectations raised by this experiment in the formation of elected district councils by the left government were nipped in the bud by the Congress government that followed. The implementation of radical decentralization measures was also made difficult by the nature of the various coalition governments.

In the process, Kerala also lost an opportunity to link decentralization with land reform. In a sense both are complementary: agriculture is an ideal domain for local development. With decentralization, along with distribution of land, the authority would also devolve to the beneficiaries of land reforms to plan the best utilization of their resources. This was the model of decentralization in left-ruled West Bengal during the 1980s. In fact, the local governments played an important role in land reforms by acting as the agencies to identify and document tenancy. In Kerala, this function was operationalized by land tribunals. The separation of decentralization from land reforms drained the political will for devolving powers.[34]

The deep conviction of EMS on the need for strong political will and mass pressure from below, in order to carry out a radical decentralization program, led to the formulation of a novel program for devolving powers to the local governments. The left government that came to power in 1996 was committed to a radical revision of the concomitant local body legislation passed by the previous Congress government. A committee, initially under Satyabrata Sen, who had come down to Kerala in 1957 to help the Communist government, was appointed to make recommendations. By the time the committee report was completed, political will and demand from below were to be generated from within the state.

For this purpose, a mass movement cutting across the political divide was initiated and became popularly known as the People's Plan Campaign (PPC). It was decided that 35 to 40 percent of the state plan budget outlay would be devolved to local governments, mostly as untied funds from the onset of the ninth five-year plan, starting in 1997. But before a local government could claim its allocation, a comprehensive plan had to be prepared, following a procedure that would ensure participation of people, transparency, and objective analysis and deliberation. A massive informal education program, spread out over a year and involving more than 100,000 participants, was organized. Millions of people participated in various planning forums. In short, instead of administrative reforms from above, social mobilization from below was the key element in Kerala's decentralization.

The PPC was successful in ensuring sustained devolution of finance, functions, and functionaries to local governments. It has since become a centerpiece of the left vision for the new Kerala. A review of the last quarter of a century of decentralization is very positive regarding the provision of public services, creation of local assets, and the reduction of poverty.[35]

Beginning of Sectarian Development Politics

Kerala's bipolar political system has been criticized for mutually negative partisan attitudes toward opponents' developmental initiatives. The genesis of this negative political approach, which characterizes the relationship between ruling and opposition political formations in the state, may be traced to the 1959 anti-communist agitation.

The political style in Kerala, whether it be of Communists, Congress, or any other political party, is a legacy of the national independence movement, which was replaced by blind opposition, personal slander, and a general negativity generated by the anticommunist agitation. Even after the formation of the ministry, many important Congress leaders, particularly those in Malabar, adopted a constructive approach to the ministry's proposals. But these traditions of constructive criticism disappeared in 1959. Even some of the left parties, such as the Revolutionary Socialist Party, had no qualms about joining with the communal and reactionary elements against the EMS ministry. The practice, set by the anticommunist agitation of 1959, of refusing to judge development issues on their merits and adopting an oppositional stand, depending on which coalition made a proposal, became characteristic of Kerala. Mutual antagonism became a barrier to development.

It was EMS who publicly came out against this degenerative trend in political style. In 1994, when the CPI(M) was an opposition party, EMS, in a public memorial lecture, raised the issue of cooperation between the two fronts in development activities of common interest, and openly contested their political positions in other areas of life and politics.[36] This new approach was named the "New Political Development Culture." With the launch of the PPC in 1996, it became a watchword. Since all political parties shared power in the local governments, such cooperation between the bipolar political formations could be effectively practiced.

Creation of Bias Against an Industrial Environment in Kerala

The false propaganda of the 1959 anticommunist agitation did severe damage to Kerala's reputation as an industrial investment destination. The budgets of the Communist ministry underlined the importance of a central public sector and private investment to overcome industrial backwardness in the state, which could allocate only limited funds for industrial investment, given its heavy social and welfare commitments. Incentives were announced to attract private investors. But only two projects were actually realized: Gwalior Rayons Factory of the Birla family in Kozhikode, and the Premier Tire Factory near Kochi. Meanwhile, the Communist ministry's attempts to reorganize traditional industries on a cooperative basis, seen as Communist takeovers, were largely scuttled.

One important reason for the lapse in investments was the pan-India campaign launched by Congress leaders, who had claimed the spread of insecurity in the state from the ministry's first days. This false propaganda reached a crescendo with the anticommunist agitation in 1959. The general belief in India and abroad, that investment in Kerala is not secure because of labor troubles, is an ideological construct generated by that anticommunist agitation. In fact, labor dispute data prove the contrary. From the late 1970s, the incidence of labor disputes measured by the density of strikes or person-days lost has been below the national all-India average and has been declining over time.[37]

It is true that the spread of unionization is much wider in Kerala, and that many sectors, unorganized elsewhere in the country, are unionized in Kerala. Unsurprisingly, the initial spread of unionization was violently countered by employers. The Communist ministry's policy barred the police from interfering in normal trade union disputes. This noninterference was decried as "anarchy" and "trade union rule" by the opposition, adding to the intensity of confrontation between capital and labor that continued to escalate until the end of the 1960s. As industrial relations matured, the intensity of confrontations declined.

Because private corporate investment from abroad or from the rest of India was quite low in Kerala, one of the challenges to Kerala's development was seen as the need for an image makeover, to remove the impression of the state's hostility to private investment.

Toward a Knowledge Economy

Kerala's challenge is to catch up with its delayed industrialization.

Though it has a relatively higher per capita income than other states, Kerala's economy is essentially based on the service sector. It is dangerously dependent on a continuous inflow of remittances and a low generation of high-income jobs, which the educated unemployed in Kerala expect. Therefore, Kerala has to choose to develop certain industrial sectors that are in tune with its natural and human resources. Knowledge-intensive and skills-based industries have been identified as Kerala's core areas of competence, and so the challenge is to attract corporate investment into these sectors and to promote a new generation of entrepreneurs in Kerala through startups promoted by educated youth.

What is required is a paradigm shift of development in Kerala. While preserving the social and welfare gains of the past, the state must also ensure rapid expansion of these new industrial sectors and quality jobs in the economy. The answer has been summed up in the concept of a "knowledge economy." This would entail rapid integration of modern science and technology with agriculture and traditional industries, promotion of knowledge, skill-based industries, and the upskilling of the educated unemployed—importantly, two to three million educated women, currently outside the labor force, who would be enabled to work from home or near home in the global digital economy.

Achieving this new Kerala model would require a total overhaul of Kerala's higher education system, in order to reach international standards and generate learning that can contribute to transforming the state into a knowledge economy. Kerala's higher education is expected to take on the role of the prime mover that was played by the lower schools in the state's earlier phase of development. Kerala looks forward to its large numbers of expatriates working in global laboratories, universities, high-end management, and technical positions to contribute to this remaking of Kerala.

There is yet another major impediment to transition to a knowledge economy: the wide gap between Kerala and other states in transport, electric transmission and distribution, and industrial park infrastructure. The social infrastructure in education and health is also insufficient to meet the current expectations of the people. Investment in these sectors has been low in Kerala when compared to other states because of its commitment to high expenditure in the social sectors. It is urgent to overcome this infrastructure deficit. For this purpose, a financial institution to mobilize from outside the budget, on government guarantee, and accelerate infrastructure investment has been formed. This has resulted in a remarkable improvement in the infrastructure.

Thus, the democratic project initiated by the first Communist ministry of 1957–1959 has moved forward, even in this dramatically changed global and national scenario. Kerala's search for democratic, equitable, and rapid development demonstrates the will for an alternative to neoliberal policies and majoritarian trends that dominate India today.

CHAPTER 10

Conclusions of the Study

The toppling of the Communist ministry in Kerala cast a long shadow over several decades of the state's history. This has to be located in the context of the Cold War that characterized the period after the Second World War. It must also be located in the dramatic and ongoing battle for social justice, which—in Kerala—has sometimes been at least partially won by ordinary people, organized and led by a remarkable group of leaders. U.S. labor attaché David Burgess might well have not appreciated how much of Kerala's history he reflected when, in 1959, he "told the CIA to go to hell."

But despite all the declassifications, the searches into archives, and the memoirs of so many activists, we still do not know most of the details behind the overthrow of the EMS ministry. Nevertheless, much has been learned.

The immediate decades after the Second World War witnessed electoral victories of left parties and formations in many Third World countries, which was part of a postwar revolutionary upsurge. All of the victories were undone through operations of the CIA. In chapter 2, we presented vignettes of six cases on three continents: British Guiana, Guatemala, Iran, Indonesia and East

Timor, Congo, and Brazil. The CIA has celebrated its role in many of these operations, as well as some unsavory actions, such as mass killings and assassinations later acknowledged by the U.S. Senate Church Committee.[1] But the CIA has never claimed Kerala as a trophy.

Some of the key elements in the typical template of CIA operations, such as military operations and assassinations, are totally absent in the case of Kerala. As we stated in chapter 1, most of the studies of toppling the Kerala EMS ministry have ignored the role of any external agency, let alone the CIA. In contrast, the focus of our study has been the role of the CIA, as well as other external agencies and movements such as the Christian Anticommunism Crusade (CACC) and the Moral Re-Armament Movement.

Kerala was of strategic importance to the U.S. Cold War strategy in Asia. U.S. leaders were already unhappy with the nonaligned foreign policy of India's government and its domestic promotion of public-sector investment with Soviet help. The United States had identified Kerala as a region for potential Communist growth from the early 1950s. We devoted chapter 3 to tracing the origins and development of the Communist movement in Kerala, and presented the background to the Communist electoral victory in 1957. Our argument regarding the distinctive nature of the CPI's roots in Kerala underlined the success of the Communists in rising to the leadership of the national (independence) movement; their praxis in dealing with the issue of caste, which won the radical elements in the social reform movements to its fold; the in-depth understanding of the agrarian question; and the building up of trade unions, peasant associations, and other mass organizations.

Contrary to their enemies' allegations, the Communists publicly took the stand of working within the national constitution and implementing a minimum program, many elements of which had been formally part of the program of the Congress Party. On the eve of the 1957 elections, the CPI had drawn up a detailed agenda for development of the state, the implementation of which we described in chapter 4. This agenda was intended to bring economic growth, at the same time ensuring the security and welfare of the people. The success of the EMS ministry in implementing such a program was something the U.S. analysts mortally feared. The United States was afraid of a domino effect on other states in India if the Communist ministry were to succeed in Kerala. It was therefore determined that the Kerala experiment had to fail.

The first point in the template of CIA toppling operations (chapter 2), was "creation of public opinion." There was no need for the CIA to undertake any direct action in this regard. In Kerala, there already existed political parties, along with the Church, that had entrenched anticommunism. Right from the ministry's swearing-in, opposition parties or Church groups raised vehement criticism and protest actions about every issue. We narrated a long list of such protests during 1957 and 1958 in chapter 5, Police excesses in reaction put the government on the defense. Most upsetting were incidents of police violence against striking workers. Nevertheless, each of these protests and agitations were withdrawn, or met with a natural end.

Despite its ups and downs, the government's popularity increased, as proved by the Devikulam by-election victory, as well as wins in other local governments. We decisively reject the explanation that the anticommunist agitation of 1959 was the high point of steadily worsening antigovernment agitations, starting with the ascension of the ministry. We instead traced the debate within the antigovernment forces—particularly in the Catholic Church—for a new strategy for toppling the government. The process of toppling the Arbenz regime in Guatemala in 1954 became a focal point of discussion among anticommunist activists in Kerala.

A number of features distinguish the anticommunist agitation of 1959 from previous protest movements: (1) The agitation was not led by the Church alone but by an alliance of community organizations including the powerful caste organizations; (2) Parallel to this agitation, a united front of political parties organized protests that charge-sheeted the government for its failures; (3) The objective of these protest movements was not partial demands for which a compromise could be reached, but the removal of the ministry itself; (4) This could happen only by the central government, using its constitutional power to dismiss the state government because of a breakdown of law and order, thereby preventing it from governing within the constitution; (5) The agitation's goal was to create just such a breakdown of constitutional machinery in Kerala.

In chapter 6, we traced the growth and spread of the agitation from the preparatory stage when alliances were formed and the propaganda machinery was readied. Police violence was provoked, and the killings scaled up the agitation. The eruption of mass hysteria and mass participation of women and children paralyzed the ministry. The threat of a march of hundreds of thousands to capture the secretariat building was the final step in the preparation for central government intervention.

The anticommunist agitation of 1959 parallels key steps in Vijay Prashad's CIA template: "Create economic chaos" and "Organize mass protests." The "green light for action" was not assassination or a coup, but dismissal promulgated by the central government. There was near perfect coordination and confidence among the major actors, despite the reluctance on the part of Nehru and a section of the national leadership of the Congress Party to ally with communal elements or dismiss a ministry that enjoyed a majority in its Assembly. One of the stated strategic lines of action by the CIA in Kerala was precisely to persuade the political leadership that there was a Communist danger in Kerala. Our analysis points to the possibility of such interventions with the help of the national level Central Intelligence Bureau (IB).

Materials we presented in chapter 8, following various documents we found in the CIA's Freedom of Information Electronic Reading Room, interweave the threads to the CIA and State Department. Based on an overview of the approximately sixty-two currently declassified or partially declassified materials, we see that the CIA's watch on Kerala was almost completely focused on preventing the CPI from expanding its base. Across ten years of excerpts, from 1950 to 1960, almost all the reports were devoted, in one way or another, to estimating the capabilities and weaknesses of the Communists and the EMS ministry. Our survey of these documents has identified more details about the role of U.S. agencies in toppling the EMS ministry. In addition, the document labeled FRUS 171 verifies our earlier suspicion that the CIA was clearly ready for covert action—although proof required the declassification of a key telegram from 1957 that only came to light in 2013.

The 1975 revelation by Daniel Patrick Moynihan and the further acknowledgment in 1979 by Ellsworth Bunker provided further proof that covert action had been at work in toppling the EMS ministry, although no details have emerged and there have even been inconsistencies in the statements by the two U.S. former ambassadors as to what they remembered. The testimony by David Burgess, recounted along with that of the ambassadors in chapter 1, gives us a bit more knowledge. But the "instructions" in Document 171, sent from the State Department to the U.S. Embassy in New Delhi, add a rich dimension. The missive to the missions in India clearly greenlights covert action to bring down the ministry, and indeed even seems to propose it—if the main perpetrators are from the Indian side. We had to wait from 2008, when we applied for access to portions that were exempted from outside viewing, until 2013, when those paragraphs were declassified and made available to us. The wait was worth it. But an empty box at the Eisenhower Presidential Library in Abilene reminds us of how much additional information might be waiting or might never be declassified.

While reviewing the CIA electronic Reading Room documents to produce chapter 8, we were struck by the entry on December 30, 1959,[2] in connection with the upcoming special election on February 1, 1960: "National leaders, including Prime Minister Nehru, now are providing the state Congress Party with the material support and direction which was previously lacking."
[3] Evidence presented in the opening paragraphs of this book

definitely points to CIA contributions to the much better "material support in the run up to the election." That could well have been the February 1, 1960, election for which preparations began near the end of 1959. But there is one more piece of evidence to present.

The financial support for the agitation, as discussed in chapter 7, also came through multiple agencies, such as the Moral Re-Armament movement and the Christian Anti-Communism Crusade, many of which were linked to the CIA, in toppling actions in other countries. The Kerala Book Stall at Madras was another such institution that played an important role in mobilizing independent intellectuals in the anticommunist agitation. There was also a large-scale financial flow to the Church and other agencies from foreign sources, details for which are not available.

The CIA's involvement in Indian political circles appeared to be directed "more than anything else in getting inside the Congress Party for purpose of information or influence."[4] In 1959 the Agency demonstrated its ability and willingness to work with India's ruling political party if it helped to pave the way for removal of a democratically elected Communist Party of India government in the southern state of Kerala. By secretly channeling funds to Congress Party officials and local anticommunist labor leaders, the CIA helped to destabilize, and ultimately bring down, the incumbent CPI administration.[5]

Finally, there remains a question: Why has the CIA not taken credit for this operation? The answer is provided in the first key document of the Kerala operation, FRUS Document 171, which states that if "Mr. Nehru or various other Indian public leaders were to become aware of any such attempts on our part they could charge us with unwarranted intervention in Indian internal affairs, and the entire effort would be counterproductive." The CIA collaborated with and worked through the national level Central IB in the Kerala case.[6]

On February 4, 1960, Allen Dulles briefed the 434th meeting of the National Security Council concerning the 1960 Kerala elections. He pointed out that although the number of seats of the

CONCLUSIONS OF THE STUDY

Communists were drastically reduced, their votes had increased. According to Dulles, as paraphrased by the note taker for the meeting: "While this election is a serious setback for the Communist Party in India, the size of the Communist vote showed that anti-Communist efforts could not be relaxed."[7]

The Special Report on Exploiting the Kerala Elections prepared by the Operations Coordinating Board on February 17, 1960, argues that the United States should secretly encourage others in using the results of the elections in Kerala, in India, and outside for propaganda purposes. The special report includes the argument: "Any exploitation of this political lesson would be vitiated if it appeared to come from the United States. However, outside India, it might be possible to make the story widely available on an unattributed basis."[8] We once again draw attention to the curious incident described in chapter 6, where shortly after the dismissal of the Kerala government R. Sankar thanked the U.S. in the press conference. The consulate denied it and ensured that it did not appear in any newspaper.

A Longer View of the Kerala Model

Looking back over the 66-plus years since the election of the EMS ministry, we noted how a pattern of alternating right and left ministries made it difficult for Kerala to fully achieve the numerous reforms in education, land ownership, public services, public health and other reforms (chapter 9). During times when the left coalition held power, at least one big reform usually took place: land reform, agriculture laborer pensions, total literacy, people's decentralized planning, plans for a "knowledge economy," and other initiatives. During periods of right-wing rule, defending the gains when out of power has been achieved by a remarkable level of mass mobilization sustained for up to five years. A key element of sustaining a mass mobilization is the inspiration from the history of the EMS first ministry which is widely known and celebrated in Kerala.

The pattern-breaking election victory of a second consecutive left coalition in 2021 may have created a groundwork for a number of new initiatives, which would imply a paradigm shift in development policy. Overcoming the infrastructure deficit in the state and high educated unemployment are given equal importance as redistributive measures. At the same time, the ascendancy of neoliberal policies globally and nationally and steady undermining of federal structures in India increases the constraints on any autonomous regional development path. They constitute a threat even to the gains that the people have earned after so much struggle and sacrifice in the past. Within the limits of the Indian federal system and neoliberal policies of the central government Kerala is attempting to fashion a new possible alternative.

Glossary and Acronyms

Alliance for Progress	U.S.-Latin America trade and development organization
ACF	Anti Communist Front
AICC	All-India Congress Committee
Alappuzha (Aleppey)	A central Kerala district
Anna	1/16 of a rupee
Ayyankali	Turn-of-the century Kerala caste reformer
Backward caste	A low caste above the former untouchables Dalits or Harijans
Brahmaswom	Joint property rights in land
Brahmin	A high-caste Hindu
Christophers	Kerala anticommunist militias
CIB	Central Intelligence Bureau (India)
CIWS	Current Intelligence Weekly Summary
Cochin	Central Kerala region
Coir	Coconut fiber, a major product of Kerala
CPI(M)	Communist Party of India, Marxist
CPK	Communist Party of Kerala
Crore	Ten million
Dalit	Oppressed one, recent name referring to former untouchables
Devaswom	Ownership of temples
Devikulam	A highlands Kerala Assembly constituency
Ezhava	A low or "backward" caste in Kerala, including coconut tree climbers
Fretilin	Revolutionary Front for an Independent East Timor
GDP	Gross Domestic Product
Harijan	Former untouchable caste member
Hartal	A general strike
HDI	Human Development Index
HUAC	House Un-American Activities Committee
IBAD	Brazilian Institute for Democratic Action
ICA	International Cooperation Administration, former name for USAID
ICS	Indian Civil Service
Janmaswom	Individual property ownership
Jatha	parade or procession
Jacobite	Kerala Syrian Christian Church

Kadhanprasangam	A Kerala folk artist performance
K-Disc 2021	Part of Kerala "Knowledge Economy" project
KIIFB	Kerala Infrastructure Investment Fund Board
Khilafath	Indian Muslim political movement ca. 1920
Kudumbashree	Kerala women's anti-poverty campaign
Kuttanad	A lowlands backwater region of Kerala
Legion of Mary	A Kerala anticommunist militia
Lakh	100,000
Lathi	Billy club, nightstick
Majlis	Parliament of Iran
Malabar	North Kerala region
Marthoma	The Kerala Saint Thomas Christian Church
Muslim League	A Kerala political party
Mysore	Kingdom (from 1399 to 1947), now a city in SW India
Nair	A Kerala second-highest caste member
Nair Service Society	A Nair caste uplift association
National Emergency	Suspension of the Indian constitution, 1975–77
NSC	National Security Council
Niranam Pada	An anticommunist militia in Kuttanad
OCB	Operations Control Board
Panchayat	Village elected council in India
PPC	People's Plan Campaign
Pulaya/Paraya	A former untouchable caste of mostly agricultural laborers
Quilon (Kollam)	A town in southern Kerala
Quit India Movement	Launched out of Congress Party demand for end of British rule, 1942
Responsible gov't movement	Movement creating bicameral government in India
RIN	Anti-colonial mutiny of the Royal Indian Navy, 1946
Ryotwari	A land tax system in British India
Scheduled Caste or Tribe	Former untouchables
Sheemakona (gliricidia)	Small tree whose leaves make green fertilizer
SDGI	Sustainable Development Goals Index
SH League	Sacred Heart League: A Kerala Catholic anticommunist organization
SNDP	Sree Narayana Dharma Paripalana Yogam: Ezhava caste uplift society

GLOSSARY AND ACRONYMS

Sri Narayana Guru	Activist for caste and other reforms via the SNDP
Tebhaga movement	Sharecroppers movement in Bengal, 1946
Telangana	Anti-landlord armed rebellion, 1946–51, in Andhra Pradesh State
Tenant-at-will	Renter not guaranteed farming rights
Tippu Sultan	Late 18th-century South India Muslim ruler
Toddy tapping	Climbing and tapping trees to make palm wine
Total Literacy Program	Kerala literacy campaign, 1992
Travancore	South Kerala region
USAID	U.S. Agency for International Development
Vimochana Samaram	Liberation Movement
Zamindari	A land tax system in British India

Notes

A complete bibliography may be found on the Monthly Review website: www.monthlyreview.org

1. Introduction: A Lingering Mystery

1. David S. Burgess interview, Association for Diplomatic Studies and Training, Foreign Affairs Oral History Project, Labor Series, 1991; Burgess, David, Interview and Memoir, Oral History Collection of the University of Illinois at Springfield, Illinois Digital Archives (idaillinois.org), 1988. Quote is on page 37.
2. David S. Burgess, *Fighting for Social Justice: The Life Story of David Burgess* (Detroit: Wayne State University Press, 2000), 96–97.
3. David Burgess, interview by C. Arthur Bradley, University of Illinois at Springfield, Norris L. Brookens Library Archives/Special Collections, 1988, http://www.idaillinois.org/digital/collection/uis/id/1229/, 33.
4. Daniel Patrick Moynihan, *A Dangerous Place* (Boston: Little, Brown , 1978), 41.
5. Ellsworth Bunker, Oral History Interview June 18 and July 17, 1979, Butler Library, Columbia University, 75–78; Paul McGarr, "Quiet Americans in India," *Diplomatic History* 38 (5) (2014):1054, https://www.jstor.org/stable/10.2307/26376622.
6. Government of Kerala, *Economic Review* (Thiruvananthapuram: State Planning Board, 1987), 2–3.
7. K. P. Kannan, *Of Rural Proletarian Struggles: Mobilization and Organization of Rural Workers in South-West India* (Delhi: Oxford University Press, 1988), 26.
8. Michael P. K. Tharakan, *Socio-Religious Reform Movements, the Process of Democratization and Human Development: The Case of Kerala, Southwest India* (London: Palgrave Macmillan, 1992), 144–72..
9. Government of Kerala, *Economic Review*, Thiruvananthapuram State Planning Board, 2023), 13.

10. P. G. K. Panikar and C. R. Soman, *Health Status of Kerala: Paradox of Economic Backwardness and Health Development* (Thiruvananthapuram: Center for Development Studies), 5, 1984.
11. Kannan, *Of Rural Proletarian Struggles*, 25.
12. Centre for Development Studies, *Poverty, Unemployment, and Development Policy: A Case Study of Selected Issues with Special Reference to Kerala*. New York: United Nations Department of Economic and Social Affairs, 1975); K. K. George, *Limits to Kerala Model of Development: An Analysis of Fiscal Crisis and Its Implications* (Thiruvananthapuram: Center for Development Studies, 1993); V. K. Ramachandran, "On Kerala's Development Achievements," in *Indian Development: Selected Regional Perspectives*, ed. Jean Drèze and Amartya Sen (New Delhi: Oxford University Press, 1997); K. P. Kannan, "Kerala 'Model' of Development Revisited," Center for Development Studies Working Paper No. 510 (Thiruvananthapuram: 2022); Govindan Parayil, *Kerala: The Development Experience: Reflections on Sustainability and Replicability* (London: Zed Books, 2000).
13. Richard W. Franke and Barbara H. Chasin, *Kerala: Radical Reform as Development in an Indian State*, Development Report No. 6, 2nd ed. (San Francisco: Institute for Food and Development Policy, 1994).
14. Patrick Heller, "Degrees of Democracy: Some Comparative Lessons from India," *World Politics* vol. 52, no. 4 (1998): 484–519, https://www.jstor.org/stable/25054127.
15. T. M. Thomas Isaac, *Kerala: Another Possible World* (New Delhi: LeftWord Books, 2022).
16. Georges Kristoffel Lieten, "Progressive State Governments: An Assessment of First Communist Ministry in Kerala," *Economic and Political Weekly* 14(1) (1979): 29–39,
https://www.jstor.org/stable/4367228; Georges Kristoffel Lieten, *The First Communist Ministry in Kerala, 1957-59* (Calcutta: K. P. Bagchi and Company, 1982); T. J. Nossiter, *Marxist State Governments in India: Politics, Economics and Society* (London and New York: Pinter Publishers, 1988); T. J. Nossiter, *Communism in Kerala: A Study in Political Adaptation* (New Delhi: Oxford University Press, 1982); Victor M. Fic, *Kerala—Yenan of India—Rise of Communist Power 1937-1969* (Bombay: Nachiketa Publications Ltd., 1970); P. M. Salim, "The First Popular Government in Kerala and Liberation Struggle 1957-59: A Historical Study" (PhD diss., Calicut University, 2013), http://hdl.handle.net/10603/210074.
17. John Pariyarath, "Coalition Governments in Kerala 1952-59" (PhD diss., Thiruvananthapuram, University of Kerala, 1978).
18. C. N. Somarajan, "Pressure Group Politics in Kerala during the First

Communist Regime of 1957–59" (PhD thesis, Thiruvananthapuram, University of Kerala, 1983).
19. S. S. Sushama Kumari, *Press and Politics in Kerala: A Study of the Role of Malayalam Dailies* (Thiruvananthapuram: University of Kerala, 2000).
20. Ajayan, T. "Dismissal of the First Communist Ministry in Kerala, and Extraneous Agencies., *The South Asianist* 5(1) (2017): 282–303. http://www.southasianist.ed.ac.uk/article/view/1652; Ajayan, T. "Midterm Election in Kerala in 1960 and the American Government," *History and Sociology of South Asia* 11(2) (2017): 212–20.
21. Indian Commission of Jurists, Report on Kerala made to the Indian Commission of Jurists by the Committee of Enquiry appointed to go into the alleged subversion of the rule of law and the consequent insecurity in Kerala during Communist regime (New Delhi: Government of India National Archives, 1960), https://www.indianculture.gov.in/archives/report-kerala-made-indian-commission-jurists-committee-enquiry-appointed-go-alleged; Alekapally, Archangel, *True Colour of Communist Rule* (*Communist Bharanathinte Thaniniram*) (Assisi Nagercoil, 1960); F. C. Joseph, *Kerala: The Communist State* (Madras: Madras Premier Company, 1959); Padmanabha Pillai Kainikkara, *The Red Interlude in Kerala* (Thiruvananthapuram: Kerala Pradesh Congress Publication, 1959); Revolutionary Socialist Party, *What Is Happening in Kerala?* (New Delhi, Kerala Pradesh Congress, 1958); Jitendra Singh, *Communist Rule in Kerala* (New Delhi: Diwan Chand Indian Information Centre, 1959).
22. EMS, *Twenty-Eight Months in Kerala: A Retrospect* (New Delhi: People's Publishing House, 1959), https://www.marxists.org/subject/india/cpi/28-months-kerala.pdf; Theyunni C. A. Menon, *Working of the Coir Co-operative Societies in Kerala State under the Coir Development Scheme* (Thiruvananthapuram: Government Press, 1959); H. Austin, *Anatomy of the Kerala Coup* (New Delhi: People's Publishing House, 1959); V. R. Krishna Iyer, *Daniel Come to Judgement, "What is Truth, said the Jesting Pilate and Did Not Wait for an Answer"* (Kozhikode: Prabhatham Printing and Publishing House, 1959); C. Unniraja, *Kerala—Intervention and After* (Thiruvananthapuram: Communist Party Publication, 1959).
23. K. Rajeswari, *Communist Rule and the Liberation Movement* (*Communistbharanavum Vimochanasavaravum*) (Ernakulam: Pen Books, 2005).
24. K. G. Gopalakrishnan, *Liberation Struggle: A Study* (*Vimochanas-amaram Oru Padanam*) (Attingal: Nakshatram Books, 1994); M. S. Sreekala, *1957–59 Varthakalkkappuram* (Thiruvananthapuram: Chintha Publishers, 2010).
25. T. M. Thomas Isaac, *The Other Side of Vimochanasmaram* (*Vimochanasmarathinte Kanappurangal*) (Thiruvananthapuram: Chintha, 2008).

26. Karen A. Winchester and James W. Zirkle, "Freedom of Information and the CIA Information Act" *University of Richmond Law Review* 21(2) (1987): 295–97, http://scholarship.richmond.edu/lawreview/vol21/iss2/3.
27. Ibid., 233.
28. Martin E. Halstuk, "Holding the Spymasters Accountable after 9/11: A Proposed Model for CIA Disclosure Requirements under the Freedom of Information Act," *Hastings Communications and Entertainment Law Journal* 27(1) (2004):103, https://repository.uchastings.edu/hastings_comm_ent_law_journal/vol27/iss1/3.
29. https://www.cia.gov/readingroom/historical-collections.
30. Matthew Connelly, *The Declassification Engine: What History Reveals About America's Top Secrets* (New York: Pantheon, 2023).
31. Halstuk, "Spymasters," 87.
32. https://www.cia.gov/readingroom/home.
33. https://www.cia.gov/readingroom/document/cia-rdp82 00457r005000450006-5; https://www.cia.gov/readingroom/docs/CIA RDP82-00457R005000450006-5.pdf.
34. https://www.cia.gov/readingroom/document/cia-rdp82-00457r005600 290003-0; https://www.cia.gov/readingroom/docs/CIA-RDP82-00457R005600290003-0.pdf; https://www.cia.gov/readingroom/docs/CIA-RDP82-00457R005000450006-5.pdf.
35. Ibid.

2. Policing the Empire: The U.S. Central Intelligence Agency

1. Philip Agee, *Inside the Company: CIA Diary* (New York: Stonehill Publishing, 1975), 8–9.
2. David Wise and Thomas B. Ross, *The Invisible Government* (New York: Bantam Books, 1964), 96.
3. See https://web.archive.org/web/20170128202042/https://www.cia.gov/news-information/featured-story-archive/2014-featured-story-archive/the-evolution-of-the-presidents-daily-brief.html.
4. Chalmers Johnson, *The Sorrows of Empire: Militarism, Secrecy, and the End of the Republic* (New York: Henry Holt Metropolitan Books, 2004), 9–10.
5. Ibid., 192.
6. Ibid., 32.
7. Ibid., 154.
8. Ibid., 124.
9. Alfred W. McCoy, *In the Shadows of the American Century: The Rise and Decline of US Global Power* (Chicago: Haymarket Books, 2017), 54; Tim Weiner, *Legacy of Ashes: The History of the CIA* (New York: Doubleday, 2007), 76.

10. Ibid., 83.
11. Quoted in David F. Rudgers, "The Origins of Covert Action," *Journal of Contemporary History* 35, no. 2 (April 2000): 249–62, esp. 249.
12. Quoted in Wise and Ross, *Invisible Government*, 99.
13. See https://www.cia.gov/about/mission-vision/; https://www.cia.gov/legacy/cia-history/,
14. Rudgers, "Origins of Covert Action," 253.
15. Wise and Ross, *Invisible Government*, 278.
16. Rudgers, "Origins of Covert Action," 255.
17. Ibid., 257.
18. Ibid., 259.
19. Quoted in ibid., 260.
20. Noam Chomsky and Edward S. Herman, *The Washington Connection and Third World Fascism—The Political Economy of Human Rights*, vol. 1 (Boston: South End Press, 1979), 50.
21. Ibid., 51.
22. Vijay Prashad, *Washington Bullets: A History of the CIA, Coups, and Assassinations* (New York: Monthly Review Press, 2020), 65.
23. Ibid., 67.
24. See https://archive.org/details/CIAAStudyOfAssassination1953/page/n1/mode/2up.
25. Duane R. Clarridge, with Digby Diehl, *A Spy for All Seasons: My Life in the CIA* (New York: Scribner's, 1997), 76.
26. Srinath Raghavan, *The Most Dangerous Place: A History of the United States in South Asia* (Gurgaon: Penguin Random House India, 2018).
27. Marshall Windmiller, "A Tumultuous Time: OSS and Army Intelligence in India, 1942–1946," *International Journal of Intelligence and Counter Intelligence* 8 no. 1 (1995): 105–24, esp. 106 and 108.
28. Ibid., 107.
29. Ibid., 112.
30. Ibid., 113–14.
31. Paul McGarr, "Quiet Americans in India," *Diplomatic History* 38 no. 5 (2014):1046–82, esp. 1051.
32. Ibid., 1052.
33. Ibid., 1053.
34. Ibid., 1055.
35. Paul Nitze, National Security Policy Paper #68: United States Objectives and Programs for National Security: A Report Pursuant to the President's Directive of January 31, 1950 (Washington, DC: Departments of State and Defense, 1950).
36. U.S. Department of State, Office of the Historian, *Foreign Relations of the United States: Milestones: 1945–1952* (Washington, DC: U.S.

Department of State, 1958).
37. Quoted in Tim Weiner, *Legacy of Ashes: The History of the CIA* (New York: Doubleday, 2007), 109.
38. Philip Reno, *The Ordeal of British Guiana* (New York: Monthly Review Press, 1964), viii.
39. Ibid., 11–13.
40. Ibid., 16; Cheddi Jagan, *The West on Trial: My Fight for Guyana's Freedom* (New York: International Publishers, 1966), 141.
41. Ibid., 139.
42. Ibid.
43. Stephen G. Rabe, *U.S. Intervention in British Guiana: A Cold War Story* (Chapel Hill: University of North Carolina Press, 2005), 42.
44. Quoted in ibid., 45.
45. Ibid., 48.
46. Ibid., 50.
47. Ibid., 57.
48. Reno, *Ordeal of British Guiana*, 30–31.
49. Rabe, *U.S. Intervention in British Guiana*, 81.
50. Robert Anthony Waters Jr. and Gordon Oliver Daniels, "When You're Handed Money on a Platter, It's Very Hard to Say, 'Where Are You Getting This?': The AFL-CIO, the CIA, and British Guiana," *Revue Belge de Philologie et d'histoire* 84, no.. 4 (2006): 1075–99, esp. 1082.
51. Robert Anthony Waters Jr. and Gordon Oliver Daniels, "The World's Longest General Strike: The AFL-CIO, the CIA, and British Guiana," *Diplomatic History* 29, no. 2 (2005): 279–307, esp. 295 and 307; Rabe, *U.S. Intervention in British Guiana*, 110.
52. Rabe, *U.S. Intervention in British Guiana*, 112.
53. Waters and Daniels, "When You're Handed Money," 1090.
54. Rabe, *U.S. Intervention in British Guiana*, 98.
55. Ibid., 99.
56. Victor Navasky, "Schlesinger and *The Nation*," *The Nation*, 26 March 2007, 6.
57. Quoted in *The Nation* editorial, "Tale of Two Books (Great Injustice Done to Jagan—Schlesinger)," *The Nation*, 4 June 1990, 763–64.
58. William Blum, *Killing Hope: U.S. Military and C.I.A. Interventions Since World War II*, 2nd ed. (Monroe, Maine: Common Courage Press, 2004), 74.
59. Blum, *Killing Hope*, 74; Stephen Schlesinger and Stephen Kinzer, *Bitter Fruit: The Story of the American Coup in Guatemala* (Cambridge, MA: Harvard University Press, 2005 [1982]), 262.
60. Blum, *Killing Hope*, 74–75.
61. Schlesinger and Kinzer, *Bitter Fruit*, xiii.

62. Barbara Chasin and Gerald Chasin, *Power and Ideology: A Marxist Approach to Political Sociology* (Cambridge, MA: Schenkman Publishing, 1974), 44; John Gerassi, *The Great Fear in Latin America* (New York: Collier Books, 1963), 241.
63. David Talbot, *The Devil's Chessboard: Allen Dulles, the CIA, and the Rise of America's Secret Government* (New York: HarperCollins, 2015), 260.
64. Blum, *Killing Hope*, 75.
65. Ibid.
66. Ibid., 77.
67. Ibid., 81.
68. Schlesinger and Kinzer, *Bitter Fruit*, 266.
69. Ibid., xvi.
70. Blum, *Killing Hope*, 65.
71. Ibid., 67.
72. "The Iranian Accord," *New York Times*, 6 August 1954.
73. Blum, *Killing Hope*, 71.
74. Dan Merica and Jason Hanna, CNN, "Declassified Document, CIA Acknowledges Role in '53 Iran Coup," 19 August 2013.
75. Quoted in Blum, *Killing Hope*, 72.
76. Ibid., 71.
77. Wise and Ross, *Invisible Government*, 147.
78. Ibid., 146.
79. Blum, *Killing Hope*, 103.
80. Wise and Ross, *Invisible Government*, 154–55.
81. Vincent Bevins, *The Jakarta Method: Washington's Anticommunist Crusade and the Mass Murder Program that Shaped Our World* (New York: Public Affairs Books, Hachette, 2020), 155; Blum, "Guatemala," 193; Peter Dale Scott, "Exporting Military-Economic Development: America and the Overthrow of Sukarno, 1965–67," in *Ten Years' Military Terror in Indonesia*, ed. Malcolm Caldwell (Nottingham, UK: Spokesman Books, 1975), 250; Carmel Budiardjo, *Surviving Indonesia's Gulag: A Western Woman Tells Her Story* (London: Cassell, 1996).
82. James Reston, "Washington: A Gleam of Light in Asia," *New York Times*, June 19, 1966.
83. Blum, *Killing Hope*, 194 and 420.
84. Bevins, *Jakarta Method*, 156.
85. Ralph McGehee, "The CIA and the White Paper on El Salvador," *The Nation* 432, no. 14 (1981), 424.
86. Bradley Simpson, *Economists with Guns: Authoritarian Development and U.S.-Indonesian Relations, 1960–1968* (Stanford, CA: Stanford University Press, 2008).
87. Richard W. Franke, "East Timor: The Responsibility of the United

States," *Bulletin of Concerned Scholars* 15, no. 2 (1983):42–58. This paper was presented at the Permanent Peoples' Tribunal on East Timor, 19–21 June 1981, Lisbon, Portugal.
88. Richard W. Franke, "East Timor: Physical and Cultural Genocide," *Anthropology and Humanism Quarterly* 6, no. 1 (March 1981):18–20.
89. https://www.usaid.gov/timor-leste/our-work.
90. http://www.columbia.edu/itc/history/mann/w3005/lumumba.html.
91. Stephen R. Weissman, *American Foreign Policy in the Congo, 1960–1964* (Ithaca, NY: Cornell University Press, 1974), 23.
92. Weissman, *American Foreign Policy*, 28.
93. Ibid., 23.
94. Stephen Weissman, "What Really Happened in Congo: The CIA, the Murder of Lumumba, and the Rise of Mobutu," *Foreign Affairs* 93, no. 4 (2014): 15 and 20. In 2023 a new and likely definitive account was published by Stuart Reid, *The Lumumba Plot: The Secret History of the CIA and a Cold War Assassination* (New York: Alfred A. Knopf. 2023).
95. Quoted in Weissman, "What Really Happened in Congo," 16.
96. Blum, *Killing Hope*, 158.
97. Ibid., 158–59; John Stockwell, *In Search of Enemies: A CIA Story* (New York: W. W. Norton, 1978), 105; David N. Gibbs, *The Political Economy of Third World Intervention: Mines, Money, and U.S. Policy in the Congo Crisis* (Chicago: University of Chicago Press, 1991), 95.
98. Weissman, "What Really Happened in Congo," 16.
99. Gibbs, *The Political Economy of Third World Intervention*, 87; Stockwell, *In Search of Enemies*, 97.
100. Weissman, "What Really Happened in Congo," 20.
101. Ibid.
102. Siddharth Kara, *Cobalt Red: How the Blood of the Congo Powers Our Lives* (New York: St. Martin's Press, 2023), 12.
103. Quoted in Bevins, *Jakarta Method*, 110; Ruth Leacock, *Requiem for Revolution: The United States and Brazil, 1961–1967* (Kent, OH: Kent State University Press, 1990), 197.
104. Bevins, *Jakarta Method*, 106–7.
105. For example, Gerassi, *The Great Fear in Latin America*, 76–99.
106. Quoted in Phyllis R. Parker, *Brazil and the Quiet Intervention, 1964* (Austin: University of Texas Press, 1964), 98.
107. Leacock, *Requiem for Revolution*, 74.
108. Ibid., 75.
109. Ibid., 225.
110. Ibid., 236.
111. Ibid., 216 and 229.
112. Ibid., 249.

113. Blum, *Killing Hope*, 171.
114. Leacock, *Requiem for Revolution*, 259.
115. Cited in Blum, *Killing Hope*, 417n76.
116. Quoted in Blum, *Killing Hope*, 171.

3. How the Communists Came to Power in Kerala in 1957

1. CIA, SN-07, "Leftist Coalition Defeats Congress Party in Travancore-Cochin, South Indian State," March 9, 1954, release date July 29, 2002, Cover Page: https://www.cia.gov/readingroom/document/cia-rdp79r00890a000200050008-2;Contents Page: https://www.cia.gov/readingroom/docs/CIA-RDP79R00890A000200050008-2.pdf, 1954a; CIA, SN-08, "Leftist Coalition Defeats Congress Party in Travancore-Cochin, South Indian State," March 10, 1954, release date December 7, 1998, Cover Page: https://www.cia.gov/readingroom/document/cia-rdp80r01443r000200180001-1; Contents Page: https://www.cia.gov/readingroom/docs/CIA-RDP80R01443R000200180001-1.pdf, 1954b.
2. K. N. Ganesh, "From Natu to Swarupam, Political Authority in Pre-Modern Kerala from the 10th to 13th Centuries," in *Reflections on Pre-Modern Kerala* (Trichur: Cosmos Books, 2016a), 97–124; A. Sreedhara Menon, *A Survey of Kerala History* (Madras: S. Viswanathan, 1984), 260.
3. K. N. Panikkar, *Caste in Kerala* (New Delhi: Primus Books, 2021); Robert Hardgrave, "Caste in Kerala: A Preface to the Elections," *Economic Weekly* (November 21, 1964), 1841–47.
4. Elamkulam P. N. Kunjan Pillai, Jenmie Sampradayam Keralathil (Mal.), (Kottayam: DC Books, 1965); EMS, *Note of Dissent, Report of the Malabar Tenancy Committee*, vol. 2 (Madras: Government Press 1940); K. N. Ganesh, "Ownership and Control of Land in Medieval Kerala—Janmam-Kanam Relations During the 16th-18th Centuries," in *Reflections on Pre-Modern Kerala*, 2016, 166–97; E. M. Sankaran Nambootiripad (EMS), "Dissent Minute," in Kuttikrishna Menon, *Report of the Malabar Tenancy Committee*, vol. 1 (Madras: Government Press,1940), 71–84.
5. Ashin Das Gupta, *Malabar and the Asian Trade 1740–1800* (London: Cambridge University Press, 1967); Rajan Gurukkal, *Rethinking Classical Indo-Roman Trade: Political Economy of Eastern Mediterranean Exchange Relations* (New Delhi: Oxford University Press, 2016).
6. Rajan Gurukkal and Raghava Varier, *History of Kerala—Prehistoric to the Present* (Hyderabad: Orient Black Swan, 2018); A. Sreedhara Menon, *A Survey of Kerala History* (Madras: S. Sreedhara, 1984), 60.
7. K. N. Ganesh, "Ownership and Control of Land in Medieval Kerala: Janmam and Kanam Relations During the 16th–18th Centuries," *Indian*

Economic and Social History Review 28, No. 3 (1991): 299–321; Michael P. K. Tharakan, "Control over Trade and Temples: Standing Army and Public Works: A Study of State Formation in Travancore 1729–1798," paper presented to the Indian History Congress, 47th Session, Srinagar, 1986 (mimeo).
8. Manali Desai, "Indirect British Rule, State Formation and Welfarism in Kerala, India, 1860–1957," *Social Science History* 29 (3) (2005): 457–88.
9. Robin Jeffrey, *Politics, Women and Well Being: How Kerala Became 'A Model'* (Delhi: Oxford University Press, 1993), 37.
10. Tharian K. George and Michael P. K. Tharakan, "Penetration of Capital into a Traditional Economy: The Case of Tea Plantations in Kerala, 1880–1950," *Studies in History* vol. 2. No.2 (1986), 99–229; Ravi Raman, *Global Capital and Peripheral Labor: The History and Political Economy of Plantation Workers in India* (London: Routledge, 2010).
11. K. P. Kannan, *Of Rural Proletarian Struggles: Mobilization and Organization of Rural Workers in South-West India* (Delhi: Oxford University Press, 1988), 51.
12. T. M. Thomas Isaac, "Class Struggle and Structural Changes: Coir Mat and Matting Industry in Kerala 1950–80," *Economic and Political Weekly* 17 (31) (1982): 13–29.
13. Jaiprakash Raghaviah, *Basel Mission Industries in Malabar and South Canara, 1834–1914: A Study of Its Social and Economic Impact* (New Delhi: Gian Publishing House, 1990).
14. T. M. Thomas Isaac, Richard W. Franke, and Pyaralal Raghavan, *Democracy at Work in an Indian Industrial Cooperative: The Story of Kerala Dinesh Beedi* (Ithaca, NY: Cornell University Press, 1998), 25.
15. Kannan, *Of Rural Proletarian Struggles*, 59.
16. Anna Lindberg, *Modernization and Effeminization in India: Kerala Cashew Workers Since 1930* (Copenhagen: NIAS Press, 2005).
17. Kannan, *Of Rural Proletarian Struggles*, 61.
18. Jeffrey, *Politics, Women*, 73.
19. T. M. Thomas Isaac and Michael P. K. Tharakan, "Sree Narayana Movement in Travancore, 1888–1939: A Study of Social Basis and Ideological Reproduction," Thiruvananthapuram Center for Development Studies Working Paper No. 214, 1986.
20. T. Varghese Jentle, "The Construction of Sadhu Janam Ayyankali and the Struggles of the Slave Castes for a New Identity in Travancore, 1884–1941," PhD diss.,English and Foreign Languages University, Hyderabad, 2016; Nisar M. and Kandasami Meena, *Ayyankali: A Dalit Leader of Organic Protest* (Vijayawada: Sahithi Books, 2013). Chentharassery, Ayyankali (Ayyankali) (Thiruvananthapuram: Prabhath Book House, 2013).

21. C. Kesavan, *Life Struggle* (*Jeevitha Samaram*) (Kottayam: DC Books, 1968), 207–11; M. K. Sanu, *Sree Narayana Guru Swami* (Irinjalakkuda: Vivekodayam Printing and Publishing Co., 1976); M. K. Sanu, *Sahodharan Ayyappan—The Sculptor of an Age* (*Sahodharan Ayyappan—Our Kalagattathinte Silppi*) (Kollam: Sree Narayana Guru Samskara Samiti, 1989); E. Madhavan, *Free Society* (*Swathanthra Samudayam*) (Thiruvananthapuram: Mythri Books, 2021).
22. Robin Jeffrey, "Travancore: Status, Class and the Growth of Radical Politics,1860–1940—The Temple Entry Movement," in *People, Princes and Paramount Power: Society and Politics in the Indian Princely States* (Delhi: Oxford University Press, 1978a), 152; T. K. Ravindran, *Eight Furlongs of Freedom, Light and Life* (New Delhi: Light and Life Publishers, 1980).
23. Jeffrey, "Travancore," 152–153.
24. EMS, 1984b, 14–20.
25. P. Appukuttan Vallikkunnu, *The Unknown EMS* ((*Ariyappedatha EMS*) (Kannur, Kairali Books, 2016), 472–95, 636–60.
26. Krishna Pillai, 1978.
27. EMS 1984; N. E. Balaram, *Communist Movement in Kerala* (*Keralathile Communist Prasthanam* (*Mal.*)) (Thiruvananthapuram: Prabhat Book House, 1990); CPI(M) 2018, 311–69. Communist Party of India (Marxist), *History of Communist Party in Kerala* (Keralathile Communist Partiyude Charithram), Part 1, Up to 1940 (Thiruvananthapuram: Chintha Publishers, 2018), 311–69.
28. K. C. George, *My Life Journey* ((*Ente Jeevitha Yathra*) (Kottayam: NBS, 1985; Paul Manalil Paul, *AJ John, Person and Period* ((*AJ John, Vyakthiyum Kaalavum*) (Thiruvananthapuram: Cultural Department, 2003), 13–104; Govindan Nair MN, *Autobiography of MN* ((*Emmente Anmakatha*) (Thiruvananthapuram: Prabhatam Printing and Publishing Co., 1984), 212–72.
29. Menon, *Kerala History*, 1984.
30. EMS, *A Short History of the Peasant Movement in Kerala* (Bombay: People's Publishing House, 1943); Prakesh Karat, "Agrarian Relations in Malabar, 1925–48," *Social Scientist* Nos. 14, 15 (Sept/Oct. 1973): 30–43 and 24–37; Chandavila Murali, *Comrade P. Krishna Pillai: A Comprehensive Study of Biography* (Thiruvananthapuram: Chintha, 2008), 105–548.
31. Murali, *Comrade P. Krishna*, 280–399; N. C. Sekhar, *Paths of Fire* ((*Agniveedhikal*) (Thiruvananthapuram: Prabhat Book House, 2010), 200–216; R. Prakasham, *History of Trade Union Movement in Kerala* (*Keralathile Trade Union Prasthanathinte Charithram*)) (Thiruvananthapuram: Prabhath Book House, 1979), 32–124.

32. Ragavan Puthupally, *Comrade R Sugathan—Political Biography* (*Sagavu R Sugathan—Rashtreeya Jeevachrithram*) (Thrissur: Current Books, 1999), 38–137.
33. Kumbalathu Sankupillai, *My Memories of Past* (*Ente Kazhinjakaala Smaranakal*) (Thiruvananthapuram: Prabhath Book House, 2006), 287–334; Raghavan Puthupally, *Revolutionary Memories* (*Viplavasmaranakal*) (Kottayam: National Book Stall, 2009), 281-82.
34. T. M. Thomas Isaac, "From Caste Consciousness to Class Consciousness: Alleppey Coir Workers during the Inter-War Period," *Economic and Political Weekly* 20/4 (January 26, 1985): 5–18.; Robin Jeffrey, "'Destroy Capitalism!': Growing Solidarity of Alleppey's Coir Workers, 1930–1940," *Economic and Political Weekly* 19/29 (1984): 1163.
35. George, *My Life Journey*; Sekhar, *Paths of Fire*, 162–99.
36. Murali Chandavila, *Comrade P Krishna Pillai a Comprehensive Study of Biography* (*Sagavu P Krishna Pilla Our Samagra Jeevacharithra Padanam* Thiruvananthapuram: Chintha, 2008), 70–100.
37. K. G. Sivanandan, *Revolutionary Memoir of Historical Throbs* (*Charithram Thudikkunna Viplava Smaranakal*) (Thiruvananthapuram: Prabhath Book House, 2020), 55–71.
38. Alathur Krishnan, *From the Valley of Veezhumala* (*Veezhumalayude Thazhvarayil*) (Thiruvananthapuram: Chintha, 1993), 6–41; Menon, *A Survey of Kerala History*, 9–18; Gopalan, *In the Cause of People*, 19–44; EMS, *Kerala: Society and Politics*, 21–26,
39. Kathleen Gough, "Palakkara: Social and Religious Change in Central Kerala," in *Change and Continuity in India's Villages*, ed. K. Ishwaran (New York: Columbia University Press, 1970), 149.
40. Joan Mencher, "On Being an Untouchable in India: A Materialist Perspective," in *Beyond the Myths of Culture*, ed. Eric Ross (New York: Academic Press, 1980), 280. A recent and more critical view of the role of the CPI in undermining the caste system in Kerala is given in Nitasha Kaul and Nisar Kannangara, "The Persistence of Political Power: A Communist Party Village in Kerala and the Paradox of Egalitarian Hierarchies," *International Journal of Politics, Culture, and Society* 36 (2023): 227–57, https://doi.org/10.1007/s10767-021-09411-w.
41. MN, *Autobiography of MN*, 359–62; Isaac and Williams, *EMS*, 159.
42. K. Madhavan, *On the Shores of Payaswani* (*Payaswaniyude Theerathu*) (Thiruvananthapuram: Prabhath Book House, 1987), 158–237; K. V. Kunjuraman, *Kelu Eettan* (Thiruvananthapuram: Chintha, 2016), 41–80; Koliyode Madhavan, *PR Nambair* (Thiruvananthapuram: Chintha, 2016), 56–72.
43. M. B. Rao, *Documents of the History of the CPI*, vol. 7: 1948–50 (New Delhi: 1976), 207; CPI(M), *History of Communist Party in Kerala*

Part 2 (Keralathile Communist Partiyude Charithram Bhagam 2) (Thiruvananthapuram: Chintha, 2018a).
44. K. C. George, *Immortal Punnapra-Vayalar* (New Delhi: Communist Party of India Publication, 1975); P. K. V. Kaimal, *Revolt of the Oppressed Punnapra-Vayalar, 1946* (New Delhi: Konark Publishers, 1994); M. T. Chandrasenan, *Punnapra-Vayalar, The Burning Chapters (Punnapra-Vayalar, Jwalikkunna Adyangal)* (Kottayam: DC Books, 1991); P. Jayanath, *Autobiography of VS (VSnte Athmarekha)* (Thrissur: Current Books, 2021), 64–108; Puthupally Raghavan, *Revolutionary Memoir (Viplava Smaranakal)* (Kottayam: National Book Stall, 2009), 896–1042; K. R. Gouri Amma, *Autobiography (Athmakatha)* Kozhikode: Mathrubhumi, 2010), 307–15; Varghese Vaidyan, *The Autobiography of Varghese Vaidyan (Varghese Vaidyante Atmakatha)* (Kottayam: DC Books, 2015), 46–65, 99–115.
45. E. M. S. Namboodiripad, *Kerala Society and Politics: An Historical Survey*, orig. *Kerala Yesterday, Today and Tomorrow* (New Delhi: National Book Centre, 1984), 162–63.
46. (Robin Jeffrey, "Matriliny, Marxism and the Birth of the Communist Party in Kerala, 1930–1940," 107–8.
47. CPI(M), *History of Communist Party in Kerala Part 3 (Keralathile Communist Partiyude Charithram Bhagam 3)* (Thiruvananthapuram: Chintha, 2019), 137–53.
48. V. Biju Kumar, "Radicalized Civil Society and Protracted Political Actions in Kerala (India): A Socio–Political Narrative," *Asian Ethnicity* 20/4 (2019); P. Govinda Pillai, "EMS as a Literary Critic and Cultural Activist," *The Marxist* 14/1-2 (Jan.–June 1998); C. Achutha Menon, *Unforgettable Memories (Marakkanavatha Anubhavangal)* (Kottayam: SPCS, 1981), 87–92; G. Janardhana Kurup, *My Life (Ente Jeevitham)* (Thrissur: Current Books, 2004), 151–76; O. Madhavan, *Live Reflections (Jeevithchayakal)* (Kottayam: National Book Stall, 1994,) 90–159.
49. SN11 CIA, *Current Intelligence Weekly Summary*, November 1, 1956, 14.

4. Reform within the Constitution: The Communist Ministry in Kerala, 1957–1959

1. EMS in *The Collected Works of EMS*, vol. 18: *1957 January to 1957 August (EMS-nte Sampoorna Krithikal)*, AKG Center for Research and Studies (Thiruvananthapuram: Chintha, 1957), 116.
2. A. M. Rosenthal, "India's Red Party Quiet in Victory," *New York Times* March 20, 1957.
3. Govinda Pillai P. Rajeev, ed. *1957 EMS Ministry History and Politics (1957 EMS Manthrisabha Charithravum Rashtreeyavum)* (Thiruvananthapuram: Chintha, 2007), 194–201.

4. H. D. Malaviya, *Kerala: A Report to the Nation* (New Delhi: People's Publishing House, 1958), 19.
5. Ronald J. Herring, *Land to the Tiller: The Political Economy of Agrarian Reform in South Asia* (New Haven: Yale University Press, 1983), 163; Marshall Windmiller, "Constitutional Communism in India," *Pacific Affairs* 31(1) (1958): 27.
6. S. Ramachandran Pillai, "EMS Namboodiripad and the Communist Government of Kerala," *The Marxist* 25 (3–4) (July–September 2009): 2.
7. Herring, *Land to the Tiller*, 164.
8. Ibid., 157.
9. Richard W. Franke and Barbara H. Chasin, *Kerala: Radical Reform as Development in an Indian State*, 2nd. ed. (San Francisco: Institute for Food and Development Policy, Development Report No. 6, 1994), 55.
10. EMS, *Kerala: Society and Politics: A Historical Survey*. (Delhi: National Book Center, 1984), 77; UNESCO, *Poverty, Unemployment and Development Policy: A Case Study of Selected Issues with Reference to Kerala* (New York: United Nations Department of Economic and Social Affairs, Document ST/ESA/29), 58.
11. EMS and Unniraja, *Is There Not Discrimination in Food Problem?* (*Bakshana Kariyathil Vivechanamille?*) (Thiruvananthapuram: Prabhath, 1959), 43.
12. Herring, *Land to the Tiller*, 165.
13. Thomas Paulini, *Agrarian Movements and Reforms in India: The Case of Kerala* (Saarbrücken: Verlag Breitenbach, Socioeconomic Writings on Agricultural Development, No. 33), 245.
14. Ibid., 246.
15. T. V. Sathyamurthy, *India Since Independence: Studies in the Development of the Power of the State*. vol. 1: *Centre-State Relations, the Case of Kerala* (Delhi: Ajanta Publications, 1985), 204.
16. Ibid., 208–9.
17. T. M. Thomas Isaac, *The Other Side of Vimochanasmaram* (*Vimochanasmarathinte Kanappurangal*) (Thiruvananthapuram: Chintha, 2008), 18–21.
18. UNESCO, *Poverty*, 69.
19. Paulini, *Agrarian Movements*, 240.
20. EMS, *Kerala: Society and Politics*, 193.
21. Malaviya, *Kerala*, 27.
22. Ibid., 29.
23. Joseph Mundassery, *Fallen Leaves Autobiography of Mundassery* (*Mundaserryude Athmakadha—Kozhinja Elakal*) (Kottayam: DC Books, 1978).
24. Malaviya, *Kerala*, 30.

25. D. Dhanuraj, *Story of 1957 Education Bill in Kerala* (Tripunithura, Ernakulam District, Kerala: Centre for Public Policy Research. Working Paper Series on Education, 2006), 9; Georges Kristoffel Lieten, "Education, Ideology and Politics in Kerala 1957–59," *Social Scientist* 6(2) (1977): 3–21.
26. Malaviya, *Kerala*, 32–33.
27. Ibid., 39.
28. Lieten, "Education," 8–9.
29. C. A.Theyunni Menon, *Working of the Coir Co-operative Societies in Kerala State under the Coir Development Scheme* (Thiruvananthapuram: Government Press, 1959).
30. T. M. Thomas Isaac, and Michelle Williams, *Building Alternative: The Story of India's Oldest Construction Workers' Cooperative* (New Delhi: LeftWord Books, 2017), 156–86.
31. E. M. S. Namboodiripad, *Twenty-Eight Months in Kerala: A Retrospect* (New Delhi: People's Publishing House, 1959), 13.
32. Malaviya, *Kerala*, 44.
33. EMS as quoted in Windmiller, "Constitutional Communism in India," 28.
34. EMS, *Twenty-Eight Months in Kerala: A Retrospect* (New Delhi: People's Publishing House, 1959), https://www.marxists.org/subject/india/cpi/28-months-kerala.pdf.
35. Windmiller, "Communism in India," 27.
36. T. J. Nossiter, *Communism in Kerala: A Study in Political Adaptation* (Berkeley: University of California Press for the Royal Institute of International Affairs, London, 1982), 157.
37. Georges Kristoffel Lieten, "Progressive State Governments: An Assessment of First Communist Ministry in Kerala," *Economic and Political Weekly* 14(1) (1979): 35.
38. Malaviya, *Kerala*, 45.
39. Ibid., 47.
40. Ibid., 50.
41. Lieten, "Progressive," 33.
42. Ibid., 34.
43. EMS, *Twenty-Eight Months in Kerala*, 49.
44. Lieten, "Progressive," 36.
45. EMS "*Twenty-Eight Months in Kerala*," 50.
46. Ghazala Mansuri and Vijayendra Rao, *Localizing Development: Does Participation Work?* (Washington, DC: World Bank, Policy Research Report, 2013); T. M. Thomas Isaac and Richard W. Franke, *People's Planning: Kerala, Local Democracy and Development* (New Delhi: LeftWord, 2021).
47. Harry Blair, "Accountability Through Participatory Budgeting in India:

Only in Kerala?," in *Governance for Urban Services: Access, Participation, Accountability, and Transparency*, ed. Shabbir Cheema (Singapore: Springer, 2020),57–76, https://doi.org/10.1007/978-981-15-2973-3_3
48. Kerala First Administrative Reforms Commission, 1957, https://arc.kerala.gov.in/node/155.
49. Kerala First Administrative Reforms Commission, 22.
50. Ibid. 19.
51. Ibid., 21,
52. Ibid., 23.
53. Ibid., 33.
54. Ibid., 35.
55. Ibid., 144.
56. Ibid., 143–55.
57. Tiki Rajwi, "Sheemakonna, once a common tree, is back in the spotlight in Kerala," *The Hindu*, July 28, 2022.
58. I. S. Gulati, "Behind the Coir Curtain:The First Communist Budget," *Economic and Political Weekly* 9(25) (June 22,1957):767–70.
59. EMS in *The Collected Works of EMS,* vol. 18: *1957 January to 1957 August* (*EMS-nte Sampoorna Krithikal*), (Thiruvananthapuram: Chintha Publishers, AKG Center for Research and Studies, 1957), 116.
60. EMS in *The Collected Works of EMS,* vol. 20: *1958–1959* (*EMS-nte Sampoorna Krithikal*) (Thiruvananthapuram: Chintha Publishers, AKG Center for Research and Studies, 1958), 92–93.
61. Ibid.
62. EMS and Unniraja, *Is There Not Discrimination in Food Problem?* (*Bakshana Kariyathil Vivechanamille?*) (Thiruvananthapuram: Prabhath, 1959), 22–23.

5. Ousting the Government: A Fruitless Two Years and a New, More Violent Strategy for the Anticommunist Opposition

1. O. V. Vijayan, *Un-Published Stories* (*Apprakashitha Kadhakal*) (Kottayam: DC Books, 2007), 46–51.
2. H. D. Malaviya, *Kerala: A Report to the Nation* (New Delhi: People's Publishing House, 1958), 19.
3. EMS, *Twenty-Eight Months in Kerala: A Retrospect* (New Delhi: People's Publishing House, 1959), 5–10, https://www.marxists.org/subject/india /cpi/28-months-kerala.pdf.
4. Government of Kerala, *Kerala Government's Reply to KPCC Memorandum* (Thiruvananthapuram: Government Press, 1958).
5. EMS, in *The Collected Works of EMS,* vol. 18: January–August 1957, (*EMS-nte Sampoorna Krithikal*) (Thiruvananthapuram: AKG Center for Research and Studies, Chintha Publishers, 1957), 116.

6. Government of Kerala, Department of Public Relations. *True Picture of the Situation in Kerala* (Thiruvananthapuram: Government Press, 1958), 52–56.
7. Fr. Joseph Vadakkan, *My Leaps and Gasps* (*Ente Kuthippum Kithappum*) (Kottayam: National Book Stall, 1974).
8. P. M. Salim, *Communist Government and Liberation Agitation* (*Communist Baranavum Vimochana Samaravum*) (Thiruvananthapuram: Bhasha Institute, 2021), 32–34.
9. Salim, *Communist Government*, 134–39.
10. Kerala Legislature, *Proceedings of the Kerala Legislative Assembly—2/12/1957 to 21/2/1957*, vol. 3, nos. 1–09 (Thiruvananthapuram: Government Press, 1957), 7–10.
11. Salim, *Communist Government*, 138–50.
12. N. K. Kamalasanan, *The Communist Warrior—Kalyanakrishnan Nair* (*Communist Porali Kalyanakrishnan Nair*) (Kottayam: NBS, 2008), 38.
13. Achutha Menon, *Budget Speech for 1957-58, Kerala Legislative Assembly* (Thiruvananthapuram: Government Press, 1957), 4–5.
14. EMS and Unniraja, *Is There Not Discrimination in Food Problem?* (*Bakshana Kariyathil Vivechanamille?*) (Thiruvananthapuram: Prabhath, 1959); C. Unniraja, *Kerala's Food Problem and Central Government* (*Keralathinte Baskshya Prashnavum Kendra Governmentum*) (Thiruvananthapuram: Prabhath, 1959).
15. Government of Kerala, *Kerala Government's Reply to KPCC Memorandum* (Thiruvananthapuram: Government Press, 1958), 82–83; Government of Kerala, *True Picture of the Situation in Kerala*, 82–83.
16. C. Thomas, "Autobiography (Athmakadha)," *Kerala Kaumudi Weekly*, September 18, 2011, 26.
17. Kerala Catholic Congress, *Memorial Submitted to the Honorable Chief Minister of Kerala by Kerala Catholic Congress on the Present School Textbooks of Kerala* (Cochin: SH Press, 1958).
18. Joseph Mundassery, *Fallen Leaves—Autobiography of Mundassery* (*Mundasseryude Athmakadha—Kozhinja Elakal*) (Kottayam: DC Books, 1978), 331–34.
19. Georges Kristoffel Lieten, "Education, Ideology and Politics in Kerala 1957–59," *Social Scientist* 6(2) (1977): 3–21.
20. A. C. Mathew, *Wheels of Memories* (*Oormayude Chakrangal*) (Kottayam: NBS, 1995), 223; Government of Kerala, *Kerala Government's Reply to KPCC Memorandum* (Thiruvananthapuram: Government Press 1958), 15.
21. K. Damodaran, *Memoir of An Indian Communist* (*Oru Indian Communistinte Ormakkurippu*) (Thiruvananthapuram: Prabhath Book

House, 1990), 45–48; A. K. Gopalan, *In the Cause of the People* (Madras: Sangam Books, 1976), 235.
22. Malaviya, *Kerala*, 126.
23. A. M. Rosenthal, "Rising Criticism Aimed at Nehru: Indian Politicians and Press Say He Missed Big Chance to Revivify His Party," *New York Times*, May 22, 1958.
24. Malaviya, *Kerala*, 122.
25. Anti-Communist Front (ACF), *The Objectives and Programs of Anti Communist Front* (*Communist Virudha Munnaniyude Lakshyavum Paripaadiyum*) (Thrissur: ACF Book Stall, 1952); ACF, *Why We Oppose Communism* (*Enthukondu Communisathe Ethirkkunnu*) (Thrissur: ACF Book Stall, 1953); ACF, *The Revolutionary Rule* (*Viplava Vazhcha*), (Thrissur: ACF Book Stall, 1954). ACF, *The Secrets of Democratic Front* (*Janaadhipathya Munnaniyude Ullukalikal*) (Thrissur: ACF Book Stall, 1954).
26. EMS, *The Anti Front and Communists* (*Virudha Munnaniyum Communistukarum*) (Kollam: Prabhat Book House, 1954).
27. O. C. D. Philip, *To Conquer Communism* (*Communisathe Jayikkanamenkil*), Aluva: SH League: JM Press, 1946); Ayyianeth, *The Bugle Call*; (Porvili) (Aluva: SH League,1953); *The Model Family* (Dambathya Maatrka) (Aluva: SH League (Mangalappuzha Seminary, 1954).
28. Kallada Peter John, *Marxism* (*Marxism*) (Mannanam: St. Joseph Press, 1956); Kallada Peter John, *Communism Top to Bottom* (*Communism Adi Muthal Mudi Vare*) (Mannanam: St. Joseph Press, 1956); Kallada Peter John, *Money! Money!* (*Panam Veno Panam*) (Mannanam: St. Joseph Press, 1956).
29. P. J. Antony, *Children of Revolution* (*Inquilabinte Makkal*) (Kottayam: SPS, 1953), 61.
30. P. T. Chacko, "Contradictions Within Anti-ism" (*Virudhathayile Vyrudhyangal*), *Deepika* newspaper, January 11, 1959a.
31. P. T. Chacko, "Contradictions Within Anti-ism" (Virudhathayile Vyrudhyangal), *Deepika* newspaper, January 20, 1959.
32. Editorial, *Deepika* newspaper, August 14, 1958.
33. J. Murikallel, "Guatemala and Kerala," Editor's page article in *Deepika* newspaper, June 21, 1959.
34. Ibid.
35. C. Unniraja, *Kerala's Food Problem and Central Government* (*Keralathinte Baskshya Prashnavum Kendra Governmentum*) (Thiruvananthapuram: Prabhath, 1959), 13.
36. Ibid., 14.
37. Ibid., 15.

6. The Fateful Months of June and July 1959: The Anticommunist "Liberation Struggle" and Dismissal of the Government

1. Jose, *The Atheists* (*Nireeswaranmaar*) (Aluva: Mangalappuzha Seminary, 1935).
2. James, *Prohibited Books* (*Nishidha Grandangal*) (Aluva: SH League, 1936).
3. C. D. Mavurus, *Communism or Socialism* (*Communism Adhavaa Samashti Vaadam*) (Mannanam: St. Joseph Press, 1937).
4. SH League, *A Question Answer on Communism* (*Communisathekkurichulla Oru Chodyothara Grandham*) (Aluva: Central Press, 1951).
5. ACF, *The Objectives and Programs of Anti-Communist Front* (*Communist Virudha Munnaniyude Lakshyavum Paripaadiyum*) (Thrissur: ACF Book Stall, 1952); ACF, *Why We Oppose Communism* (*Enthukondu Communisathe Ethirkkunnu?*) (Thrissur: ACF Book Stall, 1953); Fr. Joseph Vadakkan, *A Priest's Encounter with Revolution* (Bangalore: Christian Literature Society for the Christian Institute for the Study of Religion and Society, 1974), 40–83.
6. J. P. Thottil,, *Bishops Should Not Co-operate with Atheist Movements: Marxist United Front Dangerous* (*Nireeswara Prasthanavumayi Sahakarikkaruthe Abhivandya Methranmaar: Marxist Aikymunnani Apakadakari (Mal.)*, (Kottayam: Deepika, 1956); Peter John Kallada, *The Fake Mint of Communism* (*Communism Kallakkammattam*) (Mannanam: St. Joseph Press, 1950); Peter John Kallada, *Hindu Religion and Communism (Hindu Mathavum Communisavum)* (Mannanam: St. Joseph Press, 1956); Peter John Kallada, *Marxism* (*Marxism*) (Mannanam: St. Joseph Press, 1956); Peter John Kallada, *Communism Top to Bottom (Communism Adi Muthal Mudi Vare)* (Mannanam: St. Joseph Press, 1956); Peter John Kallada, *Money! Money! (Panam Veno Panam*) (Mannanam: St. Joseph Press, 1956); SH League, *Against Family* (*Kudumbathinte Nere*) (Aluva: SH League, 1953); P. T. Chacko, *What Is Communism?* (*Enthanu Communism?*) (Cherthala: St. Joseph Press, 1949).
7. F. Anthicaud, *Will Communism Strengthen the Workers?* (*Communisam Thozhilaalikale Samudharikkumo?*) (Thrissur: ACF Book Stall, 1957).
8. SH League, *Against Family*.
9. Narikuzhi, *The Failure of Marxism* (Marxisathinte Parajayam) (Aluva: SH League,1958); Narikuzhi, *Family Life in Marxism?* (Marxisathinte Kudumbajeevithamo?) (Aluva: SH League, 1958); Payyappilli, Balan, *Unforgettable Memories, Never Fading Faces* (Maayatha Smaranakal, Mangatha Mughangal) (Thiruvananthapuram: Chinta 1985)..
10. P. P. Alikunju, *An Open Letter to Aisha Beevi* (Aayisha Beebikku Oru Thuranna Kathu) (Thrissur: ACF Book Stall, 1954); Anie Thayyil, *Cross*

in a Measure (Edangazhiyile Kurisu) (Kottayam: DC Books, 1990); P. T. Chacko, *The Slaves in Soviet Union* (Soviet Russiayile Adimavelakkaar) (Thodupuzha: CS League, 1958); Francis Payyampally, *In the Heaven* (Swargathil) Thevara: ALF Press, 1951); Lanthaparambil, *The New Soviet Empire* (Aluva: SH League, 1957); MC, *The Turning Points in the Russian Communism* (Russian Communisathinte Vazhithirivukal) (Thiruvalla: Union Book Centre, 1958); Narikuzhi, *Family Life in Marxism?* (Marxisathinte Kudumbajeevithamo?); SH League, *Education Problem* (Vidyaabhyaasa Prashnam) (Aluva: SH League,1958)..

11. Charithrakaran, *The Red Spies—A Study on the Foreign Connections of Communist Party* (Communist Partiyude Videsabandhangaleppatti Oru Padanam) (Ernakulam: Voice of Kerala, 1959); P. V. Thampi, *Foreign Connections of Indian Communist Party* (Communist Partiyude Videsha Bandangal (Mal.)), Kerala Pradesh Congress Committee, 1962.

12. C. J. Thomas, *Bible According to Comrade Damodaran* (Saghaavu Damodharante Suvishesham) (Ernakulam: Voice of Kerala, 1959)

13. S. J. Pattanakad, *Hate Communism, Love the Communist* (Communisathe Dyeshikkuka Communistukaarane Snehikkuka) Kottayam: CSC Publications, Regal Press, 1952); see also K. M. Joseph, *The Land of Workers* (Thozhilali Rajyam) (Mannanam: St. Joseph Press, 1945); Annie Joseph, *What Happened in Hungary?* (Hungaryil Enthundayi?) (Aluva: SH League, 1956); K. M. Joseph, *The Wrong Hatred of Communism* (Thettaya Communist Virodham) (Mannanam: St. Joseph Press, 1958).

14. M. M.Thomas, Jacob Korula, and K. A.Mathew, *The Communist Rule in Kerala and Christian Responsibility* (Bangalore: Alwaye Study Conference, Christian Institute for the Study of Religion and Society, 1957), 1.

15. K. Damodaran, *Jesus Christ in Moscow* (Yesu Christu Moscowyil) (Kozhikode: Prabath Book House, 1953.

16. Fr.Vadakkan, *Jesus Christ Is Really in Moscow?* (Jesu Christu Moscowyilo?) (Thrissur: ACF Book Stall. 1953).

17. K. Damodaran, *Christian Religion and Communism* (Christu Mathavum Communisavum) (Kozhikode: Prabath Book House: Kozhikode, 1958).

18. Kesava P. Dev, *Will Indian Communist Read: Russia Praises India?* (*Indian Communistukal Vaayichittillengil Vaayikkumo?*) (Thiruva-nanthapuram: KPCC, 1954); Kesava P. Dev, *Two Communist Tactics* (*Randu Communistu Adavukal*) (Ernakulam: KPCC, 1954); Kesava P. Dev, *The Paradise of Writers* (*Saahithyakaarante Svarggam*) (Ernakulam: KPCC, 1954); Kesava P. Dev, *The Red Empire* (*Chuvappu Saamrajyathwam*)

(Ernakulam: KPCC, 1954); Kesava P. Dev, *The Paradise of Workers* (*Thozhilalikalude Parudeesa*) (Ernakulam: KPCC, 1954).
19. Kesava P. Dev, *You Are Dead* (Nee Marichu) (Kottayam: SPSS, 1956a); Kesava P. Dev, *Rain There, Umbrella Here* (Mzhayangum Kudayingum) (Kottayam: SPSS, 1956b); Kesava P. Dev, *Onam Blouse* (Onablouse) (Ernakulam: Parishath Book Stall, 1957); Kesava P. Dev, *Half a Coconut* (Our Murithenga) (Kottayam SPSS, 1959); Kesava P. Dev, *Lover of Russia* (Russiayude Kamukan) (Kottayam SPSS, 1959a).
20. Dr. A. Rasaludeen, *C. J.: The Core of a Rebel* (C.J: Dikkariyude Kaathal) (Kottayam: SPCS, 2008).
21. Jawaharlal Nehru, *Selected Works of Jawaharlal Nehru,* Vol. 30 (New Delhi: Jawaharlal Nehru Memorial Fund, 1957), 222–224.
22. *Deepika* newspaper, March 20, 1959.
23. P. P. Alikunju, *An Open Letter to Aisha Beevi* (Aayisha Beebikku Oru Thuranna Kathu) (Thrissur: ACF Book Stall, 1954); Syed Muhammed, *Muslim and Communism* (Musalmaanum Communisavum) (Thrissur: ACF Book Stall, 1954); P. Usman, *Religion and State* (Mathavum Rashtravum) (Edayoor: Islamic Books, 1958); Basherudeen Muhammed Mirza, *To Meet Communist Challenge* (Communisathe Neridan) (Kozhikode: Ahamedia Muslim Mission, 1959).
24. Quoted in Rajeswari, K. *Communist Rule and the Liberation Struggle (Communistbharanavum VimochanaSamaravum*, Pen Books, 2005), 215.
25. *Deepika* Newspaper, 19 January 1958).
26. Quoted in H. Austin, *Anatomy of the Kerala Coup* (New Delhi: People's Publishing House, 1959), 10–11.
27. Thomas Isaac and N. P. Chandrasekharan, *Manufacturing of False Consensus—A Critique of Malayalam Media 2000–2009* (Vyajasamithiyude Nirmithi—Madhayama Vimarsanam 2000–2009) (Thiruvananthapuram: Chintha Publishers, 2010), 31–32.
28. T. M. Thomas Isaac, *The Other Side of Vimochanasmaram* [*Vimochanasmarathinte Kanappurangal*] (Thiruvananthapuram: Chinta, 2008), 155–159.
29. Quoted in Thomas Isaac, *Other Side of Vimochanasmaram*, 157.
30. Quoted in Austin, *Anatomy of the Kerala* Coup, P-13.
31. Quoted in Austin, *Anatomy of the Kerala Coup*, P-99.
32. Ravi Raman, *Global Capital and Peripheral Labour: The History and Political Economy of Plantation Workers in India* (London: Routledge, 2009), 147–148.
33. Fr. Joseph Vadakkan, *A Priest's Encounter with Revolution* (Bangalore: The Christian Literature Society for the Christian Institute for the Study of Religion and Society, 1974), 40–83.
34. *Deepika* newspaper, June 2, 1959.

35. Fr. Joseph Vadakkan, *My Leaps and Gasps (Ente Kuthippum Kithappum)* Kottayam: National Book Stall, 1974), 128; see also Lonappan Nambadan, *The Autobiography of Lonappan Nambadan, A Travelling Believer* (Lonappan Nambadante Athmakatha—Sancharikkunna Viswasi) (Kottayam: DC Books, 2011), 24–26.
36. Hindu report quoted in Austin, *Anatomy of the Kerala Coup*, 50–51.
37. N. Jayadevan, *Student Movement and Kerala Politics from 1956 to 1970*, Thiruvananthapuram. PhD Thesis submitted to the University of Kerala, 1999.
38. Annie Joseph, *Six Months of Communist Rule* (Communist Sarkkarinte Aaru Masathe Bharanam) (Ernakulam: Scholar Press, 1957b), 15.
39. Deepika, *Kerala Liberation Struggle in Pictures* (Kerala Vimochanasamaram: Chithrangaliloode (Mal.)) (Kottayam: Deepika, 1959).
40. Fr. Vadakkan, *My Leaps and Gasps*,126.
41. Deepika, *Kerala Liberation Struggle in Pictures*, 1959.
42. *Malayala Manorama*, November 15, 2007.
43. Andalatt, "Liberation Struggle: The Launch of Violent Struggles in Kerala" (Vimochana Samaram: Keralathil Akrama Samarangalude Thudakkam), *Chintha Weekly*, Thiruvananthapuram, April 18, 2008, 34; Andalatt," "Liberation Struggle: Extreme Step to Recapture Power" (Bharanam Thirichupidikkan Attakai), *Chintha Weekly*, Thiruvananthapuram, March 28, 2008, 34; Andalatt, "Liberation Struggle: When Telling the Truth Becomes Dishonesty" (Vimochana Samaram: Nerothunnathe Nerikedu) *Chintha Weekly*, Thiruvananthapuram, April 25, 2008, 38–40.
44. *Indian Express*, July 26, 1959; quoted in Austin, *Anatomy of the Kerala Coup*, 53.
45. Quoted in Austin, *Anatomy of the Kerala Coup*,24.
46. Ellsworth Bunker, Oral History Interview, June 18 and July 17, 1979. New York: Butler Library, Columbia University, 78.
47. B. N. Mullik, *My Years with Nehru, 1948–1964* (New Delhi: Allied Publishers, 1972), 339–51.
48. Ibid.
49. Ibid., 352.
50. Ibid., 356.
51. *Kerala Kaumudi Newspaper*, August 29, 1959.
52. Quoted in Andalatt, "Liberation Struggle: The Launch of Violent Struggles in Kerala," 34; Andalatt, "Liberation Struggle: Extreme Step to Recapture Power,"37–39. See also Balan Payyappilli, *Unforgettable Memories, Never Fading Faces* (Maayatha Smaranakal, Mangatha Mughangal) (Thiruvananthapuram: Chintha, 1985), 126–129.
53. *Deshabhimani Newspaper*, September 27, 1959).

54. Robin Jeffrey, "Jawaharlal Nehru and the Smoking Gun: Who Pulled the Trigger on Kerala's Communist Government in 1959?," *Journal of Commonwealth and Comparative Politics* 21(1) (March 1991): 81.

7. Creating Anticommunist Hysteria: The Christian Anti-Communism Crusade and Moral Re-Armament

1. Ben H. Bagdikian, *The Media Monopoly: A Startling Report on the 50 Corporations that Control What America Sees, Hears, and Reads* (Boston: Beacon Press, 1983), 44–45.
2. Frederick Schwarz, *Beating the Unbeatable Foe: One Man's Victory Over Communism, Leviathan, and the Last Enemy* (Washington, DC: Regnery Publishing, 1996), 154.
3. Frederick Schwarz, *Communism: Diagnosis and Treatment* (Los Angeles: World Vision, Inc., 1955), 8.
4. Hubert Villeneuve, "Teaching Anticommunism: Fred C. Schwarz, the Christian Anti-Communism Crusade and American Postwar Conservatism" (PhD diss., McGill University, 2011), 235–40.
5. Schwarz, *Unbeatable Foe*, 157.
6. Quoted in Villeneuve, "Teaching Anticommunism," 237.
7. Schwarz, *Unbeatable Foe*, 158.
8. Villeneuve, "Teaching Anticommunism," 238.
9. Quoted in Villeneuve, "Teaching Anticommunism," 236.
10. Villeneuve, "Teaching Anticommunism," 241–42.
11. Schwarz, "Kerala Communists in Trouble," *CACC Newsletter*, May 1958, 2.
12. Ibid., 3.
13. Ibid.
14. Ibid.
15. Schwarz, *Unbeatable Foe*, 133.
16. Villeneuve, "Teaching Anticommunism," 504.
17. Schwarz, "Kerala: UPASI Reports More Incidents," *CACC Newsletter*, October 1957, 2.
18. Ibid., 3.
19. Quoted in Schwarz, "The Allen-Bradley Company and Kerala Update," *CACC Newsletter*, September 1958, 5.
20. Quoted in Schwarz, "Truth Daily Newspaper in Kerala, India," *CACC Newsletter* April/May 1959, 3.
21. Villeneuve, "Teaching Anticommunism," 507.
22. Schwarz, *July/August CACC Newsletter*, 1960, 4; Villeneuve, "Teaching Anticommunism," 508.
23. Villeneuve, "Teaching Anticommunism," 509.
24. Schwarz, *CACC Newsletter*, March 1959, 4.

25. Schwarz, *CACC Newsletter*, July/August 1960, 4.
26. Villeneuve, "Teaching Anticommunism," 510.
27. Schwarz, "A Taste of Victory—From Tragedy to Triumph in Kerala, India," *CACC Newsletter*, March 1960, 1.
28. Ibid., 3.
29. Schwarz, *CACC Newsletter*, November 1963.
30. Schwarz, "Hail to the Religious Women of Brazil," *CACC Newsletter*, July 1964, 1–2.
31. For example, Schwarz, *Unbeatable Foe*, 134.
32. Villeneuve, "Teaching Anticommunism," 510–11.
33. Ibid., 512.
34. Ibid., 513.
35. For example, Lawrence E. Davies, "Cross Winds on Coast: Welch, Gus Hall and Anti-Red School Leave Impact on San Francisco Region," *New York Times*, January 22, 1962; John Wicklein, "Christian Group Aims at Politics: Conservative Protestants to Work at Precinct Level," *New York Times*, February 1, 1962; "Anti-Red Funds Listed: Schwarz Tells of Collecting $1,000,000 in Campaign," *New York Times*, February 20, 1962.
36. John Wicklein, "Anti-Red Meeting Draws 3,000 Here: Schwarz Cheered for Plans for a School in City," *New York Times*, April 14, 1962; Richard P. Hunt, "Anti-Communist Says City's Hostility Is Easing: Schwarz, Head of Christian Crusade, Here to Stage Rally in Garden," *New York Times*, June 14, 1962; "Anti-Red Parley Set Here June 28," *New York Times*, June 16, 1962.
37. "Crusader Against Reds: Fred Charles Schwarz," *New York Times*, June 29, 1962; Charles Grutzner, "Anti-Red Crusade Rallies at Garden," *New York Times*, June 29, 1962.
38. United States House of Representatives (USHR), Hearings on Moral Re-Armament, 1960, 7090.
39. USHR, Hearings on Moral Re-Armament, 1960, 7091–97.
40. Archie Mackenzie and David Young, eds., *The Worldwide Legacy of Frank Buchman* (Caux, Switzerland: Caux Books: Initiatives of Change, 2008, 22.
41. Ibid., 12.
42. Ibid., 33.
43. Ibid., 19.
44. Ibid., 26.
45. Richard H. Palmer, "Moral Re-Armament Drama: Right-Wing Theatre in America," *Theatre Journal* 31(2) (1979): 179.
46. Frank Buchman, *Remaking the World: The Speeches of Frank N. D. Buchman* (London: Blandford Press, 1961), 103. Numerous editions and reprintings with changing page numbers.

47. Philip Boobbyer, "The Cold War in the Plays of Peter Howard," *Contemporary British History* 19(2) (2005): 210.
48. Pamela G. Jenner, "Propaganda Theatre: A Critical and Cultural Examination of the Work of Moral Re-Armament at the Westminster Theatre, London" (PhD diss., Anglia Ruskin University, 2016), 35–47; Palmer, "Moral Re-Armament," 175.
49. Palmer, "Moral Re-Armament," 175.
50. "Reds' Tactics Outlined: Theatre and Literature Used, Indian Tells M. R. A.," *New York Times*, June 6, 1959.
51. Moral Re-Armament, *Ideology and Co-Existence* (New York: Moral Re-Armament, 1959), 1.
52. V. C. Viswanathan, "India's Journey Towards New Governance: An Indian Perspective," in Mackenzie and Young, *Worldwide Legacy*, 149–51.
53. David Young, *Initiatives of Change in India: Observing Six Decades of Moral Re-Armament: An Assessment* (Caux, Switzerland: Caux Books, 2003), 16.
54. Viswanathan, "India's Journey," 152.
55. Muhammed Koya, *Journey (Yathra)* (Kozhikkode: Olive Publications, 2011), 136.
56. "MRA Urged to Save India from Reds: Editor Warns of Peril to Kerala, Rest of Nation," *Los Angeles Times*, December 10, 1961.
57. *Malayalarajyam*, October 9, 1959.
58. Mannath Padmanabhan, "The Changing Scene in Kerala," in Frank Buchman, *Remaking the World: The Speeches of Frank N. D. Buchman* (London: Blandford Press, 1961), 373.
59. Ibid.
60. Quoted in ibid.
61. Padmanabhan, "Changing Scene," 373.
62. USHR, Hearings on Moral Re-Armament, 7098.
63. USHR, Hearings on Moral Re-Armament, 7100.
64. Young, *Initiatives of Change*, 22.
65. Tom Driberg, *The Mystery of Moral Re-Armament: A Study of Frank Buchman and His Movement* (London: Secker & Warburg, 1964). The page numbers in the text are from this book.
66. Ibid.
67. USHR, Hearings on Moral Re-Armament, 7103–4.
68. Young, *Initiatives of Change*, 23.
69. "MRA Urged to Save India from Reds," *Los Angeles Times*, December 10, 1961.
70. Viswanathan, "India's Journey," 158–59.
71. Ibid., 161–64.

72. Ibid., 165–66.
73. Donald Janson, "Moral Re-Armament Cuts U.S. Operations," *New York Times*, August 10, 1970.
74. James K. Glassman, "Moral Re-Armament—Its Appeal and Threat: Emotion-Based Sing-Out Offers Simple Answers," *Harvard Crimson*, March 28, 1967.
75. Palmer, "Moral Re-Armament Drama," 179; Janson, "Moral Re-Armament Cuts," 30.

8. Through CIA Eyes: Information and Instructions for Toppling the Ministry

1. CIA, SN 07, "Leftist Coalition Defeats Congress Party in Travancore-Cochin, South Indian State," March 9, 1954(a), release date July 29, 2002; CIA, SN-08, "Leftist Coalition Defeats Congress Party in Travancore-Cochin, South Indian State," March 10, 1954(b), release date December 7, 1998.
2. SN 09 10, "February 1955 11-month Praja Socialist Ministry Falls in Travancore-Cochin," Cover Page, https://www.cia.gov/readingroom/document/03157466.
3. SN 04, "India's Position in the East-West Conflict," www.cia.gov/readingroom/docs/DOC_0000010593.pdf.
4. SN 05, www.cia.gov/readingroom/document/cia-rdp79s01011a000800010007-4; https://www.cia.gov/readingroom/docs/DOC_0000010597.pdf.
5. SN 06, https://www.cia.gov/readingroom/document/cia-rdp86b00269r000800080001-4; https://www.cia.gov/readingroom/docs/CIA-RDP86B00269R000800080001-4.pdf.
6. SN 11, November 1, 1956, "Reorganization of Indian States by Languages," https://www.cia.gov/readingroom/docs/CIA-RDP79-00927A001000060001-6.pdf, 9.
7. SN 12, January 24, 1957, "Indian National Elections Prospects," https://www.cia.gov/readingroom/docs/CIA-RDP79-00927A001100060001-5.pdf.
8. SN 13, January 26, 1957, "Indian Congress Party in Election Difficulties," https://www.cia.gov/readingroom/docs/CIA-RDP79T00975A002900350001-1.pdf.
9. SN 17, April 2, 1957, "Kerala Election—Office of National Estimates," Cover Page, https://www.cia.gov/readingroom/document/cia-RDP79t00937a000500030038-4.
10. SN 16, 31 March 1957, Cover Page, https://www.cia.gov/readingroom/document/03160438.
11. SN 16, 31 March 1957, Cover Page, https://www.cia.gov/readingroom/document/03160438.

12. SN 16, March 31, 1957, https://www.cia.gov/readingroom/docs/CIA-RDP79T00975A003000340001-0.pdf.
13. SN 18, "CP Gov Faces Major Problems," Part II, page 5, https://www.cia.gov/readingroom/docs/CIA-RDP79-00927A001200040001-6.pdf.
14. SN 18, 11 April 1957, "CP Gov Faces Major Problems," Cover Page, https://www.cia.gov/readingroom/document/cia-rdp79-00927a001200040001-6.
15. SN18, Part II, page 5.
16. Ibid.
17. SN 19, April 25,1957, "Communist Strength in the Indian Government," https://www.cia.gov/readingroom/docs/CIA-RDP79-00927A001200060001-3.pdf.
18. Ibid., page 3.
19. SN 20, 08 May 1957 "NSC Briefing" Cover Pages 2–3, https://www.cia.gov/readingroom/document/cia-rdp79r00890a000800070014-7.
20. Ibid.
21. (FRUS) *Foreign Relations of the United States, 1955–1957, South Asia*, vol. 8, eds. Robert J. McMahon and Stanley Shaloff, Operations Coordinating Board Report: Operations Plan for India and Nepal, Document 168, July 3, 1957 (Washington: Government Printing Office, 1987).
22. (FRUS) *Foreign Relations of the United States, 1955–1957, South Asia*, vol. 8, eds. Robert J. McMahon and Stanley Shaloff, National Security Council Report 5701, "Statement of Policy on U.S. Policy Toward South Asia (India, Pakistan, Afghanistan, Ceylon and Nepal) General Considerations," Document 5, January 10, 1957 (Washington, DC: Government Printing Office, 1987)..
23. SN 03, "State Dept. *Telegram Foreign Relations of the United States, 1955–1957, South Asi*a, vol. 8, eds. Robert J. McMahon and Stanley Shaloff Operations Coordinating Board Report. Operations Plan for India and Nepal, Document 168, July 1957 (Washington: Government Printing Office, 1987)*.* https://history.state.gov/historicaldocuments/frus1955-57v08/d168.
24. Matthew Connelly, *The Declassification Engine: What History Reveals About America's Top Secrets* (New York: Pantheon, 2023).
25. (FRUS) *Foreign Relations of the United States, 1955–1957, South Asia*, vol. 8, ed. Robert J. McMahon and Stanley Shaloff, Instruction from the Department of State to the Diplomatic Missions in India: United States Policy with Regard to Kerala, Washington, Document 171, August 1, 1957 (Washington: Government Printing Office, 1987).
26. A complete reference along with a link to online access of the pre-declassification form of Document 171 follows here: *Foreign Relations of*

the United States, 1955–1957, South Asia, vol. 8, eds. Robert J. McMahon and Stanley Shaloff. Instruction from the Department of State to the Diplomatic Missions in India. United States Policy with Regard to Kerala. Washington, Document 171, August 1, 1957. (Washington: Government Printing Office, 1987). Instruction from the Department of State to the Diplomatic Missions in India. CA–1082 Washington, August 1, 1957, Document 171. SUBJECT: United States Policy with Regard to Kerala. https://history.state.gov/historicaldocuments/frus1955-57v08/d171.
27. *FRUS*, Document 171, Opening paragraph.
28. Dwight D. Eisenhower, Handwritten Comment on Meeting Notes by Andrew Goodpaster, Jr. April 9, 1958, in *The Papers of Dwight David Eisenhower,* vol. 19, No. 647, eds. Louis Galambos and Van E. E. Daun (Baltimore and London: Johns Hopkins University Press, 1958), 829.
29. SN 22, August 25, 1957, "Nehru Warns Congress Party," https://www.cia.gov/readingroom/docs/CURRENT%20INTELLIGENCE%20BULL%5B15757496%5D.pdf.
30. SN 23, August 29, 1957, "Opposition to Communist Government," https://www.cia.gov/readingroom/docs/CIA-RDP79-00927A001400040001-3.pdf, Part II, Page 8.
31. SN 23, Part II, 7–8; Education Bill under debate.
32. SN 24 CIWS August 29, 1957, "Strength of the Opposition Not Reliably Reported," Part II, 8.
33. SN 24, September 29, 1957, "Congress Leader Gloomy," https://www.cia.gov/readingroom/docs/CURRENT%20INTELLIGENCE%20BULL%5B15757410%5D.pdf.
34. SN 25, "Indian Congress Leader Gloomy."
35. SN 25, October 8, 1957, "Consequences of Economic Crisis in India," https://www.cia.gov/readingroom/docs/CIA-RDP79R01012A009900060006-3.pdf.
36. SN 27, February 12, 1958, "CPI Membership Doubles: 56,000 members in Kerala." https://www.cia.gov/readingroom/docs/CENTRAL%20INTELLIGENCE%20BULL%5B15772432%5D.pdf.
37. SN 29, May 12, 1958.
38. SN 29, May 12, 1958, "Hungary and Other Soviet Bloc Aid to Kerala," 6 Note: 15 pages "exempt." https://www.cia.gov/readingroom/docs/CIA-RDP92B01090R000700010059-6.pdf.
39. Duane R. Clarridge, with Digby Diehl, *A Spy for All Seasons: My Life in the CIA* (New York: Scribner's, 1997), 76.
40. SN 30, "Nehru on Communism: An Awakening," https://www.cia.gov/readingroom/docs/CIA-RDP78-02771R000400010002-2.pdf, page 4.
41. Ibid., page 6.

42. SN 30, "Nehru On Communism: An Awakening," page 13.
43. "Deteriorating Political Situation," Telegram, page 3.
44. Ibid.
45. Telegram from the Embassy in India to the Department of State, August 26, 1958. "A Deteriorating Political Situation within India." FRUS Document 215.
46. CIA, *Current Intelligence Weekly Summary* (CIWS), August 28, 1958, 12.
47. FRUS, *Foreign Relations of the United States, 1958–1960*, South Asia and Southeast Asia, vol.15, eds. Madeline Chi, John P. Glennon, William K. Klingaman, and Robert J. McMahon; National Intelligence Estimate, NIE 51–58: "The Economic and Political Consequences of India's Financial Problems," New Delhi, June 7, 1958 (Washington: Government Printing Office, 1987), FRUS Document 217.
48. National Intelligence Estimate, Document 217, 5.
49. Ibid.
50. SN 32, February 21, 1959, "Soviet Bloc Concerned about Kerala," page 6, https://www.cia.gov/readingroom/docs/CIA-RDP79T00975A004300180001-4.pdf.
51. SN33, March 3, 1959, "Intl. Communism Annual Review – 1958," https://www.cia.gov/readingroom/docs/CIA-RDP81-01043R003200210001-8.pdf.
52. Intelligence Report No. 5650.75: "International Communism: Annual Review–1958–The Nonorbit Communist Parties," 73.
53. Ibid., 74.
54. Ibid., 75.
55. SN 34, March 17, 1959, "EMS ministry wins confidence vote," https://www.cia.gov/readingroom/docs/CENTRAL%20INTELLIGENCE%20BULL%5B15787508%5D.pdf.
56. "EMS ministry wins confidence vote," https://www.cia.gov/readingroom/document/03160620.
57. SN 35, April 16, 1959, "CIWS Two Years of CPI Rule in Kerala," https://www.cia.gov/readingroom/docs/CIA-RDP79-00927A00220060001-2.pdf.
58. Ibid., 6–9.
59. Ibid.
60. FRUS, *Foreign Relations of the United States, 1958–1960, South Asia and Southeast Asia*, vol. 15, eds. Madeline Chi, John P. Glennon, William K. Klingaman, and Robert J. McMahon. Memorandum: Madras telegram to Department Delhi May 25 discuss impending agitations re school closure . . . President [Prasad] to enter scene in Kerala. New Delhi, May 28, 1959. Washington: Government Printing Office, 1987. Document

231. https://history.state.gov/historicaldocuments/frus1958-60v15/d231.
61. Ibid., 1.
62. Ibid., 2.
63. SN 37, June 9, 1959, CIB Congress and Others Drive to Oust Kerala Communists, https://www.cia.gov/readingroom/document/cia-rdp79t00975a004500250001-4, CENTRAL INTELLIGENCE BULLETIN (cia.gov).
64. Ibid. Half of the page is whited out.
65. SN 38, June 15, 1959, Agitation Against CPI Government in Kerala, https://www.cia.gov/readingroom/docs/CIA-RDP79T00975A004500300001-8.pdf.
66. Agitation Against Communist Ministry, page 5, SN 38, June 15, 1959, Agitation Against CPI Government in Kerala, https://www.cia.gov/readingroom/docs/CIA-RDP79T00975A004500300001-8.pdf.
67. FRUS Document 233 Memorandum of a Conversation, Dept. of State, Washington, June 15, 1959.
68. SN 39, June 17, 1959, Anti-communist Agitation Update, NSC Briefing, https://www.cia.gov/readingroom/docs/CIA-RDP79R00890A001100060024-3.pdf.
69. FRUS, *Foreign Relations of the United States, 1958–1960, South Asia and Southeast Asia*, Volume XV, eds. Madeline Chi, John P. Glennon, William K. Klingaman and Robert J. McMahon, Memorandum of a Conversation Between the Under Secretary of State for Political Affairs (Murphy) and the Ambassador to India (Bunker), Department of State, Washington: US Relations with India, Washington, Document 75, June 19, 1959 (Washington, DC: Government Printing Office, 1987).
70. SN 40, June 23, 1959, TOP SECRET: The Situation in Kerala, https://www.cia.gov/readingroom/docs/CENTRAL%20INTELLIGENCE%20BULL%5B15787938%5D.pdf.
71. SN 40, June 23, 1959, TOP SECRET: The Situation in Kerala, https://www.cia.gov/readingroom/docs/CENTRAL%20INTELLIGENCE%20BULL%5B15787938%5D.pdf.
72. SN 40 23 June 1959 TOP SECRET: The Situation in Kerala https://www.cia.gov/readingroom/document/03191554. NSC Briefing.
73. (FRUS) *Foreign Relations of the United States, 1958–1960, South Asia and Southeast Asia*, Volume XV, eds. Madeline Chi, John P. Glennon, William K. Klingaman, and Robert J. McMahon, 411th Meeting of the National Security Council, Department of State, Washington: Anti-communist Agitations, Washington, Document 235, June 19, 1959. (Washington, DC: Government Printing Office, 1987).
74. Document 235, Editorial Note from the 411th Meeting of the National Security Council. Full citation is in the endnote just above this one.

75. SN 43 03 July 1959 CIB Nehru Probably to Act www.cia.gov/readingroom/document/cia-rdp79t00975a00460 0030001-7
76. SN 44, July 4, 1959, Nehru Anticipates Kerala Takeover, https://www.cia.gov/readingroom/docs/CENTRAL%20INTELLIGENCE%20BULL%5b15787636%5d.PDF.
77. SN 44, 04 July 1959 Nehru Anticipates Kerala Takeover https://www.cia.gov/readingroom/document/03163342.
78. SN 46, July 8, 1959, NSC Briefing—Nehru Feels He Has to Take Over, https://www.cia.gov/readingroom/docs/CIA-RDP79R00890 A001100070011-6.pdf.
79. Editorial Note: See the Document Note 235, just after June 15, 1959, of the NSC's 412th meeting, for note by Allen Dulles, who seems far behind his local station in perceiving what Nehru is reportedly considering. Dulles thinks Nehru does not want to impose rule from New Delhi, but "may ultimately be forced to take the step."
80. SN 47, July 14, 1959, NSC Briefing—Most Leaders Feel Takeover Will Occur, https://www.cia.gov/readingroom/docs/CIA-RDP79R00890A0011000 70002-6.pdf.
81. SN47 NSC briefing July 14, 1959 https://www.cia.gov/readingroom/document/cia-rdp79r00890a001100070002-6.
82. SN 48, July 20, 1959, Research Proposal—Kerala Background Info, https://www.cia.gov/readingroom/docs/CIA-RDP62-00680R000200 160042-4.pdf.
83. SN 49, July 28, 1959, Kerala decision appears near, https://www.cia.gov/readingroom/docs/CIA-RDP79T00975A004600240001-4.pdf.
84. SN 50, July 31, 1959, Nehru recommends president's rule, https://www.cia.gov/readingroom/docs/CENTRAL%20INTELLIGENCE%20BULL%5B15787723%5D.pdf.
85. SN 50, July 31, 1959. Nehru recommends president's rule.
86. SN 51, August 6, 1959, President's Rule Occurs, https://www.cia.gov/readingroom/docs/CIA-RDP79-00927A002400010001-6.pdf.
87. SN 51 www.cia.gov/readingroom/document/cia-rdp79-00927a002400 010001-6.
88. SN 52, August 8, 1959, Soviet Advises Nonviolence to Kerala Communists, TOP SECRET, https://www.cia.gov/readingroom/docs/CIA-RDP79T00975A004600340001-3.pdf.
89. SN 53, August 14, 1959, Geographic Intelligence MemorandumOffice of Research and Reports, https://www.cia.gov/readingroom/docs/CIA-RDP84-00825R000100400001-1.pdf.
90. SN 48 July 20, 1959, Research Proposal—Kerala Background Info, www.cia.gov/readingroom/docs/CIA-RDP62-00680R000200160042-4.pdf.
91. SN 53, August 14, 1959, Geographic Intelligence Memorandum –

Office of Research and Reports, https://www.cia.gov/readingroom/docs/CIA-RDP84-00825R000100400001-1.pdf
92. SN 54, August 27, 1959, Edits for a Speech in Wisconsin, https://www.cia.gov/readingroom/docs/CIA-RDP79-01048A000100070002-9.pdf.
93. SN 55, September 9, 1959, CIB CPI Consults Moscow TOP SECRET, www.cia.gov/readingroom/docs/CENTRAL%20INTELLIGENCE%20BULL%5B15787737%5D.pdf.
94. SN 56, September 12, 1959, Mutual Security Appropriations—Congress, www.cia.gov/readingroom/docs/CIA-RDP61-00357R0005001 20001-3.pdf.
95. Ibid.
96. SN 57, November 5, 1959, CIWS CPI Faces policy decision, https://www.cia.gov/readingroom/docs/DOC_0002982260.pdf.
97. SN 57, November 5, 1959.
98. SN 58, December 7, 1959, Indian Communist's Defection, www.cia.gov/readingroom/docs/CIA-RDP78-03061A0001 00010008-3.pdf.
99. SN 58, December 7, 1959.
100. SN 59, December 28, 1959, Kerala New Elections—TOP SECRET, https://www.cia.gov/readingroom/docs/CENTRAL%20INTELLIGENCE%20BULL%5B15787692%5D.pdf.
101. SN 60, December 30, 1959, Kerala elections prospects, https://www.cia.gov/readingroom/document/cia-rdp79-00927a002500110001-4, https://www.cia.gov/readingroom/docs/CIA-RDP79-00927A002500110001-4.pdf.
102. SN 60 Congress to Have Election Resources. https://www.cia.gov/readingroom/docs/CIA-RDP79-00927A002500110001-4.pdf.
103. SN 60, December 30, 1959.
104. SN 62, February 3, 1960 = 1960—10c, NSC—anti-communist coalition wins elections, www.cia.gov/readingroom/document/cia-rdp80b01676r002700020051-7, www.cia.gov/readingroom/docs/CIA-RDP79R00890A001200020007-5.pdf, www.cia.gov/readingroom/docs/CENTRAL%20INTELLIGENCE%20BULL%5B15799020%5D.pdf, https://www.cia.gov/readingroom/document/03184156.
105. SN 63, February 4, 1960, https://www.cia.gov/readingroom/docs/CENTRAL%20INTELLIGENCE%20BULL%5B15799052%5d.PDF, https://www.cia.gov/readingroom/document/03184157.
106. SN 60, December 30, 1959.

9. The Aftermath of the Dismissal of the EMS Ministry

1. Vincent Bevins, *The Jakarta Method: Washington's Anticommunist Crusade and the Mass Murder Program that Shaped Our World* (New

York: Public Affairs Books, Hachette, 2020), 238; David Michael Smith, *Endless Holocausts: Mass Death in the History of the United States Empire* (New York: Monthly Review Press, 2023), esp. chap. 5.
2. James Risen and Thomas Risen, *The Last Honest Man: The CIA, the FBI, the Mafia, and the Kennedys—And One Man's Fight to Save Democracy.* (Boston: Little, Brown, 2023). The published version of the Committee Report is: Loch K. Johnson, *A Season of Inquiry Revisited: The Church Committee Confronts America's Spy Agencies* (Lawrence: University of Kansas Press, 2015).
3. T. M. Thomas Isaac, *The Other Side of Vimochanasmaram* (*Vimochanasmarathinte Kanappurangal*) (Thiruvananthapuram: Chintha 2008), 307.
4. Ibid., 306–7.
5. Ibid., 311.
6. Krishna K. G. Murthy and Lakshmana G. Rao, *Political Preferences in Kerala* (New Delhi: Radhakrishna, 1968).
7. Ibid.
8. Kalakal Baskaran, *Ezhava Community and Communist Party* (*Ezhava Samudayavum Communist Partiyum*) (Ernakulam: Democratic Printers, 1960).
9. K. K. Madhvan, *The Black Caste and Congress* (*Karutha Vargavum Congressum*) (Ernakulam North: Voice of Kerala, 1959), 3.
10. Christian Institute for the Study of Religion and Society, *Church, Society and State in Kerala: An Evaluation Report*, Bangalore, 1960.
11. Isaac, *The Other Side*, 319–20.
12. Ibid., 319.
13. Muhammed C. H. Koya, *Journey* (*Yathra*) (Kozhikkode: Olive Publications, 1959).
14. B. N. Mullik, *My Years with Nehru, 1948 to 1964* (New Delhi: Allied Publishers, 1972), 363.
15. Ibid, 364–65.
16. UNESCO, *Akshara Keralam: The Kerala Total Literacy Programme* (Kerala Saksharatha Samithi, 1992).
17. Dr. Jaya Mehta and Vineet Tiwari, *From the Realm of Necessity to the Realm of Freedom* (New Delhi: Aakar Books, 2023).
18. Kerala Development and Innovation Strategy Council, *Strategy Paper: Comprehensive Programme for Employment of the Educated Unemployed in Kerala*, vols. 1, 2, 3 (Thiruvananthapuram: Kerala Development and Innovation Strategy Council, 2021),
19. T. M. Thomas Isaac, *Kerala: Another Possible World* (New Delhi: LeftWord Books, 2022), 47.
20. Ronald J. Herring, *Land to the Tiller: The Political Economy of Agrarian Reform in South Asia* (New Haven: Yale University Press, 1983), 211.

21. Thomas Paulini, *Agrarian Movements and Reforms in India: The Case of Kerala* (Saarbrücken: Verlag Breitenbach, Sozialökonomische Schriften zur Agrarentwicklung, 1979), 337.
22. K. N. Raj and Michael Tharakan, *Agrarian Reform in Kerala and Its Impact on the Rural Economy: A Preliminary Assessment* (Geneva: International Labor Organization: World Employment Programme, Working Paper 49, 1981).
23. A. V. Jose, "The Story of Social Spending: A Revisit to the Kerala Model of Development—Part II," *Kerala Economy*, 2/1 (2021).
24. T. N. Krishnan, "Wages, Employment and Output in Interrelated Labor Markets in an Agrarian Economy—A Study of Kerala," *Economic and Political Weekly* 26(26) (1991): 82–96.
25. Reserve Bank of India, *Handbook of Statistics on Indian States* (Mumbai, 2022).
26. K. P. Kannan, *The Welfare Fund Model of Social Security for Informal Sector Workers: The Kerala Experience* (Thiruvananthapuram: Center for Development Studies, Working Paper No. 332, 2002); C. P. John, *Social Security and Labour Welfare with Special Reference to Construction Workers in Kerala* (Thiruvananthapuram: Centre for Development Studies, Discussion Paper No. 65, 2004).
27. Philip Cherian, *Quarter of a Century* (*Kaal Noottandu*) (Kottayam: DC Books, 2021), 183–95; R. K. Bijuraj, *Political History of Kerala* (*Keralathinte Rashatreeyacharithram*) (Kottayam: DC Books, 2021), 216–17.
28. Niti Aayog, *School Education Quality Index (SEQI) 2019* (New Delhi: Government of India, 2019). Niti Aayog is the think tank of the Indian national government that replaced the planning board.
29. Niti Aayog. *The School Education Quality Index (SEQI) 2019.* (New Delhi: Government of India, 2019).
30. World Vision India, *India Child Well-Being Report, 2021* (New Delhi: 2022).
31. Kerala State Planning Board, *Economic Review: 1987* (Thiruvananthapuram: KSPB, 1988).
32. Niti Aayog. *India National Multidimensional Poverty Index Baseline Report* (New Delhi: Government of India, 2021).
33. K. K. George, *Limits to Kerala Model of Development: An Analysis of Fiscal Crisis and Its Implications* (Thiruvananthapuram: Centre for Development Studies, 1993).
34. K. N. Harilal and K. K. Eswaran, "Agrarian Question and Democratic Decentralization in Kerala," *Agrarian South: Journal of Political Economy* 5(2–3) (2016):292–324.
35. T. M. Thomas Isaac and Richard W. Franke, *People's Planning: Kerala, Local Democracy and Development* (New Delhi: LeftWord, 2021).

36. EMS, *Politics and Kerala's Economic Planning: Mathai Manjooran Memorial Lecture on Development Problems of Kerala* (Thiruvananthapuram: Chintha, 1992).
37. Jayan Jose Thomas, "Labor and Industrialisation in Kerala," *Indian Journal of Labor Economics* 46(4) (2003): 575–92.

10. Conclusions of the Study

1. U.S. Senate, Church Committee, "Report, Foreign and Military Intelligence, Book I, Final Report of the Select Committee to Study Governmental Operations with Respect to Intelligence Activities" (Washington, DC: U.S. Government Printing Office, April 26, 1976); Loch K. Johnson, *A Season of Inquiry Revisited: The Church Committee Confronts America's Spy Agencies* (Lawrence: University of Kansas Press, 2015).
2. CIA, *Current Intelligence Weekly Summary*, December 30, 1959, Part 2, page 2, https://www.cia.gov/readingroom/docs/CIA-RDP79-00927A002500110001-4.pdf.
3. Ibid.
4. Paul McGarr, "Quiet Americans in India," *Diplomatic History* 38(5) (2014): 1054.
5. Ibid.
6. FRUS, *Foreign Relations of the United States, 1955–1957, South Asia*, vol. 8, eds., Robert J. McMahon and Stanley Shaloff, "Instruction from the Department of State to the Diplomatic Missions in India: United States Policy with Regard to Kerala," Document 171, August 1, 1957, (Washington, DC: Government Printing Office, 1987); see also T. Ajayan, "Dismissal of the First Communist Ministry in Kerala, and Extraneous Agencies," *South Asianist* 5(1) (2017), 298–300.
7. FRUS, Document 250, *Editorial Note*, February 4, 1950, https://history.state.gov/historicaldocuments/frus1958-60v15/d250; see also T. Ajayan, "Midterm Election in Kerala in 1960 and the American Government," *History and Sociology of South Asia* 11(2) (2017): 218.
8. FRUS, Document 254, *Report Prepared by the Operations Coordinating Board,* February 17, 1960, https://history.state.gov/historicaldocuments/frus1958-60v15/d254.

Index

Achuthanandan, V. S., 113
Adenauer, Konrad, 159, 167
Administrative Reforms Committee (ARC; Kerala), 96–99, 104, 128
AFL-CIO (American Federation of Labor-Congress of Industrial Organizations), 39, 41
Agee, Philip, 24–25
Agrarian Bill, 109–10; becomes law, 228; opposition to, 130
Agricultural Labor Welfare Fund, 231
Ahrens, Richard, 149
Aiyar, C. P. Ramaswami, 76
Aiyar, V. R. Krishna, 107, 132
Ajayan, T., 15
Alcoholics Anonymous, 162
Alexander, T. C., 18
Alliance for Progress, 57, 58
All-India Catholic Bishops Conference (Bangalore, 1958), 128
All India Congress Committee (AICC), 130, 200
All-India Newspaper Editors Conference (1959), 133
All India Student Federation, 112
All Kerala Trade Union Conference (1935), 70
Amnesty International, 59
Andhra State (India), 79
Angamali (Kerala), 135–36, 144
Anglo-Iranian Oil Company, 48, 219
Anti-Communist Front (ACF; Kerala), 115, 124
Antony, P. J., 115
Arbenz, Jacobo, 43–47, 118–19, 218, 243

Arévalo, Juan José, 43, 118
Asan, Simon, 223
assassinations, 31
atheism, 124, 125
Ayyankali, 67
Azad, Maulana, 187
Azhikode, Sukumar, 127

Bagdikian, Ben, 148
Bala Jana Sakhyam (Alliance of Children), 138
Bevins, Vincent, 219
Birla, G. D., 179
Birla, Madhav Prasad, 120
Bolívar, Simón, 43, 118
Bolsonaro, Jair, 59
Bombay Plan, 104
Bosch, Juan, 25
Bradley, Harry, 150–51
Brahmins (caste), 63
Brazil, 56–59, 156–57
Brazilian Institute for Democratic Action (IBAD), 57
bribery, 119
Britain: Guiana under, 38–42, 120, 121; Indian Independence Movement against, 33; Iran and, 48; Travancore-Cochin under, 64
British Guiana, 36–37; Christian Anti-Communism Crusade in, 156; as example for Kerala, 120, 121 (*see also* Guyana)
Brizola, 157

Buchman, Frank, 159; in India, 164–65, 167; Moral Re-Armament founded by, 162–63; Oxford Group founded by, 161–62; Padmanabhan on, 166
Bunker, Ellsworth, 134; on CIA aid to Congress Party, 10; on CIA working with CIB, 142; on overthrow of Kerala government, 202–3, 212, 245; on U.S. aid to India, 195–96
Burgess, David, 32, 212–13; on CIA, 9–-11, 26, 241, 245
Burnham, Forbes, 37, 39, 40; becomes prime minister of British Guiana, 42

caste system, 63, 66–67; anticommunism and, 128–30; Communist Party of India on, 80; in Kerala, 95–96; in land reform, 85; public mediation within, 104; Vaikom Satyagraha campaign against, 67–68
Castillo Armas, Carlos, 46, 47, 118
Castro, Fidel, 25
Catholic Church: anticommunism of, 124–26; anticommunist militias organized by, 106–7; anticommunist organizing by, 115–16; in Devikulam election, 113; Education Bill opposed by, 110, 128,

131–32; on education in Kerala, 91; in Guatemala, 47, 48, 218; Kerala's schools under control of, 89; on Moral Re-Armament, 166

Caux (Switzerland), 165–66

Central Intelligence Agency (U.S.): Agee on secret activities of, 24–25; in Brazil, 57, 58; in British Guiana, 36–42; Burgess on, 9, 10; on Communist victory in Kerala, 177–81; "Consequences of Communist Control Over South Asia." report by, 176; covert actions by, 20–21, 27–32, 241–42; democratic governments overthrown by, 218; Doolittle report on, 34–35; Freedom of Information Act on, 17–18; in Guatemala, 44–45, 118; Indian Central Intelligence Bureau and, 32–34, 142; on Indian elections of 1954, 174; in Indonesia, 50–53; information sources within, 16–19; in Iran (1953), 48–50; in Kerala election of 1960, 213, 216–17; Kerala government overthrown by, 242, 244–47; Kerala monitored by, 188–89, 212; Kerala's government overthrown by, 11–12, 15, 205–6; National Clandestine Service of, 219; on Nehru, 193–95; opposition in Kerala funded by, 134; origins of, 25–27; public opinion targeted by, 147, 243; role in Kerala of, 145; strategy for Kerala of, 183–88; on Travancore-Cochin elections of 1954 and 1957, 79, 174

Central Intelligence Bureau (India), 19, 142–43; on Chinese and Soviet responses to overthrow of Kerala government, 208; CIA and, 32–34, 244; on Kerala as communist showpiece, 197–99; on Kerala election of 1960, 211–12; in Kerala's ministry of 1960, 224–25; on overthrow of Kerala government, 201–2

Chacko, P. T.: in Caux, 165, 166; in dispute with Menon, 129–30; in dispute with Sankar, 226; on Education Bill, 110, 115–17

Chadayanmuri, George, 223

Cherian, K. M., 166, 171

Chiang Kai-shek, 33

Child Development Index (CDI), 233

Chile, 24

China: border incursions into India by, 210; on overthrow of Kerala government, 207–9; Revolution in, 33

Chomsky, Noam, 30

Christian Anti-Communism Crusade (CACC), 22; in Brazil, 58; in British Guiana, 41; decline of, 158–59; donations to, 150; history of, 148; in Kerala, 147, 156, 246; *Keraladhwani* published by, 153–55, 157–58; Moral Re-Armament and, 160–61
Christians: in elections of 2004 to 2019 in Kerala, 227; votes by, 222–23; *see also* Catholic Church
Christophers (organization), 106–7, 113, 131–32
Church Committee (U.S. Senate), 29–30, 219, 242
Churchill, Winston, 38–39, 48
Clarridge, Duane R. "Dewey," 32, 192–93
coconuts, 65–66
Colbert, James, 156
Cold War, 25; State Department policy objectives during, 34–35
collective bargaining, 230–31
Communist Party (Guatemala), 43, 46
Communist Party (Indonesia; PKI), 50, 51
Communist Party of India (CPI): on caste system, 95; CIA on, 209; decline in votes from Christians for, 222–23; after dismissal of Kerala's government, 144; elected to power in Kerala, 14, 21; in election of 1960, 219–20; formation of, 69; in Indian Assembly election of 1960, 220–24; Kerala as showpiece for, 197–99; Operations Coordinating Board report on, 181–82; police actions against unions allied with, 112–13; split in, 226; in Travancore-Cochin elections of 1952 and 1957, 78–80; Travancore independence movement supported by, 76–78; U.S. State Department on, 176–77; on violence in Kerala, 145; wins Kerala election of 1957, 81–82; during World War II, 74
Communist Party of India (Marxist), 226
Communist Party of Kerala, 242–43; comes to power, 21; on education, 89–90; in election in Devikulam, 113–14; in election of 1960, 210–11; formation of, 69; National Security Council on, 61; opposition to, 21–22; overthrow of, 22; in Travancore-Cochin, 62; during World War II, 74–75
Congo, Republic of, 54–56
Congress for Cultural Freedom (organization), 127
Congress Party (India): anti-communism of, 129; CIA

on, 178, 196; CIA aid to, 10, 246; decline of, 190; on Education Bill, 110, 232; in Kerala, 61; after Kerala election of 1960, 212, 226; in Kerala election of 1960, 210, 217; in Kerala's ministry of 1960, 224–25; on land reform, 84; in opposition to Agrarian Bill, 109; in overthrow of Kerala government, 202, 204–5; split within, 226; Student Congress of, 137; in Travancore-Cochin elections of 1954 and 1957, 79, 175; on Travancore general strike (1946), 77
Congress Socialist Party (CSP; India), 69–72
crime, 105–6
Cuba, 25

da Gama, Vasco, 63–64
Dalits (caste), 222
Damodaran, K., 69, 126
decentralization, 96–99, 235–36
Decree Against Communism (Pope Pius XII), 124
Deepika (newspaper), 136
Democratic Publications (publisher), 127
Desai, Morarji, 187, 191
Dev, P. Kesava, 126, 127
Devan, M. V., 127
Devikulam (Kerala), 113–14, 117, 119

Dey, 191
Dhebar, U. N., 130, 187, 189–91
District Administration Bill (1974), 235
Dominican Republic, 24–25
Doolittle, Jimmy, 34–35
Driberg, Tom, 168–69
Dulles, Allen, 34, 189, 214; on British Guiana, 39; on Congo, 55; on Guatemala, 44–45; on Iran, 48; on Kerala, 197, 203–4, 246–47
Dulles, Clover, 45
Dulles, John Foster, 45
Dwight D. Eisenhower Presidential Library, 213–16

East Timor, 53–54, 218–19
education, 89–91, 231–33; in British Guiana, 38; in Kerala, 67; for knowledge economy, 239; role of students, 137–38
Education Bill (1957), 110–11, 117, 231–32; Catholic Church opposition to, 125, 128, 131–32; CIA on, 189, 195; political opposition to, 130, 131
Eisenhower, Dwight David: CIA under, 34–35; on Kerala, 189; Operations Control Board created under, 174; visits India, 213
Eisenhower administration: CIA covert actions during, 27; on Kerala, 180–81
elections: in British Guiana,

37–42; in Devikulam, 113–14, 117, 119; for Indian Assembly of 1960, 220–22; in Kerala of 1957, 81–82; in Kerala of 1960, 210–13, 217, 219–20; in Kerala of 1965 and 1967, 226; in Travancore-Cochin (1952, 1954 and 1957), 78–80, 174–75
EMS, see Namboodiripad, E. M. S.
Ezhava (caste), 128, 130, 144

fair-price shops (Kerala), 102
The Final Revolution (play), 171
Finlay, James, 135
First Century Christian Fellowship (organization), 160
fiscal policy, 100–101
fishermen, 75–76
Flory, 140
food, 107–9
The Forgotten Factor (play), 163, 165
Freedom of Information Act (FOIA 1966), 17–18; declassification under, 182–83; Executive Order on withholding of documents under, 215

G-2 unit (U.S. Army), 32
Galbraith, John Kenneth, 169
Gandhi, Indira, 121, 133; Bunker on, 203; CIA aid to, 10; on education in Kerala, 232; as president of All India Congress Committee, 130
Gandhi, Mohandas K., 33, 68, 142; Buchman meets, 165
Gandhi, Rajmohan, 168–72
George, K. C., 223
George, K. M., 192
Ghosh, Ajay K., 79, 177, 211
gliricidia (Sheemakonna) shrubs, 99–100
Gopalakrishnan, K. G., 15
Gopalan, A. K., 72
Gordon, Lincoln, 56, 57
Gough, Kathleen, 73
Goulart, João, 57, 157
Gouri, K. R., 83, 84
Govindan, M., 126, 127
Graham, Billy, 148
Greece, 24
Gregorious, Mar, 169–70
Guatemala, 218; assassinations in, 31; lessons for Kerala in, 118–19; overthrow of government of, 43–48, 243
Gulati, I. S., 100–101
Guyana (British Guiana), 36–42, 120, 121
Gwalior Rayons Factory, 238

Harijans (caste), 209–10
hartal, 123, 135
Harvest Evangelism, 41
Health Index (HI), 232
Herman, Edward, 30
Herring, Ronald, 84, 85
Herter, Christian, 214

INDEX

The Hindu (newspaper), 165
Hitler, Adolf, 162
Hoffnung (play), 167, 169, 170
Honduras, 45
House Unamerican Activities Committee (HUAC), 148–50, 159
Howard, Peter, 170
Human Development Index (HDI), 233
Hungary, 125
Hydarali (sultan), 64

Ideology and Co-Existence (booklet), 160, 164, 167–68
Immerman, Richard H., 45
Independent Student Organization, 137
India: Assembly election of 1960 in, 220–22; border incursions by China into, 210; Independence Movement in, 33; Moral Re-Armament movement in, 164–65; Schwarz on communism in, 149; United States aid to, 195–97; during World War II, 74–75
Indian Gospel Mission (IGM), 151
Indonesia, 24, 50–51, 218; coup and massacre in, 51–53; East Timor and, 53–54
Indonesian Communist Party (PKI), 50, 51
industrial investment in Kerala, 237–38

infant mortality rate (IMR), 13
Initiatives of Change (Moral Re-Armament; organization), 160, 172
International Cooperation Administration (ICA), 181, 182, 184, 202
Iran, 48–50
Iyer, V. R. Krishna, 82

Jagan, Cheddi, 36–37, 39–42, 120, 156
Jagan, Janet Rosenberg, 36–37
Jeffrey, Robin, 145
Jha, Aditya Nath, 143
Johnson, Chalmers, 26–27
Johnson, Lyndon, 17
Joseph, Annie, 139
Joseph, O. J., 223

Kadhaprasangam (performance art), 127
Kara, Siddharth, 56
Katari, 187
Kattampally (Kerala), 109
Kelappan, K., 112, 144
Kennan, George, 29–30
Kennedy, John F.: on British Guiana, 41; CIA covert actions under, 27; Operations Control Board disbanded by, 174
Kennedy, Robert, 51
Kennedy administration, 57
Kerala (India): caste system and inequality in, 95–96; caste system in, 66–67; Christian

293

Anti-Communism Crusade in, 156; CIA covert action in, 60; CIA on Communist victory in, 177–81; CIA overthrow of government in, 11–12; CIA strategy for, 183–88; CIB on overthrow of government of, 201–2; CIB's role in ministry of 1960 in, 224–25; as communist showpiece, 197–99; crime and violence in, 105–6; decentralization in, 96–99; dismissal of government of, 143–46; economy and trade of, 65–66; education in, 89–91; election of 1957 in, 81–82; election of 1960 in, 210–13, 217, 219–20; ending tenant evictions in, 83–84; history of, 62–64; industrial investment in, 237–38; labor in, 92, 94; land reform in, 85–89, 228–30; monitored by CIA, 188–89; movement to unite, 78; MRA World Assembly in (1962), 170–71; Nehru on, 194; overthrow of government of, 204–10; police in, 92–94, 112–13; politics from 1960 to present, 225–28; society and economy of, 12–14; state archives of, 19–20
Kerala Agrarian Relations Bill, 84–85, 88
Kerala Book Stall, 246
Kerala Congress (organization), 158, 226
Kerala Congress Party, 200
Keraladhwani ("The Voice of Kerala"; newspaper), 153–55, 157–58
Kerala District Councils Bill, 99
Kerala Infrastructure Investment Fund Board (KIIFB), 227
Kerala Kaumudi (newspaper), 133, 144
Kerala Model of Development, 14
Kerala Panchayat Bill, 99
Kerala Pradesh Congress Committee (KPCC), 131, 200
Kerala Students Union (KSU), 112, 137–38
Kerala University, 89, 91
Kinzer, Stephen, 45
knowledge economy, 239–40
Koya, C. H. Muhammed, 165, 166, 225
Krishnamachari, T. T., 187
kudikidappukars, 87
Kudumbashree Women Neighborhood Group, 227

labor, in Kerala, 92, 94, 230–31, 238
labor unions, 70–71; in British Guiana, 39, 41; collective bargaining institutions and, 230–31; general strike of 1938 by, 71–72; in Indonesia,

INDEX 295

51–52; in Kerala, 92, 238; police actions against, 112–13
land reform: Agrarian Bill on, 109–10; in British Guiana, 38; decentralization and, 235; in Guatemala, 44; in Kerala, 85–89; in Kerala, in 1971, 228–30
Left Democratic Front (LDF), 226–28
Legion of Mary (organization), 107
Liberation Day (June 12, 1959), 131
Liberation Samithi (Committee), 131
Lieten, G. K., 95
Lovestone, Jay, 39
Lumumba, Patrice, 30, 54–56, 219

Mackay (colonel), 135
Madras (India), 191–93
Malabar (India), 70, 75
Malaviya, H. D., 113
Malayala Manorama (newspaper), 132–33, 141, 166
Malayalam newspapers, 132–34
Mannam, *see* Padmanabhan, Mannath
Matthai, John, 91, 104
Mathrubhum (newspaper), 132–33
McGarr, Paul, 33–34
Meany, George, 41
Mehta, Ashok, 141

Mencher, Joan, 73
Menon, A. R., 82
Menon, C. Achutha, 82
Menon, K. A. Damodara, 129–30
Menon, K. B., 104
Menon, Krishna, 205
Menon, M. Gopalakrishna, 142
Menon, Panampally Govinda, 121, 132
Mindszenty, József (cardinal), 125
minimum wage legislation, 230
Mobutu Sese Seko, 56
Moral Re-Armament (MRA; organization), 22, 147, 159–61; critiques of, 168–69; decline of, 163–64, 172–73; after election of 1960, 169–70; in India, 164–65; in Kerala, 246; Namboodiripad and, 165–68; Oxford Group becomes, 162–63; World Assembly of (Kerala, 1962), 170–71
Mosaddegh, Mohammad, 48–49, 219
Moynihan, Daniel Patrick, 10, 134, 212, 245
Mullik, B. N., 142–43, 225
Mundassery, Joseph, 82, 90
Murphy, Robert D., 202
Muslim League, 110, 129, 210, 212, 223–26
Muslims, 68, 129, 223–24; in elections of 2004 to 2019 in Kerala, 228

Nair, Chandrasekhara, 18
Nair, M. N. Govindan, 72, 81, 82
Nair, Madhavan, 180
Nairs (caste), 110, 128
Nair Service Society (NSS), 109–10, 128, 129
Namboodiripad, E. M. S. (EMS), 14, 78; on anticommunist conventions, 115; on caste system, 95, 96; CIA on, 178–79; CIB and, 143; CIB on overthrow of, 201–2; decentralization under, 96–97, 99; dismissal of Kerala's government under, 144; on Education Bill, 131; elected as Chief Minister of Kerala (1957), 81, 82, 104; elected as Chief Minister of Kerala (1967), 226; fiscal policy under, 100–101; Kerala unit of Communist Party of India formed by, 69; on land reform, 85–86; Moral Re-Armament and, 165; Nehru's demands accepted by, 141; on newspapers, 133; on political cooperation, 237; on private industrial investments, 101; tenant evictions ended by, 83; uniting of opposition to, 200
Narayana Guru, Sree, 67
Narayanan, K. R., 144, 145
Narayanan, Shriman, 103–4

National Security Act (1947), 25, 28
National Security Council (U.S.), 28; on British Guiana, 41; CIA under, 29; on Communist Party in Travancore-Cochin, 61, 62; on Kerala election of 1960, 211; on overthrow of Kerala government, 205; psychological warfare in Guatemala by, 46; on Soviet activities in India, 199; on Travancore-Cochin election of 1954, 174
Navasky, Victor, 42
Nehru, Jawaharlal, 121; on anticommunist violence, 145; Buchman meets, 165; CIA on, 178, 186, 189, 191, 193–95, 245, 246; on decline of Congress Party, 190; Jagan meets with, 120; on Kerala, 130, 198, 203–6, 219; in Kerala election of 1960, 210, 213; on South Indian Book Trust, 127; visits Kerala, 123, 138, 140–41; visits U.S., 213
New Political Development Culture, 237
newspapers, 132–34; *Keraladhwani,* 153–55
New York Times, 15–16; on British Guiana, 40–41; on Indonesia, 52; on Iran (1954), 49
Niranam Army (Niranam Pada; organization), 107

INDEX

NITI (National Institution for Transforming India), 232
Nitze, Paul, 34

Office of Strategic Services (OSS), 32–33
one-anna agitation, 111–12, 116–18
Operations Coordinating Board (OCB; U.S.), 181–83, 247
Oxford Group (organization), 160, 162

Padmanabhan, Mannath (Mannam): in Caux, 166; fundraising by, 135; Moral Re-Armament and, 165–71; as Nair leader, 128; "Save India Day" declared by, 145
Pahlavi, Mohammad Reza (shah, Iran), 49
Panchayats (village boards), 98–99
Pant, Govind Ballabh, 142–43
Pant, Pandit, 191, 198–99
Pasternak, Boris, 126
Pathrose, K. V., 223
Patil, S. K., 10, 187, 191
Pavanan, 144–45
Pawley, William, 34–35
Penn-Lewis, Jessie, 161
People's Food Committees, 102
People's Plan Campaign (PPC), 236, 237
People's Progressive Party (British Guiana), 37–42, 120, 121
Philbrick, Herbert, 158
Philip, Boobbyer, 163
Pillai, P. Govinda, 125
Pillai, P. Krishna, 69, 71, 72, 212
Pillai, Pattom Thanu, 225–-226
Pius XII (Pope), 124
Plantation Labor Act (Kerala), 94
plantations, 88–89
police, in Kerala, 92–94, 112–13; in violent incidents, 135–37, 140, 243
Ponnuse, Rosamma, 221
Pope, Allen, 50–51
poverty, 233
Praja Mandalams (organization), 70
Praja Socialist Party (PSP), 109, 210–12
Prasad, Rajendra, 170, 206, 207
Prashad, Vijay, 30–32, 216, 217, 244
Premier Tire Factory, 238
Progressive Student Organization, 137
psychological warfare, in Guatemala, 46–48
Punnapra-Vayalar uprising (1946), 75–78
Punnoose, P. T., 223
Punnose, Rosamma, 113

Rabe. Stephen, 38–39
Radhakrishnan, 187

Radical Group, 72
Rajeswari, K., 15
Ralph, McGehee, 53
Ram, Dhani, 209
Reagan, Ronald, 158
redistributive development strategy, 102
religion, in British Guiana, 41
Reston, James, 52
Revolutionary Socialist Party (RSP), 109, 237; newspaper of, 133; Progressive Student Organization of, 137
Rice Deal Scam, 108
Rodney, Walter, 36
Romualdi, Serafina, 39
Roosevelt, Kermit, 48–50
Rosenthal, A. M., 81, 82
Roy, B. C., 187
Roy, M. N., 126
Roy, William, 135
rubber, 65
Rusk, Dean, 42
Ryotwari settlement, 70

Sanjevi, Tirupattur Gangadharam, 33
Sankar, R.: becomes Chief Minister of Kerala, 226; as Kerala Pradesh Congress Committee president, 129, 130, 142, 145
Sanu, M. K., 127
Sarvis, Charles, 152–53
Savage (Governor of British Guiana), 39
Schlesinger, Arthur, 42

Schlesinger, Stephen, 45
School Education Quality Index (SEQI), 232
Schwarz, Fred, 148–53, 158; in British Guiana, 156; death of, 159; *Keraladhwani* published by, 153–55
second-generation problems, 234
Sekhar, N. C., 69
Sen, A. K., 191
Sen, Satyabrata, 236
Shahidi (general), 48
Sheemakonna (gliricidia) shrubs, 99–100
Shrimali, 191
Sluis, Joost, 156
Smith, Bob, 162
Smith, Walter Bedell, 45
Social Scout Movement (SSM), 106
Société Générale (firm), 54–55
Solomon, P. S., 223
Somarajan, C. N., 20
Somoza, Anastasio, 45
South Indian Book Trust, 127, 192
Soviet Union, 49, 125, 126; activities in India by, 199; on overthrow of Kerala government, 206–9
Sreekala, M. S., 15
Sree Narayana Dharma Paripalana Yogam (SNDP; organization), 128, 129, 222
Stalin, Joseph, 125
State, U.S. Department of: *Communism in the Free*

INDEX

World report by, 176–77; policy objectives of, 34–35; on removal of Kerala government, 245
strikes: general strike of 1938, 71–72; Travancore general strike (1946), 76–77
Student Congress, 138
Student Federation (SF), 137, 138
students, 137–38
Suharto, 51–54
Sukarno, 24, 51, 52
Sushamakumar, S. S., 20
Sustainable Development Goals Index (SDGI), 233
Sutter, George, 135

A Taste of Victory (film), 155–56
taxes, 66; on plantations, 88–89
tea, 65, 176
teachers, 90–91
Thimayya, K. S., 187
Thomas, C. J., 126–27
Thomas, George, 150–53, 155–58
Thomas, M. M., 125
Thomas, T. V., 94, 223
Thomas Isaac, T. M., 15
Thornhill, Alan, 163
Tippu (sultan), 64
trade unions, *see* labor unions
Travancore (India), 76–77
Travancore-Cochin (India), 61, 62, 119–21; CIA on election of 1954 in, 174–75

Travancore Labor Association (TLA), 70–71
Travancore State Congress, 69–70
Trivandrum Martyrs Column, 139
Trujillo, Rafael, 25
Truman, Harry, 25
Truman administration, 29
Truth Commission (UN Commission for Historical Clarification), 47–48, 218
Tudeh Party (Communist Party; Iran), 48–49

Ubico, Jorge, 43
Udayabhanu, A. P., 222
United Democratic Front (UDF), 226, 227
United Democratic Front of Kerala (UDF), 210–11
United Fruit Company, 44–45, 219
United Nations Commission for Historical Clarification (Truth Commission), 47–48, 218
United States: aid to India from, 195–97; Brazil and, 57–58; decline of Christian Anti-Communism Crusade in, 158–59; in Indonesian massacre, 52–54; on overthrow of Kerala government, 208–9
United States Information Service (USIS), 145, 184, 188; Madras office of, 191–93

Unniraja, C., 120, 121
Up with People (organization), 172

Vadakkan (priest): on Angamali violence, 135; Anti-Communist Front founded by, 115, 124; in debate with Damodaran, 126; on fundraising, 135; on picketing by women, 139; Social Scout Movement founded by, 106
Vaikom Satyagraha campaign (1924), 67–68, 72
Varantharapally (Kerala), 106
Vijayan, O. V., 103
Villeneuve, Hubert, 157–58
Vimochana Samithi (Liberation Committee), 140–43, 216
Vishwa Deepam (The Light of the World; newsletter), 151, 157

Voice of Liberation (radio station), 46–47

wages, in Kerala, 230–31
water transport, 111–12
Weissman, Stephen, 55, 56
Whitman, Ann, 45, 214
Wilson, Bill, 162
Wolf, Leonard G., 159–60, 167–68
women, 138–40; in Brazil, 157; under Communism, Catholic Church on, 125; in Kerala's population, 13
World War II, 74–75

Young, David, 168, 170, 171

Zamindari settlement, 70